CAMBRIDGE LIBRARY COLLECTION

Books of enduring scholarly value

History

The books reissued in this series include accounts of historical events and movements by eye-witnesses and contemporaries, as well as landmark studies that assembled significant source materials or developed new historiographical methods. The series includes work in social, political and military history on a wide range of periods and regions, giving modern scholars ready access to influential publications of the past.

Despatches and Correspondence of the Marquess Wellesley, K. G.

Richard, Marquess Wellesley (1760–1842) became one of the most controversial politicians of his generation during his time as Governor-General of Bengal (1798–1805). Although this period saw him achieve territorial gains in India, the financial cost was considered too high and many in London disagreed with the changes he made in Bengal. In 1809, after his return to Britain, he was appointed ambassador to Spain during the height of the Peninsular War (1808–1814) between France and an alliance of Britain, Spain and Portugal. His younger brother Arthur, the Duke of Wellington, was one of the key generals during this campaign. This collection of papers, published in 1838, covers this brief but dramatic period of Wellesley's career, after which he was appointed foreign secretary. Its editor, the political activist and historian Robert Montgomery Martin (1800–1868), also edited five volumes of Wellesley's Indian correspondence (also available in this series).

T0371116

Cambridge University Press has long been a pioneer in the reissuing of out-of-print titles from its own backlist, producing digital reprints of books that are still sought after by scholars and students but could not be reprinted economically using traditional technology. The Cambridge Library Collection extends this activity to a wider range of books which are still of importance to researchers and professionals, either for the source material they contain, or as landmarks in the history of their academic discipline.

Drawing from the world-renowned collections in the Cambridge University Library, and guided by the advice of experts in each subject area, Cambridge University Press is using state-of-the-art scanning machines in its own Printing House to capture the content of each book selected for inclusion. The files are processed to give a consistently clear, crisp image, and the books finished to the high quality standard for which the Press is recognised around the world. The latest print-on-demand technology ensures that the books will remain available indefinitely, and that orders for single or multiple copies can quickly be supplied.

The Cambridge Library Collection will bring back to life books of enduring scholarly value (including out-of-copyright works originally issued by other publishers) across a wide range of disciplines in the humanities and social sciences and in science and technology.

Despatches and Correspondence of the Marquess Wellesley, K. G.

During His Lordship's Mission to Spain as Ambassador Extraordinary to the Supreme Junta in 1809

RICHARD COLLEY WELLESLEY
EDITED BY
ROBERT MONTGOMERY MARTIN

CAMBRIDGE
UNIVERSITY PRESS

CAMBRIDGE UNIVERSITY PRESS

Cambridge, New York, Melbourne, Madrid, Cape Town,
Singapore, São Paolo, Delhi, Tokyo, Mexico City

Published in the United States of America by Cambridge University Press, New York

www.cambridge.org
Information on this title: www.cambridge.org/9781108168977

© in this compilation Cambridge University Press 2011

This edition first published 1838
This digitally printed version 2011

ISBN 978-1-108-16897-7 Paperback

THE

DESPATCHES AND CORRESPONDENCE

OF THE

MARQUESS WELLESLEY, K. G.

DURING HIS LORDSHIP'S MISSION TO

SPAIN

AS AMBASSADOR EXTRAORDINARY

TO THE

SUPREME JUNTA IN 1809.

———————

EDITED BY

MONTGOMERY MARTIN.

———————

LONDON:

JOHN MURRAY, ALBEMARLE-STREET.

MDCCCXXXVIII.

INTRODUCTION.

THE Despatches and Correspondence of the Marquess
Wellesley during his Embassy to Spain in 1809 were printed
for both Houses of Parliament, and recorded in the journals
of the day. They are now collected together and arranged
chronologically, as containing matter calculated to illustrate
the history of the period when England commenced her
active interference in Spain on the expulsion of Ferdinand
the VII. and the occupation of a great part of his kingdom
by the French. It is necessary to state that this special
Embassy originated in a proposition made by Mr. Canning,
then Secretary of State for the Foreign Department, in the
spring of the year 1809, to the Marquess Wellesley. Mr.
Canning stated that it was intended to send a large armament to Spain, and to place it under the orders of Sir Arthur
Wellesley. By command of his Majesty George the 3rd,
Mr. Canning offered to the Marquess Wellesley the station
of Ambassador Extraordinary to the Supreme Junta, with
a view to an efficient negotiation, which would render the
operations of the army under Sir Arthur Wellesley of solid
benefit to the cause of the allied Powers.

The Marquess Wellesley was subsequently informed by
Mr. Canning that the destination of the armament had been
changed from Spain to the Scheldt. His Lordship then
tendered his resignation of the proposed mission; stating
that, under such circumstances, he apprehended, that he
could not render any useful service to his country.

At the earnest desire of Mr. Canning, however, his Lord-ship consented to accept the Embassy to Spain; and his proceedings in that country are detailed in the following pages.

His Lordship's return from Spain was caused by the com-mands of his Majesty George the 3rd, who nominated him to the office of Secretary of State for the Foreign Depart-ment on the change of the administration, which ensued upon the death of the Duke of Portland.

The Editor has annexed to these documents a speech delivered by the Marquess Wellesley (then Earl of Morning-ton) in the House of Commons in 1794, as illustrative of the opinions which he entertained relative to the general princi-ples, designs, and power of France, so strongly exemplified in the invasion of Spain.

SUBSTANCE

OF THE

EARL OF MORNINGTON'S SPEECH

IN THE

HOUSE OF COMMONS,

ON TUESDAY, JANUARY 21st, 1794,

On a Motion for an Address to his Majesty at the commencement of the Sessions of Parliament.

MR. SPEAKER,

IF the present conjuncture of our affairs afforded us a free option between war and peace; if the necessity which originally compelled us to engage in the present contest had ceased, and the question for our deliberation on this day were merely, whether we should return to the secure and uninterrupted enjoyment of a flourishing commerce, of an overflowing revenue, of tranquil liberty at home, and of respect and honour abroad; or whether, on the other hand, we should wantonly commit to the doubtful chance of arms all those accumulated blessings; no man could hesitate one moment in deciding on such an alternative. To us more especially no other guide would be necessary than our own recent experience. Within our own memory, the country has passed with such rapid steps from the lowest state of adversity to the utmost degree of opulence, splendor, and power, that all our minds must be furnished with whatever useful lessons are to be drawn from either fortune. We all know, and have felt what may be lost by the calamities of war, and what may be gained by a wise improvement of the advantages of peace. But whether I revert to the grounds and origin of this war, whether I look forward to the probable issue of the contest, or fix my attention on the inevitable effects of any attempt to abandon it in the present crisis, my judgment is driven to the painful, but irresistible conclusion that no such alternative is now before us. Our choice must now be made between the vigorous prosecution of our present exertions, and an ambiguous state neither of open hostility, nor of real repose; a state in which we should suffer most of the inconveniences of war, in which we should enjoy none of the solid advantages of peace, in which, even if we could purchase at the expense of our honour and of our faith a short respite from the direct attacks of the enemy, we could never for a moment feel the genuine sense of permanent security; unless we could contemplate without emotion the rapid progress of the arms and principles of France in the territories of our allies; unless we could behold without anxiety the rapid approaches of the same danger threatening the British dominions; unless we could sit at ease with the axe suspended over our heads, and wait with tranquillity of mind the moment, when these formidable enemies, after the extinction of every element of order and regular government in their own country, after the subjugation of every foreign power whose alliance might assist us in our last struggles, strengthened by additional resources, animated by the prospect of new plunder, and flushed with the triumphant success of their prosperous crimes should turn their whole force against the British Monarchy, and complete their victory over the interests of civil society by the final destruction of that fair fabric of government, under which these happy kingdoms have so long enjoyed the inseparable advantages of substantial liberty, settled order, and estab-lished law.

No part of the speech from the Throne more fully meets my sentiments on this important question than that in which His Majesty recommends it to us to bear in mind the true grounds and origin of the present war. We cannot have forgotten, that before the French had declared war against us, we had seen in their conduct views of aggrandizement, projects of ambition, and principles of fixed hostility against all established government: and we had been convinced, that unless the foundation of our complaints should be removed by a total alteration in their system with respect to foreign nations, war on our part would become at length inevitable. We cannot have forgotten, that instead of endeavouring to remove our just apprehensions, their explanations afforded fresh motives of jealousy, and their conduct aggravated every cause of offence; until at length, they interrupted all negociation by a sudden declaration of war, attended by circumstances of unex-ampled perfidy and violence. At that time we declared at the foot of the throne, " that we considered whatever His Majesty's subjects held most dear and sacred, the stability of our happy Constitution, the security and honour of His Majesty's Crown, and the preservation of our laws, our liberty, and our religion, to be all involved in the issue of the present contest; and we pledged ourselves, that our zeal and exertions should be proportioned to the importance of the conjuncture, and to the magnitude and value of the objects for which we had to contend." Impressions conceived after such deliberate examination, assurances so solemnly pledged in the face of the nation and of all Europe will not be abandoned by the wisdom and firmness of this House upon such suggestions as have hitherto been offered in this debate. Before we can be justified in relinquishing the principles by which our proceedings have hitherto been governed, we shall require satisfactory proof, either that the impressions which we had originally conceived of the views of France were erroneous; or, that by the course of subsequent events, the success of the war is become desperate and impracticable; or, that from some improve-ment in the system and principles which prevail in France, and in the views and characters of those who now exercise the powers of Government there, the motives of justice and necessity which compelled us to enter into the war, no longer con-tinue to operate.

On each of these propositions separately, and on the combined result of the whole, I shall endeavour to bring this question to a fair issue.

Although the question of the original justice and necessity of the war was so fully examined in the last session of Parliament, yet to relinquish the blessings of peace is a measure of such serious and grave importance, that I am confident we shall not be unwilling, during any period of the contest, carefully and anxiously to revise the grounds on which it was adopted. In the present moment, however superfluous it may appear to search for any additional justification of our conduct, or to endeavour to throw any new light on a question already so well understood, yet it cannot but prove satisfactory to us, that a variety of occurrences since the commencement of the war, and many new and striking proofs have concurred to confirm the wisdom and justice of our decision, not merely on general grounds, but precisely on the very grounds on which it was originally founded. If I could bring to your bar the most malignant, the most active, and the most able enemy of the British name in the National Convention, the author of the most scandalous official libels against the views, interests, and power of Great Britain, the author of the most inflammatory speeches tending to provoke the war in which we are engaged, the author of the declaration of war itself, and the inventor of all the pretences by which it has since been palliated both in France and in England; if I could bring him to a cross-examination in your presence, confront him with his own reports, speeches, and manifestoes, as well as with those of his colleagues in office, and comparing the result of the whole with concurrent and subsequent events, convict him and his associates of falsehood, treachery, and prevarication in all their pretended explanations of their own designs, as well as in all their affected complaints of the supposed views of His Majesty's Councils, I am persuaded that you would not reject an investigation, the issue of which must tend to confirm the confidence of the nation in the original justice of our cause : such is the nature of the proof which I am about to offer to you.

Brissot, the leader of the Diplomatic Committee, Brissot, the main-spring of the French Government at the breaking out of the war, falling into disgrace and danger, addressed to his constituents a defence of all his measures, in which he reveals the whole secret and mystery of the French Revolution, and makes an open confession of the principles by which France was directed in her intercourse with other powers, of the means which she employed, and of the ends which she pursued. From the unquestionable testimony of this production, from the evidence of the principal actor in these transactions, I propose to examine the truth of our complaints, the justice of the conduct of France, and the validity of the arguments which have been used on either side.

The views which we attributed to France previous to the war, were views of aggrandizement and ambition connected with the propagation of principles incompatible with the existence of any regular government.

The particular acts by which those views had been manifested, were 1st, the decree of the 19th of November, in which France made (according to her own language) a grant of universal fraternity and assistance, and ordered her generals every where to aid and abet those citizens who had suffered, or might suffer hereafter in the cause of (what she called) liberty. Her sense of liberty, as applied to England, was shewn by the reception of seditious and treasonable addresses, and by the speeches of the President of the National Convention expressing his wish for the auspicious institution of a British Convention, founded, as such an institution must have been, upon the destruction of every branch of our happy Constitution.

2nd. The conduct of France, in incorporating the territories of other powers with her own, under colour of voluntary acts of Union, pretended to have been freely voted by the people; particularly in the cases of Savoy, and of the Netherlands, of both which countries France had assumed the sovereignty.

3rd. The opening of the Scheldt, in direct violation of the most solemn treaties guaranteed by France herself; and, lastly, her general designs of hostility against Holland.

When the decree of the 19th of November was complained of here, the Executive Council replied, that, "It would be injurious to the National Convention to charge them with the project of protecting insurrections."

Brissot, in his confessions, is pleased to admit, that, "the decree of the 19th of November was absurd and impolitic, and justly excited uneasiness in foreign cabinets." You shall now hear the wise, politic, and conciliatory exposition of the principles of France, which he opposes to that decree. "What was the opinion of enlightened men, of men who were Republicans before the 10th of August, who desired liberty, not only for their own country, but for all Europe? They thought that liberty might be established every where, by exciting* those for whom government is administered against those who administer it, and by proving to the people the facility and advantages of such insurrections." This theory of universal liberty founded upon universal insurrection, this system of exciting the

---

* Les Administrés contre les Administrans.

people against all regular government of whatever form, against all authority of whatever description, this plan for the instruction of the mob in the advantages of disorder, and in the facility of outrage and plunder, is deliberately applauded by Brissot, as the established doctrine of the most moderate men in France, to which no one could object on account of its absurdity and impolicy, or of its tendency to excite uneasiness in foreign cabinets.

You may perceive that the authors of the decree of the 19th of November, and the *enlightened Republicans* of whom Brissot speaks, were equally animated by the great principle of *desiring liberty* (as they are pleased to style it) *for all Europe;* their only difference consisted in the mode of carrying their common views into speedy and effectual execution. This will appear more clearly in the passages which I shall now read to the House: "But how can the people be led to that point? By zealous efforts to spread the spirit of liberty among them. This system was pursued at first. Excellent pamphlets from the pen of Condorcet had prepared all people for liberty. The understandings of the Belgians ought to have been enlightened by good writings, we ought to have sent missionaries among them." The House will find no difficulty in understanding what is meant by good *writings* (I say nothing of *missionaries*) when the *letters of Condorcet* are quoted as models of perfection. We are not unacquainted with the style of those "excellent pamphlets from the pen of Condorcet by which all people were to be prepared for liberty." We cannot be so ungrateful as to have forgotten the delicacy with which he suggested to the people of England, "that the French Revolution was an object both of their fears and desires, that a Parliamentary Reform would be proposed in this House, and that from thence the passage to the complete establishment of a Republic would be short and easy." Such are the means, so reconcileable with the faith of nations, so compatible with the amicable intercourse to be maintained with foreign powers, which Brissot, the reporter of the Diplomatic Committee, proposed to employ for the introduction of the principles of universal confusion into the bosom of every independent state. The disappointment of these benevolent views, and the failure of this great design, are lamented by him in terms so forcible, and so pathetic, as to display at once the stupendous magnitude of this scheme of destruction, and the frantic zeal with which it was pursued. "Oh! how grievous it is! for a man who has seen the Revolution advanced to a degree, to which, four years ago, it would, perhaps, have been madness to have thought of carrying it; how grievous it is! to see that Revolution falling back, while every thing was contending in its favour! Shall then all the benefit of our experience be lost to the general cause of liberty, to other nations, and to future Revolutions? Tears of blood should flow from the eyes of all Republicans; liberty, which might so easily have been extended, until it should have known no other bounds than those of the world, must now submit to a doleful confinement within the limits of France."

Some doubt might, perhaps, have been thrown upon the authority of the evidence which I have produced to the House, if it had appeared to attribute to the Government of France principles incompatible with their general system, and not conformable to the conduct of their agents and ministers in the different foreign countries; but when we find, that the public acts and language of all the agents of France correspond with the designs here ascribed to their employers, this circumstance at once corroborates the testimony to which I have alluded, and exhibits in itself a striking instance of the uniformity and consistency of the system in all its parts.

In America (a Government which, I am persuaded, the noble Earl* who has

---

* Lord Wycombe.

spoken in this debate, will concur with me in thinking, does not require to be improved by any infusion of French principles) Citizen Genet was appointed Resident by Brissot and Le Brun: he there commenced his operations by the institution of a Jacobin Club; he publicly insulted the magistrates; disputed the acts of Government; opened what he was pleased to call a consular tribunal under the authority of the French Republic for the condemnation of prizes within the territory of America; enforced the execution of its sentences by acts of open violence; and at length, the powers and privileges of the Consul acting under his orders having been annulled by the President of the United States, and his proceedings having been checked, as being contrary to the law of nations and to the rules by which the relations of independent states are governed, citizen Genet presents a remonstrance to the Secretary of State, in which he gravely says, "that he does not recollect what the worm-eaten writings of Grotius, Puffendorff, and Vatell say on these subjects; he thanks God that he has forgotten what those hireling civilians have written on the rights of nations, in times of universal slavery; but he knows that his conduct has been agreeable to the spirit of the French Constitution, of the American Constitution, and of the rights of man, which are for ever engraven on his heart, and from which he learns, that an appeal must lie from the President, who is a mere ministerial officer, to the Sovereign people of America."

Thus this disciple of Brissot takes upon himself to supersede every maxim of the law of nations by doctrines drawn from the Constitution of France; and not content with that outrage, he arrogates to himself the right of interpreting the Constitution of America by reference to the same polluted source, and affects to depose the President of the United States from his Constitutional authority, under colour of the sacred rights of man, and of the indefeasible sovereignty of the people.

Citizen Descorches, employed by the same party at Constantinople, proceeded in the same spirit; he established Jacobin Clubs, and held primary assemblies for the propagation of the true faith of liberty among the Janisaries at the Porte. Thus from Mr. Jefferson to the Reis Effendi, from the President of the United States of America to the Grand Seignior, from the Congress to the Divan, from the popular form of a Republic to the most unmixed military despotism, every mode and gradation of lawful authority, or of established power, was the object of deliberate, systematic, and uniform attack. There is another feature of this project which I cannot omit, because it so nearly concerns the security of some of the most valuable possessions of the British empire. We are told by Robespierre, that a part of the general scheme of Brissot and his associates was to free and arm all the negroes in the French Colonies in the West Indies. Brissot, instead of attempting to refute this charge, takes merit to himself for the ingenuity and simplicity of the invention; he says, that "by the simple operation of purifying the Colonial system of the French Islands, he would have accomplished the destruction of all the British Colonies in the West Indies." He adds, "That this is a secret of which few have any idea." Those who have given their attention more particularly to the case of the African Negroes, will be the first to feel the complicated horror of this detestable project of massacre and desolation. An abrupt emancipation of the slaves in the West Indies, accompanied with the circumstance of putting arms into their hands, would instantly occasion a scene of bloodshed and misery, which our imaginations could scarcely conceive, if it had not already been realized in the Island of St. Domingo under the auspices of the commissioners appointed by Brissot and his party. There cannot be a more striking instance of the general tendency of the views of those who governed France at the time of the declaration of war; it contains an epitome of that extensive conspiracy against the order of society and the peace of mankind, which we have already considered in detail.

With this compendious example of the ruinous projects of those who provoked the present war, I shall conclude this part of the argument, conceiving that I have shewn to the House, that the mischievous spirit of the decree of the 19th of November, denied by the Executive Council, has been avowed, acknowledged, and defended by Brissot, the champion of all their principles and the author of all their plans; that his exposition of this destructive spirit has been confirmed by a variety of concurrent circumstances; and that the arguments, by which the difference of opinion between the contending parties in France with respect to the decree of the 19th of November has been maintained, serve only to prove more strongly their unanimous agreement in the main principle of destruction, on which that decree was founded.

The principle of the incorporations, or re-unions of the different territories annexed to the dominions of France, (which is the next great feature of the system by which we were menaced,) as well as the means employed to obtain those re-unions, are fully explained by Brissot. In examining this part of the subject, I beg to call the attention of the House particularly to the gross prevarications and contradictions of the author of the declaration of war, as well as to the shallow artifices employed by the Executive Council, in the hope of concealing the ambitious views of France from the eyes of Europe.

First, with respect to Savoy and Nice. Brissot, in a Report made to the National Convention, on the 12th of January, 1793, in the name of the Committee of General Safety, a report intended to prepare them for the approaching war, and professing to contain a full and candid discussion of all the complaints of Great Britain, uses these words, "The unanimous wish of all the communities of Savoy legitimates the union with that country." Thus writes Brissot before the commencement of the war; observe how frankly and honestly he has since confessed the truth. "Cambon wanted to unite every thing, that he might sell every thing; thus, he FORCED the union of Savoy, and of Nice."

With regard to the Netherlands, Brissot tells us in his confessions, that Cambon the French Minister of Finance forced that measure also with two views; the compulsory introduction of assignats into that opulent country, and the universal plunder of property; he introduces Cambon and his party reasoning with the Convention upon the manner of negociating an union with the free and sovereign people of Belgium, in the following words. "The mortgage of our assignats draws near its end: what must be done? Sell the church property of Brabant; there is a mortgage of two thousand millions (eighty millions sterling). How shall we get possession of them? By an immediate union! Men's minds are not disposed to it. What does that signify? Let us make them vote by means of money. Without delay therefore they secretly order the Minister of Foreign Affairs to dispose of four or five hundred thousand livres, (20,000l. sterling) to make the mob of Brussels drunk, and to buy proselytes to the principle of union in all states.

"But even these means, it is said, will obtain but a weak minority in our favour. What does that signify? Revolutions, said they, are made only by minorities! It is the minority which has made the Revolution of France."

Thus you see, that the union of these vast territories with all their immense population, wealth, and commerce was considered by the French Minister of Finance as nothing more than a mere financial operation, for the purpose of supporting the sinking credit of his assignats. The sacred regard paid to the general will of the people in the doctrines respecting minorities, cannot have escaped the observation of the House. Something has been said already of the means employed to obtain the free consent of the people to these unions. On this subject, we have full information from Brissot. " Do you believe the Belgians were ever imposed upon by those votes and resolutions made by what is called acclamation for their union, for which corruption paid in part, and fear forced the remainder? Who at this time of day is unacquainted with the springs and wires of their miserable puppet-show? Who does not know the farces of primary assemblies, composed of a President, of a Secretary, and of some assistants, whose day-work was paid for? How could they believe themselves free and sovereign when we made them take such an oath as we thought fit, as a test to give them the right of voting?

" What could the disarmed Belgians object to all this, surrounded as they were by seventy thousand men? They had only to hold their tongues, and to bow down their heads before their masters! They did hold their tongues; and their silence is received as a sincere and free assent."

Brissot states, with equal force of language, the ruinous effects of all these measures; he says, " despotism and anarchy are the benefits which we have transplanted into this soil; we suppressed at once all their ancient usages, all their prejudices, all the ranks and orders of their society; we proscribed their priests; we treated their religious worship with open marks of contempt; we seized their revenues, their domains, and their riches for the profit of the nation; we carried to the very altar those hands, which they regarded as profane.

" Doubtless, these operations were founded on* true principles; but those principles ought to have had the consent of the Belgians, before they were carried into practice."

Have then the "true principles" of France been misrepresented or exaggerated in this House? Is it possible for the most honest and enthusiastic indignation, which the scenes exhibited in France have raised in any British heart, to vent itself in terms of more severity, than those which Brissot had used in expounding, what he justly calls, the true principles of the French Republic? Now let us again confront Brissot's confessions with his report in the name of the Committee of General Defence, on the 12th of January, 1793. " Shall I recall the accusation of having invaded the Netherlands, of having dictated laws, and made a Constitution for that country? We make a Constitution there! read the instructions given to our Generals! to assemble the people, to consult their wish, to enable them to express it freely, to respect it when expressed; such was our tyranny! The Belgians themselves form, and alone will form their Constitution; but in order to lead them to that point, it is necessary to tie up the hands of the malevolent, of Austrian emissaries, who would excite sedition; and this is the cause of some necessary acts of authority, this is the foundation of the Revolutionary power, which is nothing more than a guardian of liberty in her infancy, and which ceases to exist, as soon as she has attained the age of maturity. We pillage Belgium! when we only desire to be voluntarily reimbursed for the expences of a war, where the blood of our brothers is counted for nothing." So far Brissot, and the Committee of General Safety; I now entreat the House to hear the language of the Executive Council: " France calls back to freedom a people, which the Court of Vienna had devoted to slavery; her occupation of the Low Countries shall only continue during the war, and the time necessary to the Belgians to ensure and consolidate their liberty, after which, let them be independent and happy. France

---

* Sur les Principes.

will findher recompence in their felicity. When that nation shall be found in the full enjoyment of liberty, when its general will can lawfully declare itself without shackles, then if England and Holland still attach some importance to the opening of the Scheldt, they may put the affair into a direct negociation with Belgia. If the Belgians, by any motive whatever, consent to deprive themselves of the navigation of the Scheldt, France will not oppose it; she will know how to respect their independence, even in their errors. After so frank a declaration, which manifests such a sincere desire of peace, his Britannic Majesty's Ministers ought not to have any doubts with regard to the intention of France."

It is difficult to determine whether the prevarications of Brissot, the reporter from the Committee of the General Safety, or the subterfuges of the Executive Council, are most worthy of animadversion; both are so gross and flagrant, that I cannot aggravate by any comments the impression which they have already made: but when we recollect that the audacious violation of the law of nations and of the acknowledged rights of our allies by the opening of the Scheldt was justified upon no other ground than the maintenance of the *natural rights* of the *free* people of Belgium; when we recollect, that the final adjustment of that important question was postponed by France until the time when the *liberty* of the Belgians should be *secured and consolidated,* and when the *general will of the people could lawfully declare itself without shackles,* the tyranny exercised by France over the Netherlands, and the violence and corruption employed to procure the Union, cannot fail to excite the general indignation of this House. Most of us indeed were not deceived by the *frank* declaration of the Executive Council of France; but those few amongst us who seemed to be deceived by it at that time, and who under that deception maintained the justice of the pretences of France, must find additional motives of resentment and indignation in the recollection of the imposture, which was so successfully practised at least upon them: if they had been possessed of the information which I have detailed to the House, I am persuaded that they would never have proposed to us to carry to the foot of the Throne an Address, containing the paragraph, which I shall now read to you, relative to the navigation of the Scheldt.*

" We must further remark, that the point in dispute seems to us to have been relieved from a most material difficulty, by a declaration of the Minister of Foreign Affairs in France, that the French nation gave up all pretensions to determine the question of the future navigation of the Scheldt."

The insult and mockery of that declaration is now so evident, that I cannot suppose it possible that any person should retain the opinion, that the Executive Council ever had a sincere intention of relinquishing at any time the pretensions of France to determine the question of the navigation of the Scheldt, or any other question which might affect her operations in the Netherlands: the object of a declaration so inconsistent with the whole system pursued by France in the Netherlands could only be to delude this country with false pretences of moderation, until it might be convenient to discover in the face of day, and to enforce by the sword against every nation in Europe the inordinate scheme of ambition, of which the re-union of Belgium and the opening of the Scheldt formed but an inconsiderable part.

The designs of France against Holland may be inferred from her general views of aggrandizement, and particularly from the established maxim of her policy, *that France ought to know no other barrier to the eastward than the Rhine;* a maxim avowed by Brissot, by Dumourier, and at different periods by almost every person

---

* Address moved by C. Grey, Esq., on the 1st of February, 1793.

who has acted a leading part in the government of France since the massacre of the 10th of August. But the correspondence between Dumourier and Pache the Minister of War, which has been published, and of the authenticity of which no doubt can be entertained, has placed the hostile views of France against Holland in so strong and so clear a light, that it would be injustice to the argument to rest it entirely upon the general grounds already stated. It has been contended, that the rejection by the Executive Council of Dumourier's proposal to invade Holland in the month of November, 1792, was a strong proof of the pacific disposition and of the good faith which prevailed in the Councils of France at that time : but it appears that on the 30th of November, Dumourier, in a letter addressed to the Minister of War, communicated in detail a plan for the immediate invasion of Holland, and stated the previous conquest of Holland to be essential to the great object of driving the Austrian and Prussian armies beyond the Rhine. One of the principal arguments which he alleges in favour of this operation is founded in the hostile views which he attributes to Holland, and in his apprehension that if he should move towards the Rhine before he had effected a Revolution in Holland, his rear might be exposed to a sudden attack from the Dutch. It appears that the Minister of war *expressly warrants the neutrality of the Dutch in the beginning of December* to Dumourier. But notwithstanding that assurance, the question between the immediate invasion of Holland, and a movement towards the Rhine is argued throughout the whole of the official correspondence *merely upon grounds of expediency ;* the doubt being only, whether the operations of Dumourier's army in the month of December should commence, or terminate with the invasion of Holland ; this will appear more clearly from a passage in the last orders from the Minister of War to Dumourier on this subject, dated December the 6th, 1792. "Thus, if the army of Belgium should attack Holland, and not pass the Rhine, the Austrians will be able to attack Bournonville, and to force him to abandon the banks of the Moselle ; Custine might be endangered. These motives have deter- mined the Executive Council, and they have resolved (as a measure of urgency,* and which ought to take the lead of the invasion of *Holland*† which you propose) that you shall dispose the three armies under your orders, in the manner in which you judge the most proper for driving the Austrians from the countries compre- hended between the Meuse, the Moselle, and the Rhine."

This letter leaves no doubt on my mind, that if the French could have succeeded in driving the Austrians and Prussians beyond the Rhine early in December, 1792, they would without scruple have fallen upon Holland, although by the confession of the Minister of War in the month of December, the Dutch had given them no ground of offence.

Such are the various proofs and occurrences which tend to confirm those impressions of the designs of France, in consequence of which we thought it our duty to enable his Majesty to augment his forces previous to the declaration of war.

The aggression of France, which was the immediate cause of the war, forms another material branch of the argument ; it was attempted to be justified under the pretence of certain alleged acts of hostility, particularly the stopping the export of corn to France in the month of November, 1792 : that measure was defended by my Right Hon. Friends near me on the ground of their knowledge, that warlike preparations were then actually making in France. Upon this subject, Brissot's testimony is not only ample and unequivocal, but it proves that prepara-

---

* Une mesure d'urgence.
† Qui devoit devancer l'invasion de la Hollande.

tions had been commenced at an earlier period, and were proposed to be carried to a much greater extent than could have been supposed by any person in this country in the month of November. He tells us, "that as early as the month of October, the possibility of war with the maritime powers was foreseen, and the Diplomatic Committee and the Committee of General Defence had warned Monge the Minister of Marine of this circumstance. Considerable sums of money were put into his hands; he had promised* to collect stores and provisions from all quarters, to repair all the ships and frigates; he had promised a fleet of 30 sail of the line for the month of April, and 50 sail of the line by the month of July; he had promised to cover the sea with frigates for the protection of commerce, to send succours to St. Domingo and Martinique, an express law passed in October enjoined this." While France was thus preparing an armament against the maritime powers, what should we have thought of the conduct of our Ministers, if they had suffered the export of corn to that country, and thereby had contributed to accelerate the equipment of those formidable fleets which the Minister of Marine had engaged to provide? It ought not to be forgotten, that the same Government of France which had ordered preparations for equipping a fleet in the French ports as early as the month of October, thought it decent in the month of January, to make the armaments preparing by his Majesty a principal ground of complaint, and to insist as the ultimatum of France, that England should disarm: a more insulting proposal under all the circumstances of the case as I have now stated them was never made by one independent nation to another.

But while we are inquiring in this House into the immediate cause of the war, we may derive some useful information on that head from the contentions and divisions which have disturbed the Councils of our enemies. In the Act of Accusation against Brissot and his party, one principal charge is, "the proposal from the Diplomatic Committee by the organ of Brissot to delare war abruptly against England, war against Holland, war against all the powers which had not yet declared themselves."

During the trial of Brissot, Chaumette says in the Jacobin Club, "Every patriot has a right to accuse in this place the man who voted the war; and the blood which has been shed in the Republic and without the Republic in consequence of it shall be their proofs and their reasons."

Robespierre in his Report, on the 17th of November, 1793, says, "With what base hypocrisy the traitors insisted on certain pretended insults said to have been offered to our Ambassador!"

Brissot, on the other hand, replies, "Who has been the author of this war? The anarchists only, and yet they make it a crime in us."

Thus, amidst the animosities and dissensions which preceded the last revolution in Paris, the heinous crime of having provoked the war with England is mutually imputed by one party to the other. Robespierre imputes it to Brissot; Brissot retorts it upon Robespierre; the Jacobins charge it upon the Girondists; the Girondists recriminate upon the Jacobins; the mountain thunders it upon the valley; and the valley re-echoes it back against the mountain; for my part, I condemn them both—the share of this guilt, which belongs to Brissot and his associates, is already known to you; they who murdered Brissot and his associates upon the scaffold were not only the most active promoters of the decree of the 19th of November, and of the several unions, but the principal agents in all the odious vexations exercised over the people of the Netherlands, and not one voice among them was raised against the measures which immediately led to the war. There-

* S'approvisionner de tous les cotès.

fore I repeat it, whatever be the crime of having drawn down upon their own country the indignation of Great Britain and of her numerous allies, and of having fomented a general war in Europe, I charge that crime equally upon both these sanguinary factions. But who is the British subject that shall acquit both these sanguinary factions of the crime which they mutually impute to each other? and by charging it upon the Councils of his own Sovereign, shall impair the confidence of an united people in the justice of their cause, and weaken the energy of their exertions in the prosecution of this arduous contest?

Unless I am wholly deceived in the authenticity and application of the proofs which I have adduced, I cannot suppose that any such person will appear in the course of this debate; and I must conclude, that these proofs, added to the arguments employed last year, have confirmed the original justice and necessity of the war upon the most solid and secure foundation.

If then the original justice of our cause, instead of appearing to be in any degree weakened, has received additional force and confirmation from the whole course of subsequent events, it must be both our right and our duty (a right which a high-spirited people will not easily concede, and a duty from the discharge of which they will not shrink) to prosecute the war without remission, unless it can be made to appear that all our efforts must be vain and fruitless, and that our enemies are not only formidable, but invincible by any force which we can bring to act against them. But although the events of the last campaign have undoubtedly proved that France in her present situation is a formidable enemy, so far from proving her to be invincible, I shall contend that the general result of the campaign, both in its effects upon our own situation and upon that of the enemy, has been such as to afford a reasonable expectation of ultimate success.

What was our situation at the commencement of the last campaign? France was in full possession of the Netherlands, and by the operation of the revolutionary power under the decree of the 15th of December, 1792, was rapidly adding to her own resources not only all the ordinary resources of that wealthy country, but the property of the church, of the nobility, of all the corporations, the personal property of the prince, and of all his adherents. Upon the first produce of this immense booty, Dumourier had calculated that he could support an army of an hundred thousand men for ten months. By the possession of the port of Ostend, France commanded the commerce both of Holland and England, and had the means of interrupting the intercourse between us and our allies. By the possession of Antwerp and the measures which she had taken relative to the navigation of the Scheldt, she had the means of annoying Holland in that quarter; the possession of Liege gave her the command of the Meuse, and furnished her with great advantages in any operation which she might meditate against Maestricht. Mentz was also in her hands, and the commerce of the Rhine was consequently entirely at her mercy. She had a powerful army ready to enter the territory of Holland at the first moment of the war, with the avowed object not merely of conquest, but of effecting a revolution in that country upon her own destructive principles; and in the Mediterranean she had a formidable fleet, which had struck all the Italian States with such consternation, as had given her the absolute controul over the commerce of that sea, and the undisputed command of whatever resources could be drawn from the countries which border upon it. This was our situation at the opening of the campaign. It was no doubt truly serious, and such as would not have tempted us to undertake a war, if peace could have been maintained consistently with our safety and honour. It might reasonably have been expected, that with such advantages on her side, the general balance of events would have been greatly in favour of France at the conclusion of the first campaign, especially when it is considered that the policy which has been adopted by this country of keeping both her naval and military establishments at the lowest possible scale in time of peace must necessarily confine the extent, and weaken the vigour of her efforts in the early periods of war.

Prophecies of a much more gloomy complexion were uttered in this House; we were told (nearly in the language of one of the extracts which I have read from Brissot) that the sea would be immediately covered with the armed vessels of our enemy, and that our commerce would be exposed to depredation in every quarter; we were told in the same tone, that perhaps after five or six years of war, the Netherlands might be evacuated as the price of peace. What is our situation now at the conclusion of the first year of the war?

Holland has been saved; the importance of this event in the present situation of Europe may be estimated by the designs which France has uniformly entertained against that country since the time of her success in the Netherlands. Robespierre, lamenting that Dumourier did not invade Holland immediately after the conquest of the Netherlands, says, "If we had invaded Holland, we should have become masters of the Dutch navy; the wealth of that country would have been blended with our own, her power added to that of France, the Government of England would have been undone, and the Revolution of Europe secured." The nature of the Revolution intended in Holland is now well known. When the invasion of that country was projected, Cambon is said to have declared, that "as the Dutch had no church lands to offer France for her indemnification in the war, the Dutch Revolution must be made on new principles; it must be a revolution of strong boxes and purses." The decree which passed about the time Dumourier entered Holland is a sufficient commentary on this expression; it shews, that if the French had succeeded in that expedition, they would have struck the most fatal blow that commercial credit has ever received.

But the protection of Holland was of great importance in another view. From the moment that France had declared war against the Dutch, Dumourier repeatedly states, that the conquest of Holland was essentially necessary for the purpose of maintaining the possession of the Netherlands in the hands of the French; he says, that "without Holland the Netherlands must soon fall; and with Holland he entertained no doubt of being able to oppose an effectual barrier to the progress of the Austrian and Prussian armies." The recovery of the Netherlands therefore was intimately connected with the protection of Holland. Whatever opposition was made to the force under the command of Dumourier in Holland, must in this view of the subject be considered as a combined operation with the attack of the Prince of Saxe-Cobourg upon the armies of Valence and Miranda on the banks of the Roer and of the Meuse. It is certain, that the brillant successes of the Austrians would have been at least retarded, if the gallant defence of Williamstadt and of the passage of the Maese had not changed the progress of Dumourier, and prevented him from effecting a junction with the armies opposed to the Prince of Cobourg at an earlier period, and under circumstances of greater advantage. It is unnecessary to state, that the seasonable assistance afforded by this country to the Dutch, was *alone* the circumstance which encouraged and enabled them to make so vigorous an effort in that critical conjuncture of their affairs. The recovery of Flanders, thus connected on the one hand with the defence of Holland, was on the other hand an object of equal importance to the permanent security of the Dutch frontier. It was also material to the prosecution of the war in many other respects. It deprived our enemies of resources, which, according to the account given by Cambon, were become necessary to the support of their declining finances, and added what was thus taken from them to the strength of our Allies. Brissot says, that "the evacuation of Belgium tarnished the glory of the French arms, and retarded" what he calls "the liberty of Europe." The Netherlands recovered under such circumstances have not only been maintained throughout the campaign, but an impression has been made upon the frontier of France by the capture of Valenciennes, Condé, and Quesnoy. Against these successes are to be set the raising of the sieges of Dunkirk and Maubeuge. Making the utmost allowance for each of those failures, and comparing the circumstances of our situation on the side of Holland and Flanders in the month of February, 1793, with their actual state, it cannot be denied, that the campaign in Flanders has been productive of the most considerable acquisitions both in point of territory and resource, which this country and her allies ever obtained in that quarter in any single year of our most prosperous wars. On the Rhine the recapture of Mentz, and the progress made in Alsace after the distinguished action of Weissembourg, afforded effectual protection to the frontier of Germany during the greater part of the campaign, and operated as a powerful diversion of the force of the enemy. Notwithstanding the sudden irruption of the French by means of the requisition of the mass of the people (a measure, the effects of which upon the internal situation of France I shall have occasion to examine more particularly before I sit down), our general situation is far more favourable than at the opening of the campaign. Although the French have regained a considerable part of the country from which they had been driven in the course of the summer, they have as yet been contending with us for our conquests, and not for any advantages which they did not possess before the commencement of the war. While our allies retain Mentz, it must be admitted, that after all the extraordinary exertions of the enemy their situation is much more disadvantageous than it was in the month of July. In the territories of the King of Sardinia the French have made no additional progress. On the side of Spain they have suffered considerable losses. The blockade of the French fleet in the port of Toulon, by an inferior force, was highly creditable to the naval honour of this country; and in the circumstances attending the evacuation of that town, one of the most severe blows was given to the naval power of France which has ever been struck in the whole history of our marine, and the command of the Mediterranean was at once transferred from the hands of France into our own. If the fleets of the enemy have offered no opportunity to our's of obtaining any brilliant success, let us compare the actual state of our trade and commerce with those gloomy predictions to which I have already alluded, and with the captures made from the enemy. On this subject I must again refer to the authority of Brissot, which is corroborated by our own accounts: he says, "In the month of March all our privateers were destroyed by the English in the Channel. In the month of April our trading vessels were taken by English frigates at the very mouths of our rivers: our ships could not go into the Mediterranean without danger; and yet we had a fleet there of 15 ships of the line."

If we look to the result of the campaign abroad, the prospect is equally favourable; the fishery of Newfoundland, from which the French have been driven, has always been considered as a most valuable object; we know that it has formed one of the most contested articles in most of our negociations of peace since the commencement of the present century: the acquisition of this fishery in the first campaign of the war must operate as a material check to one source of the naval power of France. In the West Indies, the importance of the Island of Tobago, which we have acquired, may be estimated, when we recollect, that it was the only one of all her conquests which France retained at the peace of 1783, after the calamities of the American war. In the island of St. Domingo we are in possession of Nicola Mole, the most advantageous post with a view to the command of the windward passage, and of Jeremie, the part of the island which has suffered the least from the ravages of Brissot's commissioners. In the East Indies, the French have been expelled from all their possessions, excepting Pondicherry, the capture of which could not (according to the latest advices) long be delayed. The acquisition of the fort of Mahé on the coast of Malabar is of the greatest advantage to our new territories on that coast, both with a view to the commerce and good government of those countries; in a political view it is obviously of considerable importance that the French should not continue to hold a possession which afforded them the means of so direct and easy an intercourse with Tippoo Sultan.

Thus, Sir, I have endeavoured to give a summary view of the events of the campaign; it does not belong to me to enter into any reply to the critical observations which have been made upon the conduct of particular expeditions, or upon the general disposition and application of our naval and military force. That argument will not be declined by those whose situation in his Majesty's Councils renders them most competent to treat it with effect. But from what lies within the observation of every man, we may collect that the general result of the last campaign has not only exceeded our first expectations, but including all the advantages which the combined armies have obtained on the continent of Europe, including the blow which has been struck against the naval power of France, and the acquisitions which we have made both in the East and West Indies and at Newfoundland, the general result of the last campaign has not been surpassed in effective advantage either with a view to indemnity, to ultimate security, or to the intermediate means of distressing the enemy during the continuance of the war by any campaign in which this country has been engaged since the revolution. And in this part of the argument it must never be forgotten that this is the first campaign of the war. No man would attempt to deny that such a success as we have obtained in the course of this year against France, would have been deemed of decisive importance in the most brilliant periods of the French monarchy. If therefore our success is now to be undervalued, it must be from an opinion that under the present circumstances and situation of France, her resources are so inexhaustible, her strength is so absolutely unconquerable, that what would have been esteemed a promising impression against any other state that ever existed, and against herself in other times, must now be considered as wholly nugatory and ineffectual. Let us examine whether we have any reasonable ground to apprehend that this enemy, whom we know to be so formidable, is really invincible; let us not be deterred by the magnitude of her temporary exertions from looking closely into the means by which they have been supported; let us search the real foundations of her apparent strength, and comparing them with the nature and sources of our own power, let us decide upon the true and solid principles of political economy, and upon the established maxims of all human government, whether both the probability of our ultimate success, and the necessity of our present exertions are not greatly increased by the extraordinary and unprecedented character of that system under which the powers of Government are now exercised in France.

At the entrance of this arduous and extensive argument I feel myself embarrassed by two difficulties of a very opposite kind :—To apply to the Government now prevailing in France the epithets which such a scene would naturally suggest; to call it a system of rapine, extortion, and fraud, under the colour of a lawful revenue; of arbitrary imprisonment under the false pretence of liberty; of murder under the name of justice; a system which unites despotism with anarchy, and atheism with persecution, and to adduce no particular facts and proofs in support of such a charge, might well be deemed idle declamation and empty invective: on the other hand, to attempt to bring before you all the shocking and disgusting scenes by which every part of this charge might be confirmed, would lead to a detail wholly unfit for the ears of a British House of Commons. I shall endeavour with the utmost care to avoid both these extremes; but if, from the very nature of the dreadful transactions on which it is my duty to comment, I should sometimes fall into either, the indulgence of the House will not be refused either to the natural sentiment of indignation which the view of such crimes must excite, or to my anxiety to draw from them conclusions which may be justly and usefully applied to the subject of our present deliberation. It is my intention to advert only to such of the fundamental principles, and of the leading branches of this monstrous system of Government, as will furnish the most certain grounds for any possible estimate of its real force, and of its probable duration. But although every fact which I shall adduce will be directed to this particular point of the argument in the first instance from the same facts, other considerations will arise, and other conclusions will be drawn not less applicable in my opinion to the general question of this day.

The same circumstances which explain the nature of that power with which we have to contend, will also explain the causes of whatever difficulties we may have encountered in the contest, and enable us to judge whether they are to be surmounted by perseverance : the same circumstances will also serve to shew whether the further extension of the system now prevalent in France is to be considered as a matter of indifference, or as an object of terror by the other powers of Europe, and particularly by Great Britain; and whether it be or be not an essential and inherent quality of that system to extend itself abroad, as the only security for its existence at home. These and other inferences will be made from whatever detail I may be permitted to lay before you, in endeavouring to give you a faithful picture of the true state and condition of France at the present moment.

On the 31st of May, a revolution took place in the Government of France, as extraordinary in its circumstances, and as sudden and violent in its effects, as any of those convulsions by which that unhappy country has been afflicted at any period of the late disturbances. By a repetition of precisely the same violences which had been used to bring about all the former revolutions, through the terror which the Jacobin Club inspired, and by the absolute dominion which the Municipality of Paris has invariably exercised over the pretended National Assemblies, a few individuals of no distinguished talents, of the most desperate and profligate characters, despised until that moment even in France for the wild extravagance of their principles, and detested even there for their sanguinary and vindictive spirit, drove from the government a powerful majority of the Convention, consisting of men who, although equally guilty of the crimes and calamities of their country, were at least supported by whatever remained of landed or commercial interest in the nation, by a great majority of the departments, and by all the principal cities and manufacturing towns. Above an hundred and forty members of the Convention were expelled by force from their seats in one day; many of them were immediately imprisoned, and since that time, those who have not perished on the scaffold, have either fled the country or destroyed themselves, from the terror of suffering the same indignity and cruelties which they had already exercised on others, and which they would have exercised on their present antagonists, if the victory in this desperate contest had taken a different inclination.

I shall not dwell in this place upon the instability of any engagement which could have been entered into with a Government subject from its nature to such sudden, total, and repeated changes, both of men and of measures ; I will only request you to bear this general observation in mind, and to apply to it a subsequent part of the argument.

The party which had triumphed by such means, recollecting that the Convention had been chosen for the express purpose of new-modelling the Constitution, although little or no progress had been hitherto made in that work, hastily, in the course of three weeks after their accession to power, put forth a most extraordinary production under the title of a new Constitution.

This new version of the natural rights of man contains a digest of every visionary notion of political liberty which has appeared in the speculations of the most wild of all the French philosophers, mixed with some principles and regulations which bear the appearance of regard for the lives, liberties, and properties of the people. Whatever may be the absurdities of this system, it at least serves to shew what were the principles of Government which the present rulers of France asserted to be not only indispensably necessary to the happiness of the people, but founded in strict right; and in this view it may be a matter of curiosity to compare this Constitution with the subsequent measures of those who framed it. Not only the extravagant principle of individual suffrage, but its natural consequence, the principle of individual legislation, were enacted in their fullest extent; the laws were to be submitted to the sanction of the primary assemblies, and to derive their validity and binding force from the individual assent of above twenty millions of men. It was particularly enacted, that all regulations affecting civil and criminal justice, the nature, amount, and collection of public contributions, and all alterations in the current coin or circulating medium, should require the previous sanction of the whole collective body of the people; certain objects of inferior importance were to be determined by the decrees of the representative body without any reference to their constituents; the representative body was to be changed annually; the Executive Council, in which was solely vested whatever executive authority was suffered to remain in the state, was to be selected by the Convention from a list framed by the electoral assemblies of the people, one half of which list was to be renewed every six months; the municipal officers were to be chosen absolutely by the people in the departments. In order to render the administration of criminal justice independent of the executive or legislative authority, it was enacted, that the judges in all the ordinary courts of justice should be annually chosen by the electoral assemblies; and that there should be a court of general appeal, the judges of which should be elected in the same manner. Certain leading principles were solemnly recognised both in the declaration of rights and in the concluding part of the Constitution, which is entitled the guarantee of the rights of man—these principles were, "that no man should be judged and punished until he had been heard; that punishments should bear a due proportion to crimes; that the right of property was that right which belongs to every citizen, of enjoying and disposing of according to his pleasure his goods, his income, the fruits of his labour and of his industry; that no person could be deprived of the least portion of his property without his own consent, unless under the pressure of a public necessity legally proved, and under the condition of a just and previous indemnity; that the right of petitioning ought in no case to be interdicted, suspended, or limited; that the people have always the right to review, reform, and change the Constitution; and finally, that the Constitution guarantees to the whole people of France liberty, safety, property, the public debt, the free exercise of religious worship, the right of petitioning, and the right of assembling in popular societies." And for the better security of the people against any violation of these rights and privileges, it was declared, "that the oppression of a single member of the society was to be deemed the oppression of the whole body; and that whenever the Government should violate the rights of the people, insurrection became both the most sacred right, and the most indispensable duty not only of the people at large, but of every portion and division of them."

This formal recognition of some principles of incontestible truth, mingled with many of the most incoherent dreams, and many of the most pernicious doctrines which ever occurred to the most enthusiastic zealot, or to the most wicked conspirator in the cause of absolute and unqualified democracy, was tendered to the people in the several departments for their acceptance; and, if we are to believe the reports made to the Convention, was actually accepted by a large majority. The acceptance of this model of perfection, which was to secure for ever the happiness and prosperity of France, was solemnly celebrated by a civic feast on a day aptly chosen for such a ceremony, on the anniversary of the massacre of the 10th of August, when the last Constitution to which the people of France had sworn was overthrown by force, when magistrates were murdered for executing the laws, citizens for defending property, and troops for obeying the orders of those to whom by law they owed obedience. But mark the sequel of this solemnity. The dissolution of the Convention, the necessary and immediate consequence of this new Constitution, would have destroyed the power of the now reigning party: many other branches of this Constitution would have been equally incompatible with the duration of their authority: not only therefore those articles which related to the form of the executive power and to the election of the legislature were left unexecuted, but the whole Municipal Constitution, and every article in any degree favourable to personal liberty, to life, or to property, were continually violated without scruple and without disguise. Until the 10th of October, the entire system of the indefeasible inalienable rights of man, from which nothing can derogate, which admit of no modifications of expediency, which neither bend to times nor circumstances, nor even to the practical happiness of society, was formally and openly suspended; and in defiance of the sovereign people, a new and unheard-of species of government was established, which, growing out of the theory of impracticable liberty, was to be maintained by the practice of the most unmitigated tyranny. A decree was passed, by which the whole executive authority of the state was thrown into the hands of the Committee of Public Welfare. Provision was made for the rapid execution of what are termed revolutionary laws, and for the direction and employment of a revolutionary army, in order to repress every symptom of a counter-revolutionary spirit; and among the great fundamental articles of this counter-constitution, it was decreed, that the corn and grain in the several departments should be seized at the discretion of the new Government; and that garrisons should be placed in all counter-revolutionary towns, to be paid and maintained at the sole charge of persons of property. This decree was proposed expressly for the purpose of punishing " not traitors only, but even those who dared to be indifferent to the cause of the existing Government, who had the audacity to be passive, and to do nothing for the sovereignty of the people:" it was said, "that such persons must be governed by the sword, since it was impossible to govern them by the maxims of justice:" it was said, "that the Constitution of the 10th of August, 1793, was not sufficiently violent to repress such dangerous attempts against liberty :" it was said, "that revolutionary laws could never be executed, unless the government itself was constituted in a revolutionary manner." Such was the origin, and such is the form of that monster in politics, of which, as the very notion involves a contradiction of ideas, the name cannot be expressed without a contradiction in terms,—a *Revolutionary Government !* a Government which, for the ordinary administration of affairs, resorts to those means of violence and outrage which had been hitherto considered, even in France, as being exclusively appropriated to the laudable and sacred purpose of subverting all lawful and regular authority. The sense of the epithet *revolutionary*, which is so lavishly applied by the Convention to every part of this new system, requires some explanation. An extract from the proceedings of the National Convention will serve to exemplify the manner in which that singular phrase is understood and admired by the most unquestionable authority in the science of revolutions. Barrere makes a report respecting the situation of the Republic in the month of December, he reads a variety of despatches from the National Commissioners in various parts of the Republic, and at length he produces a letter from Carrier, one of the Commissioners of the Convention, dated Nantz, December the 10th. This letter, after giving an account of a successful attack against the Royalists, concludes with the following remarkable words : "This event has been followed by another, which has however nothing new in its nature. Fifty-eight individuals, known by the name of Refractory Priests, arrived at Nantz from Angers. They were shut up in a barge on the river Loire, and last night they were all sunk to the bottom of that river. What a revolutionary torrent is the Loire !"—You expect perhaps to hear, that the disgusting relation of this inhuman action raised some emotions of horror, if not of compassion in the audience ; you expect to hear, that the Convention manifested their resentment at this abuse of the revolutionary language ; but does any symptom of such sentiments appear ?—No ! after having listened to this *interesting* report, the Convention votes the following resolution :—" The National Convention, highly satisfied with the report of Barrere, orders it to be printed, inserted in the Votes, and sent to all the armies."

Highly satisfied with this figurative illustration of the style and title of that gracious and mild Government which they had so lately instituted, they order it to be proclaimed and published over the whole territory of the Republic, to conciliate the affections of a free people, and to animate the enthusiasm of a brave and generous army. Here you learn the full force and energy of their new phraseology. The Loire is a revolutionary torrent because it has been found an useful and expeditious instrument of massacre, because it has destroyed by a sudden and violent death fifty-eight men, against whom no crime was alleged but the venerable character of their sacred function, and their faithful adherence to the principles of their religion. But this event is truly said to have nothing new in its nature ; I dwell upon it for the application of the phrase, not for the singularity of the fact : every proceeding since the commencement of the troubles in France which has been dignified by the title of Revolutionary is marked with similar characters of violence or blood. The seizure of the property of the clergy and of the nobility was a Revolutionary measure ;—the assassinations of Foulon and Berthier at Paris, and of the King's guards at Versailles in the year 1789 were Revolutionary measures : all the succeding outrages, the burning of the title-deeds and country houses of all gentlemen of landed property, the numberless confiscations, banishments, proscriptions, and murders of innocent persons—all these were Revolutionary measures—the massacres of the 10th of August, and of the 2nd of September—the attempt to extend the miseries of civil discord over the whole world, the more successful project of involving all Europe in the calamities of a general war, were *truly* Revolutionary measures ;—the insulting mockery of a pretended trial, to which they subjected their humane and benevolent Sovereign, and the horrid cruelty of his unjust, precipitate, and execrable murder, were *most* Revolutionary measures : it has been the art of the ruling faction of the present hour to compound and to consolidate the substance of all these dreadful transactions in one mass, to concentrate all their noxious principles, and by a new process to extract from them a spirit, which combines the malignity of each with the violence of all, and that is the true spirit of a Revolutionary Government.

Some of the general principles and fundamental maxims maintained by the founders of this Government are so curious, that it is impossible to pass them over in silence. They represent, that in a revolutionary state *civil liberty* (including the personal freedom, the interests, and the happiness of individuals) is but a secondary object, the principal end of such a Government being (what they call) *public liberty*, which, according to their definition, does not consist in the personal freedom of individuals, but in the unrestrained and arbitrary exercise of the Supreme Executive Power. They assert that under the existing circumstances *liberty must be considered to be in a state of war*, not with foreign powers merely, but with her numerous enemies in the bosom of the Republic : it follows as a consequence of this principle, that those who act under the commission of liberty may for her sake imprison, plunder, and destroy by the sword the inhabitants of France, according to the rights of war as exercised by belligerent powers in an enemy's country. This abstract idea of liberty at war with the properties, the lives, and the personal freedom of the people however incomprehensible to a nation accustomed to feel the practical and substantial advantages of a free constitution, is the favourite doctrine of Robespierre, to which the Convention has subscribed with the warmest zeal : connected with this is the main and leading maxim upon which their whole system turns : it is expressed in terms which, although originally derived from the proceedings of this House, will appear to you, Sir, somewhat singular in their application ; it is, " that terror should be the order of the day ;" and that (for the purpose of enforcing a general observance of this order) " the salutary movement of terror should be circulated from one extremity of the Republic to the other by means of a rapid execution of the Revolutionary laws." Here then you perceive that terror is not only the avowed instrument but the sole end of what in this new system is called by the name of law. The Government openly renounces the antiquated error of founding itself in the affections, the interests, and the happiness of the people, and publicly declares with a boldness unparalleled in the history of usurpation, that it neither possesses, nor expects, nor desires any other security for the maintenance of its power than abject fear, and general consternation.

To diffuse this consternation as widely as possible, and to remove every obstacle to the rapid circulation of that sentiment which was so essentially necessary to the vigour and action of the administration, an operation was performed, which may be considered as the preliminary step to the general introduction of the whole plan. In open violation of the principles solemnly sanctioned in the Constitution, whereby the absolute choice of the municipal officers is reserved to the people, Commissioners were sent into every city, town, and village of France, *to regenerate the municipalities ;* that is, to substitute in the place of municipal officers, chosen by the inhabitants under their forms of election, other officers named according to the sole and arbitrary will of these commissioners.

But even this was not sufficient ; the right of assembling in popular societies, which had been deemed of such importance, as to hold a place in that part of the constitution which is entitled *the guarantee of the rights of man*, being found inconvenient in a Revolutionary state, was also set aside without scruple ; and the same commissioners had orders to *regenerate all the popular societies.* This work of regeneration was performed differently according to the exigency of the particular case ; in some places the obnoxious persons were imprisoned, in others they were executed, and in all they were replaced, as I have already stated, by persons named at the discretion of the Commissioners. In many instances however the aversion to the new tyranny was found so obstinate and incurable, that the Commissioners were actually obliged to send to Paris for good Sans Culottes warranted by the Jacobin Club, and to appoint them to fill the municipal offices and the popular societies. The extract which I shall now read from a letter of one of these Commissioners, will give a summary view of this extraordinary stretch of arbitrary power, and of the principles with which it was connected :—"Herault Schelles, in a letter dated Plotzheim, Nov. the 27th, gave an account of his measures for restoring the Republican spirit in the department of the Upper Rhine. He had regenerated the popular societies and committees ; organized the movement of terror ; created a central Committee of Revolutionary activity ; detached a Revolutionary force from the army to traverse the whole department ; erected a Revolutionary tribunal ; and was preparing a feast, and celebrity of reason, a remarkable conquest in that part of the country over profound ignorance and inveterate fanaticism." Thus, Sir, was erected a Government, which in its form, in its avowed principles, and in its general spirit is not only incompatible with the existence of all just and rational liberty, but directly contradictory to all those opinions which have been so industriously inculcated in France, and to every doctrine which has been (to use their own phrase) consecrated in either the new or the old version of the Rights of Man. Thus was established, and thus is now exercised a Government, which is, in the strictest sense of the words, the most atrocious and the most degrading tyranny that has ever trampled on the liberties, and sported with the happiness of a great nation.

If this description seems to be exaggerated, look at the practice, look at the details of this Government ! View its operation and effect upon all those means, by which the great ends of civil society are to be accomplished !

Enquire from what sources and through what channels it draws the public revenue ? how it affects the systems of agriculture and commerce ? with what attention to the internal prosperity of the country it levies and maintains the public force ? what provision it makes for the pure and equal administration of justice ? how it regards religion, that great basis of every moral and civil duty ? and as the result of all these considerations what is the real condition of all the inhabitants of France, with respect to the security of liberty, of property, and of life ? and consequently, what must be the disposition and temper of the people ? what the permanent strength of the state under all its actual circumstances ? and what the stability of that power, which now menaces, and holds at defiance the united force of Europe ?

At the accession of the Revolutionary Government, the expenditure of France stood, as far as can be gathered from an account of three months at the end of the year 1792, at the enormous rate of twelve millions sterling per month. The resources of the country had already been greatly injured by former mismanagement · agriculture and internal trade had already suffered by the first attempts towards the establishment of that gigantic system of military force, which has since been carried to such an excess ; foreign commerce had already much declined ; and both public and private credit had been greatly embarrassed by the quantity of assignats in circulation ; an evil of such magnitude, that even as early as the month of November, 1792, the plunder of the Netherlands was proposed by the Minister of Finance, as the only remedy which could avert the impending danger.

Since the revolution of the 31st of May the expenditure has been so much encreased that according even to the accounts laid before the Convention itself, the expence of the month of August was above *eighteen millions sterling* : and there is reason to believe that the real charges of the succeeding months may have exceeded that sum. But as the *levée en masse*, or compulsory levy of the mass of the people took place about that time, by which it is stated that five hundred thousand additional men have been raised, the maintenance of so vast an army must be such an encreased charge, as seems to justify the supposition that eighteen millions sterling may be taken as the average of the present monthly expenditure of the Revolutionary Government. This would make an *annual expenditure of two hundred and sixteen millions sterling*, a sum which nearly approaches to the amount of the whole national debt of England.*

The total ordinary revenue of France before the war was stated to be about 600 millions, or about 25 millions sterling, arising from duties on imports, taxes upon real and personal property, stamp duties, and duties on registry of deeds, bills of exchange, notes of hand, &c.

The total collective income of all the individuals in France is stated in the financial reports of the present Government to be one hundred and twenty millions sterling, of which one-third is said to arise from commerce; so that if the account here given be correct, (and there is every reason to credit it,) it appears that the annual expenditure of the Government of France at present exceeds the total collective income of the individuals of the country by the enormous sum of 96 millions sterling: or, in other words, that there is an annual waste of ninety-six millions of the aggregate capital of France by the expenditure of the government alone, besides what is consumed by the expenditure of private individuals. To supply an expenditure infinitely exceeding the prodigality and extravagance of any government that ever yet appeared in the world, the Revolutionary Government had recourse at first to the practice of encreasing the mass of paper money. They declared, that they had no other means of sustaining the pressure of the present war, than by the creation of an additional quantity of assignats upon the pledge of the *National Property* ; consisting of the ancient church lands, the estates of the Crown, the resumed grants or sales of Crown lands, and the estates real and personal of the emigrants, and of all persons executed for state crimes. But they have been compelled to confess, that this resource of assignats cannot be available to any thing like the extent to which it was carried by their predecessors; and both from their language and their measures there is every reason to believe that they are convinced it cannot long be available at all. There is not a single speech or report upon the subject of finance, in which the quantity of assignats already in circulation is not represented as a grievance of the most urgent nature. In one of the reports they declare, that assignats are become their only instrument of commerce and measure of value; they give them the favourite title of *Revolutionary Money;* and then they describe their effect, which is indeed of the genuine revolutionary character; they say, " *assignats grind the poor, cheat the rich, foment avarice, and nourish every species of ruinous speculation.*"†

Upon this reasoning, they determine that it is absolutely necessary to diminish

---

* The deficiency between the total receipt of revenue, ordinary and extraordinary, and the total expenditure of France, according to the monthly accounts was, in French livres—For April, 1793, 460,000,000; May, 315,000,000; June, 192,000,000; July, 253,000,000; August, 400,000,000; September, supposed from encreased expence, 400,000,000; total, £2,020,000,000. This makes the deficiency for a year, upon a computation drawn from six months from April to September at the exchange of 30, or 10*d*. English per French livre—about £166,640,000. sterling.

† The total number of assignats created, has been—5,100,000,000; en caisse, on the 1st of May, 485,000,000; issued about 4,615,000,000; burnt to 1st of August, 840,000,000, remained, 3,775,000,000; royal assignats demonetisés, 558,000,000;

the quantity of assignats in circulation, and they enter upon a variety of projects and experiments for that purpose, which together form a system of finance so absurd and iniquitous in its principle, and so rapidly destructive in its operation, that its existence, in an age conversant with every question of political economy would be incredible, if it were not capable of proof by reference to the authentic reports of the several committees, and to the decrees of the Convention. One of their first steps was to forbid, under the colour of a Republican zeal for the extinction of every trace and vestige of the monarchy, the circulation of all assignats of above an hundred livres bearing the image of the late King. This outrageous act of public fraud is attempted to be justified by a most singular train of reasoning. Twelve or fifteen hundred millions of livres, (that is, about 50 or 60 millions sterling) they say, are due on account of arrears by the purchasers of national domains; and six or seven hundred millions of livres (that is, from 25 to 30 millions sterling) are due on account of arrears of taxes; they therefore permit these *dismonied** assignats, as they call them, to be received at the public treasury in payment of either of these classes of arrears, provided such payment be made before the 1st of January, 1794.† It is evident that this relief could have only a partial operation; it makes no provision whatever for the case of that numerous description of persons who might be in possession of royal assignats of above the value of an hundred livres, and yet might not be indebted to the public treasury to that amount. But this was followed by a proceeding still more violent; on the 14th of December it appeared that there remained royal assignats of above 100 livres outstanding to the amount of 178 millions of livres, a sum exceeding seven millions sterling. Cambon, in reporting upon the subject treats this sum as a mere trifle; he adds, that none but aristocrats could at that period be the holders of royal assignats, and no body could feel any regret at seeing them perish in such hands; besides, the Republic would gain 50 or 60 millions (or about 2,500,000l. sterling) by this new operation. Upon this ground, a decree passed on the 14th of December, declaring that after the 1st of January 1794 no royal assignat of above an hundred livres shall either be circulated or received in the treasury on any account; that all holders of any such assignats after that day shall be bound to bring them to the municipalities to be burnt; and that after the 1st of February any holder of such an assignat shall be deemed a suspected person, and exposed to the vengeance of the Republic. This decree can be considered as nothing less than a direct act of bankruptcy; to what precise amount must have depended on the value of the assignats paid into the treasury between the 14th of December 1793 the day on which the decree passed, and the 1st of January 1794 the time limited for receiving such assignats at the treasury. Cambon states the gain to the Republic would be about 25,000,000l. sterling. We may therefore at least take the amount of the bankruptcy of the Republic upon his calculation.

The next proceeding which I have to state is of a still more extraordinary complexion: on the 24th of August 1793, a subscription was opened for a loan at 4 per cent. interest for the purpose of taking up assignats. This loan was called by a singular epithet the *voluntary* loan, to contra-distinguish it from the *forced* loan, by the plan of which it is accompanied in the same report, although the details of

---

in circulation on the 1st day of August, 1793, 3,217,000,000; or above 130 millions sterling.

N. B. This sum is exclusive of forged assignats to a great amount.

* Demonetisés.

† This decree passed on the 31st of August, 1793.

that plan were not formally enacted until the 3d of September. Few or no voluntary subscribers having appeared, (as might naturally be expected in a country
where there is no public credit, and no security for any property, and least of all
for any property in the public funds,) the companion of the voluntary loan was
now brought forward, and a decree was passed, exacting from the people of France
a *forced loan* of one milliard, or forty millions sterling, being one-third of the total
collective annual income of all the individuals in France according to the statement of the Convention itself. The object of this measure is stated expressly to
be to diminish the mass of assignats, and to bind the rich citizen to the fate and
to the success of the revolution. This loan is to be levied on " all income arising
from property in the public funds, from private annuities, from interest of capital
employed in commerce, in banking, or generally in profitable business of any
kind. But this is not enough ; even what is called *idle capital* is not exempt.
Idle capital is defined to be " any sum exceeding his half-yearly income, which an
egotist may have laid by either in his strong box, or at his banker's, or in the hands
of persons indebted to him." This unproductive property is estimated to produce
five per cent. interest, and according to that rate is to be reputed as income, and
to be made liable to the tax: any profit made upon capital employed before the
year 1793 is also be rated at five per cent. and subjected to the tax. A commission
is appointed to ascertain every man's income, and every man is bound to give in
the name and dwelling-place of all his creditors. No interest is allowed upon this
forced loan, and no part of it is to be repaid until the term of two years after the
peace, when attested receipts of payments on account of the loan are to be admitted
in the purchase of national domains. The rate of this tax is as follows : on all
yearly income not exceeding a thousand livres, or forty pounds sterling, one-tenth
is to be taken. The tax then encreases progressively one-tenth upon each one
thousand livres, or forty pounds sterling, until where the income reaches ten thousand livres, or four hundred pounds sterling, two hundred and twenty pounds are
absorbed by the tax. All income *above four hundred pounds sterling is to be taken
absolutely and entirely* ; so that the first basis of calculation on which this measure
is founded is, that for the present year no man in France shall have an income of
more than one hundred and eighty pounds.*

There are however certain deductions allowed to bachelors 40*l.* income free
from the tax, to every married man 60*l.* and the *ample* allowance of forty pounds
for the maintenance of his wife, and the same for each of his children ; and all
those who may choose to take charge of an old man, or of the wife or child of a
defender of the country are to be allowed the same addition of forty pounds free
income. What may be the expence of maintaining the wife or child of a defender
of the country is difficult to compute ; probably the intention of this regulation
was to afford a pretext to the Jacobins and to their friends for evading this grievous
tax. I leave it to the House to decide, what the operation of this tax must be
upon the higher classes affected by it ; and what relief it would be to a man† of

---

* The tax is calculated as follows in sterling money :

Income.—1st, 40*l.*; Tax.—4*l.*   Do. 2d, 40*l.* ; do. 8*l.*   Do. 3d, 40*l.*; do. 12*l.*
Do. 4th, 40*l.*; do. 16*l.*   Do. 5th, 40*l.* ; do. 20*l.*   Do. 6th, 40*l.*; do. 24*l.*   Do. 7th,
40*l.* ; do. 28*l.*   Do. 8th, 40*l.* ; do. 32*l.*   Do. 9th, 40*l.* ; do. 36*l.* Do. 10th, 40*l.*;
do. 40*l.*—Total Income 400*l.*   Total Tax, 220*l.*—180 Remainder.   The whole sur-
plus income above 400*l.* goes to the tax.

† In the model of the declaration of income annexed to the decree, the form is
drawn for a married citizen of 5,800*l.* a year, arising from landed property, an-

ten, of five, or of one thousand pounds a year who should be reduced, at one blow to an income of one hundred and eighty pounds; to be allowed forty pounds for the maintenance of his wife, and the same sum for each of his children. In reasoning upon this part of the question the Convention declare, that they would not have "confiscated the whole income beyond four hundred pounds, if this measure were to be permanent; because it could never enter into their views to place any bounds to the emulation, or to the industry of the people; but it was their object, leaving to every man the enjoyment of the fruits of his labour, to reduce to the level of equality by* *gentle* ways those fortunes which had risen above it." They add, however, "that it is indeed true, that this measure will be very partial in its operation; it must fall most heavily on men of property; but they deserve no mercy; if they have the obstinacy to hoard up their unproductive capital in their coffers, they must suffer the penalties due to such a robbery committed against the rights of society, and against the beneficial circulation of cash; for what is the injury to egotists in the forced loan? Let them carry their money to the voluntary loan before the month of January; it will be received in discharge of the sums due on account of the forced loan, and interest will accrue upon it, payable at the convenience of the state. In this light the forced loan is a benefit to egotists; although it may restrain their luxury for a time, it compels them to draw a profit from their idle capital; and economy is a virtue which ought above all others to be cherished in a Republic."

Here, Sir, is such an advantageous proposal, as was never before made to men of property of all descriptions: those who have large incomes arising from landed estates, property in the funds, or capital profitably employed, are *invited* to pay in the course of four months, nearly the whole anticipated receipt of twelve into the public treasury on account of the voluntary loan, and are assured, that the time will come, when they shall receive interest for their money. Those monied men, who from motives of prudence, have not thought fit to embark their property in the uncertain funds of a distracted state, are also *invited on the ground of economy,* to pay into the treasury on account of the voluntary loan, 5 per cent. upon that which produces them nothing at the risk of entirely sinking the sum so advanced, and upon the faith of a precarious and illusory promise, that they shall receive in the interval a per centage insufficient to indemnify them for their immediate loss.

But if any person should be so negligent of his own interests, and so forgetful of the true principles of domestic economy as to reject this invitation to contribute all his means of present subsistence to the voluntary loan before the month of January, he is compelled to pay the whole to the forced loan by the month of March, without the prospect of receiving any interest at all, or of being repaid his principal until the period of two years after the peace: and if he should not be able to pay the sum at which he is rated, by the month of March, his property is liable to seizure, and when the sum is levied, he forfeits it absolutely to the state, and entirely loses his right of repayment. Thus (say the Commissioners of Finance in their report on this subject) "the forced loan allies itself with the volun-

_____

nuities in the funds, capital employed in commerce, in contracts with government, &c. He is supposed to support his father, wife, a child, an old man, and the child of a defender of the country; he is charged for the tax the sum of 5,420*l.* Remainder 380*l.* The payment to the forced loan does not exempt any man from the taxes which have been imposed for some time on all real and personal property, and which are very heavy.

* Voies douces.

tary loan; thus these two salutary operations are intimately mixed and blended together, and reciprocally support each other. Such are the measures which ought to date their origin from the epoch of a constitution, which consecrates and guarantees the true principles of society. The legislators have recorded in the first article of their decree upon the forced loan their homage to the constitutional principle of respect for property; for by this tax they only take every man's income, and by allowing him to retain his capital they leave him all that he possessed in reality before." These, Sir, are the gentle ways of equality; these are the lessons by which the people of France have learnt the intimate and natural alliance between compulsion and consent, and this is the nature of that hommage which the revolutionary government has paid to the rights of property in this great financial operation. Notwithstanding that the public debt had been gua-- ranteed by the constitution of the 10th of August, 1793, the funds,* are by this scheme subjected to tax; the fundamental principle of the whole commercial system, which consists in the application of the profits of one year to support the enterprizes of the next, is overturned at one blow by this violent confiscation of so large a proportion of the annual income arising from profitable capital. The injustice and mischief of this project in its general operation on other branches of property have sufficiently appeared in explaining the regulations and doctrines on which the decree is founded. The effects of so sudden and violent a reduction of income in all the classes above 400l. a year, must extend equally to all the lower classes† also; it must be as severely felt by the poor, as by the rich who are the immediate objects of the exaction. All the servants, dependants, tradesmen, workmen or labourers, who have been used to draw their maintenance either from the benevolence, or from the necessary demands of such persons of property, must instantly be ruined by the failure of that source from which they derive their only means of subsistance. The only just observation in the whole course of the voluminous reports on this measure is, *that it is not of a nature to be renewed;* it is evident, that whatever might be its produce in the first year, such must be its rapid and ruinous effects, that even if it were to be renewed in another year, it could not be productive.

It was stated by Cambon, late in the month of November, that although this tax

---

* The forced and voluntary loans were accompanied by a decree for consolidating the public debt; this was done by compelling all the public creditors to enter their demands in one book, and by confounding every class of them, so that the order and priority of their claims on the state might not be distinguishable hereafter. Thus it was said "the debt will be *republicanised,*" and it is added, "this operation of *republicanising* the debt will facilitate the means of *taxing it;*" these measures together, namely the voluntary loan, the forced loan, the republican debt, and the taxed funds are called by the commissioners "a *Jubilee of Revolutionary Finance.*"

† By referring to the scale of this tax it will be seen that the distress would be scarcely less felt by the middle ranks of society, consisting of persons of 400l. a year, and of an income below that sum; it is remarkable that in the first plan for the forced loan laid before the Convention, it was proposed to exempt from the tax all income below 400l. a year; the plan was extended in consequence of a report from the Commissioners of Finance stating, that such an exemption would reduce the produce of the tax so considerably, as to render it wholly insufficient for the purposes of the government.

had been collected at Paris, where the movement of terror may be supposed to be most active, very little had been received in the several departments.

The means which have been employed for enforcing this and other extortions, I shall have occasion to consider presently, as well as the total amount of the sums which they are said to have brought into the national treasury.

In the same spirit with this general forced loan, local loans have been levied in different parts of the republic, which however have not on that account been exempted from the general contributions. At Bordeaux, during the regeneration of that city, large sums were raised in order to punish, what is styled, the *malevolence of the rich, and the crime of egotism*; a crime which, as nearly as any definition of it can be collected from the proceedings of the Convention, consists in the possession of property, and the application of it to the use of the possessor, or to any other purposes than those which the rapine of the present tyrants of France is pleased to prescribe. At Strasburg, a loan of twenty millions of livres, (nearly a million sterling) was levied exclusively upon the rich, by St. Just, one of the National Commissioners. Some proceedings of this nature were so violent as to have been made matter of complaint in the Convention. It was stated to the Convention on the 30th of September, that one of the National Commissioners in the department of Loiret, imposed arbitrary taxes unauthorized by law upon the citizens. A particular case was adduced, and a motion was made that the taxes so imposed should be repealed, and the commissioner reprimanded. It was answered, that the Convention would not embarrass the proceedings of their commissioners for the sake of aristocrats and counter-revolutionists; and the Convention accordingly, upon a special case stated of a tax levied without authority of law by the arbitrary power of one of their own commissioners stifled all enquiry, and passed to the order of the day. Complaint having been afterwards made that the revolutionary taxes were not paid into the public treasury; it was decreed, that the produce of all taxes levied upon citizens in any part of the republic by incompetent authority should be paid into the public treasury; and that those who had collected such taxes in the several departments should be accountable to the public for the sums which they have received. This decree contained no provision whatever for refunding any part of these illegal exactions to the persons aggrieved, while it gave the sanction of the Convention to such unwarrantable oppression, by applying the profits arising from it to the use of the State as a regular and legitimate article of revenue.

Such being their mode of diminishing the mass of circulating assignats, the next leading branch of their financial system was the effort made for procuring gold and silver. It will appear rather extraordinary to the House, that the first measure taken with this view should have been the proscription of these metals. A letter is received from Fouché, commissioner in the central and western departments in which you may perceive the first symptoms of a growing indignation against gold and silver. He says, " Gold and silver have been the causes of all the calamities of the republic; I know not by what weak complaisance those metals are still suffered to remain in the hands of suspected persons; let us degrade and vilify gold and silver, let us drag these deities of monarchy in the dirt, and establish the worship of the austere virtues of a republic." He however adds, " I send you seventeen chests filled with gold, silver, and plate of all sorts the spoil of churches and castles : you will see with peculiar pleasure two beautiful croziers, and a ducal coronet of silver gilt."

This ingenious idea of vilifying and degrading valuable effects by seizing them for the use of the Revolutionary Government, is not lost upon the French Minister of finance. A few days after the receipt of this letter, a Citizen appears at the bar, and desires to be permitted to exchange certain pieces of gold and silver bearing the image of the tyrant for Republican paper. This patriotic and disinterested offer, as you may imagine, was gladly accepted by the Convention; but upon a motion being made, that honourable mention of this transaction should be inserted in the votes, the Chancellor of the Exchequer rises with the utmost indignation to oppose so monstrous a proposition—he delivers a most eloquent and vehement invective against gold and silver; he says, " In a short time the world will be too happy if we should deign to receive pieces of metal bearing the effigy of tyrants in exchange for Republican assignats; already the whole nation rejects and despises those corrupting metals, which tyrants originally brought from America for the sole purpose of enslaving us. I have in contemplation the plan of a sumptuary law, by which I will drive that vile dung once more into the bowels of the earth." What was the sumptuary law by which the Chancellor of the Exchequer proposed to accomplish this salutary reform ? Here is that excellent law : " All gold and silver metal, in specie or plate, all jewels, gold and silver lace, or valuable effects which shall be discovered *buried in the earth*, or concealed in cellars, walls, rubbish, floors, or pavements, hearths, or chimneys, or *in any secret place shall be seized and confiscated for the use of the Republic ;* and the informer shall receive a twentieth part of the value of whatever he shall discover, to be paid in assignats." Concealment alone is the crime on which this law attaches, without even any of the ordinary pretences of aristocracy or disaffection. In consequence of this decree, every place in which it was possible to conceal treasure is searched with the utmost rigour ; the privacy of every house is violated ; every cellar and garden is dug up ; and the Chancellor of the Exchequer with the most unrelenting spirit of persecution pursues the objects of his hatred and contempt even to the bowels of the earth, where he had threatened to drive them.

About the same time a law was passed appointing Commissioners, for receiving on behalf of the nation, the gold and silver plate, and every other valuable article which had been consecrated to the use of religious worship in any part of the country. This leads me to a most distinguished feature of the Revolutionary Government ; I mean the formal abolition of religion. It may appear extraordinary that I should introduce in this part of the argument a subject which from its serious and awful nature might seem to demand a separate and distinct considera- tion. But in order to shew the system which I am describing in its true colours, I am compelled even in the distribution of this detail to follow the course of the extravagant follies, and of the eccentric crimes which distinguish the Revolutionary Government not more by their absurdity and magnitude, than by their novelty and singularity ; for this reason I must class the abolition of religion under the head of revenue. The main object of this measure was certainly to obtain a new resource by seizing the salaries of the clergy, and by plundering the ornaments of the churches. There was however another collateral object inseparably connected with the first, namely, to strengthen the foundations of the Revolutionary Government, and to reconcile the minds of the people to the crimes of their tyrants by destroying the first elements of all moral principle, by dissolving the firmest bond of civil society, and by subverting the strongest bulwark of lawful authority.

The plan for the accomplishment of these combined objects was deliberate and systematic, and pursued from beginning to end with the utmost regularity, consistency, and vigour. The ground-work of this scheme had indeed been long laid ; it may be traced in the seizure of the church-lands, in the oath exacted from the clergy by the civil constitution of 1792, and in the persecution and massacre of those who had the virtue and courage to reject that oath, and to sacrifice their fortunes, and expose their lives, for the sake of the established religion. The fury of that persecution had been nearly exhausted before the 31st of May, and the Revolutionary Government found no priests in possession of salaries from the State, but those who had submitted to the constitutional oath. The first step taken was, to reduce the salaries of the priests to an allowance scarcely sufficient for their subsistence. Soon after, all disguise was thrown off, and the Convention on the one hand excited the people by a public address to despise their clergy as an useless and unnecessary burthen, and on the other openly proposed rewards to such priests as should voluntarily renounce not their salaries only, but the duties of their sacred office. The Commissioners in the several departments received instructions to enlighten the public mind, and to encourage the abdication of the clergy. Some extracts from the addresses of the clergy, and from the letters of the National Commissioners will best explain the true spirit of these proceedings : an address dated the 30th of October from the Curate of Villos de Luchon says, " Legislators, I come to make a public confession, and to declare my repentance. Why should we spare established prejudices ? For my part, I believe that no religion in any country in the world is founded in truth. I believe that all the various religions in the world are descended from the same parents ; they are all the daughters of Pride and Ignorance. I believe that Heaven is nothing more than the happiness which attends virtue on earth. I render this solemn homage to Truth. Universal morality is become my gospel ; and henceforth I mean to draw my texts from thence alone, and to preach in no other cause than that of liberty, and of my country. Fanaticism will not now listen to me ; but by habits of truth men will be converted to reason ; and we may hope that soon priests of all religions will comprehend the triumph of philosophy and of the liberty of nations, and acknowledge the difference between the functions of the priesthood and the duties of honesty and virtue." Upon receiving this address, the Convention decrees, " that all similar addresses of renunciation of the ecclesiastical character, and of the functions relating to it shall be lodged with the Committee of Public Instruction, which is ordered to take effectual measures for rendering all such public acts useful to the history of the revolution, and to the public education." This proceeding does not satisfy the eagerness of Thuriot : he observes, that " he has no doubt that the new creed will soon efface all memory of the old :" But in order that truth may be carried into every part of the republic with more promptitude and effect, he moves, " that all similar letters should be translated into all the provincial idioms." Not satisfied even with the hope of propagating these liberal doctrines in the provinces, he carries his benevolence beyond the limits of France. He says, " It is not sufficient to enlighten one part of Europe : this is a case in which it may be right to soften the rigour of the French laws respecting foreigners : it should be the duty of the Convention to assume the honourable office of diffusing truth over the whole earth." And upon his motion it is decreed, " that all renunciations of the functions of religion shall be translated into all foreign languages." In the same month the Archbishop of Paris enters the Convention accompanied by a solemn procession of his Vicars, and by several curates of Paris : he makes a speech, in which he renounces the priesthood in his own name and in the name of all his attendants ; and he declares, that he does it, " because he is convinced that no national worship should be tolerated, excepting the worship of Liberty and Equality." The votes of the Convention mention, that the archbishop and his curates were received and embraced with transport by the whole Convention ; and that the archbishop was solemnly presented with a red cap : before he left the Convention several members who were clergymen imitated his example, by adopting his creed. The day concludes with a speech from

Julien of Toulouse, a Member of the Convention, and a Minister of the Protestant Church : he says, " For twenty years I have exercised the functions of a Protestant Minister; I declare that I renounce them for ever. In every religion there is more or less of quackery (great applauses). It is glorious to be able to make this declaration under the auspices of reason, of philosophy, and of that sublime constitution which has already overturned the errors of superstition and monarchy in France, and which now prepares a similar fate for all foreign tyrannies. I declare that I will no longer enter into any other temple than the Sanctuary of the Laws ; that I will acknowledge no other God than Liberty, no other worship than that of my country, no other Gospel than the Republican Constitution : such is my profession of moral and political faith. I shall cease to be a Minister of the Protestant Church; but I shall think myself equally bound to advise, exhort, and instruct my fellow citizens in the Jacobin Clubs, and in the public squares ; there I will preach, and there I will inspire them with the love of liberty and equality : I will soon lay upon the table my letters of ordination, of which I hope you will have the kindness to make an Auto da Fe." The letters of the National Commissioners are full of the same zeal : Lequinio and Laignelot Deputies of the Convention write to that Assembly, from Rochefort on the 2d of the same month, in these words : " We pass from miracle to miracle : soon our only regret will be that no more miracles remain to be performed. Eight Priests of the Catholic persuasion, and one Minister of the Protestant Church, unfrocked themselves on the day of the last decade in presence of the whole people in the Temple of Truth, heretofore called the Parish Church of this Town : they abjured the errors which they had so long taught, and they swore henceforth to teach nothing but the great principles of morality, and of sound philosophy ; to preach against all tyrannies political and religious, and at length to display the light of reason to mankind. The whole people, Protestants and Catholics, swore to forget their ancient superstition. In this town there will no longer exist more than one mode of preaching morality; there will exist but one temple, that of Truth : but one repository for the remains of the dead, whose resurrection has been perpetually preached by Superstition for the torment of the living. The Rights of Man and several other Constitutional Laws are to be substituted in the room of the mysterious ornaments of the Churches. We thought it right to recompense the courage of these philosophical Priests, who have been the first to shake off the yoke of Superstition : We have accordingly granted to each of them for their lives a pension of fifty pounds a year. Every thing goes on smoothly here : the people of their own accord approach the torch of reason, which we hold up to them with an air of mildness and fraternity. The Revolutionary Tribunal which we have established quickens the motions of the Aristocrats ; and the Guillotine strikes the heads of traitors to the ground."

The same commissioners in another letter say, " The people of Rochefort triumph over all prejudices ; they now exchange their gold for assignats ; and we have no doubt that their example will soon be followed throughout all France ; and that soon the whole people renouncing the ancient habits which they had contracted under the royal Government will demand the suppression of all money in specie, as they have already destroyed every remnant of presbyterian mummery. We announce to you with great satisfaction, that the popular society of Rochefort has selected from its own body several preachers of morality, who are gone upon a vicarial mission into the villages and hamlets of the neighbouring district. We are informed that these apostles of reason make proselytes wherever they go. If this measure had been adopted at the commencment of the Revolution, we should never have heard of La Vendèe."

c

Boisset, another commissioner gives an account of his operations in the department of Ardêche, la Drôme, du Garde, and Herault. He says, " Fanaticism is destroyed ; Catholics and Protestants forgetting their former animosities unite in the same worship,—that of liberty and the laws. The altars of Christianity are replaced by altars more holy. The whole people will soon assemble before them, each Decade to render homage to Liberty."

Wherever the priests could not be induced by corruption to abjure their profession ; wherever the people did not willingly approach the torch of reason and truth, the most rigorous measures of persecution were adopted. Dumont one of the National Commissioners announces to the Convention, " that, in order to destroy fanaticism he arrests all priests who celebrate religious ceremonies on Sundays." He adds, " that he includes all those monsters called priests in his general list of proscription ; and that he has made several captures of those infamous bigots." This letter was greatly applauded in the Convention. But the zeal of the municipality of Paris was most eminently distinguished in every period of this impious and cruel persecution. The conduct of that body merits peculiar attention, not only because it had so large a share in producing the Revolution of the 31st of May, but because it is likely to have an equal influence in any future convulsion.

The Municipality of Paris decreed, " that all churches and temples of religious worship of whatever denomination existing at Paris should be instantly shut ; that the priests and ministers of the different religions should be responsible for any commotions on account of religion which might happen in consequence of this decree ; that any person requiring the opening of a church or temple for the celebration of religious worship of any kind should be put under arrest as a suspected person ; and that the Revolutionary Committees should be invited to keep a watchful eye over the clergy of every denomination."

In consequence of this decree the cathedral church of Nôtre Dame at Paris and all the parish churches were shut up for some time, until they could be regenerated and purified from every taint of Christianity. The cathedral church was formally dedicated to reason and truth by a decree of the convention passed at the instance of the Municipality of Paris ; other churches underwent a similar purification : many were dedicated to reason, many to truth, some to probity and the nation, some to liberty and equality, but all, without exception, were alienated from the service of God.

Nor was it merely against Christianity that these efforts were directed : on the 12th of November a Jewish Rabbi is introduced into the council general of the commons of Paris ; he makes an offering of the ornaments of religious worship employed in his synagogue ; they are received with the warmest applause ; and this interesting scene is recorded in the following words :

" The Council General, in testimony of its sense of the disinterested conduct of the citizen Benjamin Jacob heretofore a Jew, resolves, that civic mention shall be made of his name in their votes. On this occasion the members of the Council vied with each other in giving the fraternal kiss to this respectable philosopher."

On the same day a report was received from the popular society of the Section of the Museum announcing that they had " executed justice upon all the books of superstition and falsehood ; that breviaries, missals, legends, together with the Old and New Testament, had expiated in the fire the follies which they had occasioned among mankind." A book of registry was opened at the town hall, for receiving the declarations of those who wished to give proofs of their civism by abjuring the functions of minister of any sect of· any religion. All this passed at Paris under the eye of the Convention, not only without their opposition, but with their formal approbation and concurrence.

In order to take the lead in completing the salutary work in which they had hitherto borne so active a part, the Council General of Paris decreed, "that a civic feast should be celebrated in the heretofore cathedral church, and that a patriotic hymn should be chaunted before a statue of liberty, to be erected in the place of the heretofore Holy Virgin."

You remember the circumstances of that extravagant orgy to which this decree was the prelude; you remember the introduction of the Goddess of Reason into the Convention, the fraternal ardor with which she was embraced by the president in the chair, by the secretaries at the table, and by all the members present, and the piety with which she was afterwards publicly worshipped by the whole legislature of France in the cathedral church, or (to use their own language) in the regenerated Temple of Reason and Truth : there the Archbishop of Paris officiated in his new character, with a red cap on his head, and a pike in his hand ; and with that sacred weapon, which he bore as the symbol of the united deities of Reason and Liberty, having destroyed or defaced whatever emblems of the Christian religion had escaped the first purification of the regenerated Temple, he terminated this auspicious ceremony by placing the bust of the regicide Marat on the altar of God. To perpetuate the memory of this solemn act and celebrity of atheism, the Convention voted that a colossal statue should be erected upon the ruins of all the emblems of monarchy and religion. The impiety of the sections of Paris seems to have received new vigour from this august ceremony. A deputation from the section of Unity was soon after received in the Convention ; the deputies were laden with the spoil of one of the richest churches at Paris ; to this acceptable offering they added an address full of energy, in which they congratulated the Legislature, "that reason had gained so great a victory over superstition ; that a religion of error and of blood was annihilated ; a religion, which for eighteen centuries had occasioned nothing but evils upon earth ; and yet it was pretended to be of divine origin !"

Here the address enumerated several different epochs of Christianity, in which murders and massacres have been committed. It continued in these words :

" Such are the works, such are the trophies of this religion ; may it be obliterated from the face of the earth ! happiness will then return ; mankind will live like friends and brothers : from this auspicious moment history, whose painful task has hitherto been to record the crimes of religion, shall have nothing to commemorate but virtue and happiness. We swear that we will tolerate no other worship than that of reason, liberty, equality, and the republic." It appears by the votes, *that the whole Convention joined in this oath* ; and the President made the following reply to the address ;

" In a single moment you have annihilated the memory of eighteen centuries of error ; your philosophy has offered to Reason a sacrifice worthy of her acceptance, and fit to proceed from a true republican spirit. The Assembly receives your offering and your oath in the name of the country."

These proceedings in the Convention and Municipality were seconded by *good writings* industriously circulated among the people by the means ordinarily employed for the propagation of every favourite doctrine.

In one of them appears the true spirit and principle of this reform : it is there maintained in plain and direct terms, "that provided the idea of a Supreme Being be nothing more than a philosophical abstraction, a guide to the imagination in the pursuit of causes and effects, a resting-place for the curiosity of enquiring minds, a notion merely speculative, and from which no practical consequences are to be applied to human life, there is no great danger in such an idea : but if it is to be made the foundation of morality ; if it is to be accompanied by the supposition, that there exists a God who presides over the affairs of the world, and rewards or punishes men for their actions on earth according to some principle of retributive justice, there can be no opinion more prejudicial to the interests of society.   That the idea of a supreme Deity is a despotic idea, and must be so in all times ; that mankind can never be really liberated or republicanised, so long as they shall preserve such a notion ; that beings who adore an invisible master will easily believe that he may accomplish his ends by earthly agents ; and reasoning by analogy, they must conclude the necessity of some system of ranks and orders of society, and finally of some regular government among mankind ; and thus the servitude of the understanding will enslave every moral and political principle "

From the mouths of the principal actors in this extraordinary scene I have brought before you the scope and aim of their design : It was not (as we have been told on this day) to purify their own established mode of worship, and to clear it from the errors of the Church of Rome.   Protestants were invited to unite with Catholics in the extinction of the Protestant as well as of the Catholic religion ; Protestants as well as Catholics were denied the liberty of assembling for the purpose of public worship ; Protestant as well as Catholic churches were shut up ; and those who dared to celebrate religious worship of any kind were arrested, and treated as suspected persons.   Christianity was stigmatized through the organ of the President of the Convention amidst the applauses of the whole audience as a system of murder and massacre, which could not be tolerated by the humanity of a revolutionary government.   The Old and New Testament were publicly burnt as prohibited books.   Nor was it even to Christianity of any denomination that their hatred was confined.   Even Jews were involved in this comprehensive plan ; their ornaments of public worship were plundered, and their vows of irreligion recorded with enthusiasm.   The rigour of the laws respecting foreigners was relaxed, in order that impiety might be universally propagated for the general benefit of all mankind.   The existence of a future state was openly denied, and modes of burial devised for the express purpose of representing to the minds of the people, that death was nothing more than an everlasting sleep ; and to complete the whole project, doctrines were publicly circulated under the eye of the government, maintaining that the existence of a supreme God was an idea inconsistent with the liberty of man.   And yet a noble Earl * in this debate has lamented that the French government should have met with any interruption in their laudable efforts for the destruction of despotism and superstition !   I trust those expressions were inconsiderately used : we are not yet sufficiently enlightened in this House to consider an attack against Christianity, and even against the belief and worship of a God, as a laudable effort to destroy superstition.   So very little has the noble Earl examined this subject, that the most striking feature of this whole system has entirely escaped his observation.   It is a circumstance well deserving of attention, that as the anarchy which prevails in France is accompanied by all the evils of despotism, so their atheism bears all the most odious features of superstition.   Their enthusiastic worship of those abstract ideas of liberty and equality which they have substituted in the place of God, their bigotted infidelity, their intolerant zeal for the propagation of atheism, and their furious spirit of persecution against every mode of religious worship have not been surpassed, and have seldom been equalled in the most

* Lord Wycombe.

sanguinary periods in which misguided and fanatical superstition has ever disgraced the cause of religion.

But since the noble Earl has, it seems, connected these impious proceedings with certain political principles, I beg his attention to what I shall now offer on that subject, with the view of showing to the House the intimate alliance between all the parts of the French system, and the various modes in which they all mutually aid and co-operate with each other.

The Abbé Seyes, the author of the original declaration of rights and one of the committee for framing the Constitution of the 10th of August 1793, in making his solemn abjuration of religion, explains to the Convention the cause and the progress of his conversion ; he says, " my wishes have long desired this triumph of reason over superstition. I repeat now what I have always felt, and often declared, that I know no other worship than that of liberty and equality, no other religion than the love of humanity, and of my country. When the vigour of my understanding first cast off the melancholy prejudices by which my youth had been afflicted, at that moment the energy of insurrection entered into my heart. If since that time I have submitted to bear the chains of the church, it has been under the pressure of the same force which equally subjected all free spirits to the chains of the monarchy. The day of the revolution necessarily dissolved all those odious bonds."

In one and the same moment the mind of this great man was touched by the benignant influence of atheism, and by the sacred flame of insurrection, and was at once miraculously relieved from all sense of civil obedience to his King, and of religious duty to his God. Never was so comprehensive a system unfolded to the world by an exposition so clear, so unequivocal, and so compendious. The noble Earl and the House may learn from these few words, whether it was superstition or religion, despotism or monarchy against which the violence of the Jacobin faction was levelled, and why they thought atheism the most secure foundation on which a revolutionary government could be established.

Such were the proceedings by which the abolition of religion was attempted in France : But for the honour of human nature, they did not answer the expectations of those who had digested the plan, and had been most active in providing the means for its execution. Disciplined in crimes, and accustomed to every scene of rapine, injustice, and cruelty, the people of France could not yet be induced to renounce for ever the consolations of religion. The provinces, almost without exception, were scandalized at the audacious profligacy of the government, and even at Paris the strongest symptoms of the same sentiment appeared. Robespierre himself was alarmed ; and the Jacobin Club thought it prudent to declare, that under all the existing circumstances they admitted the idea of a God. Apprehensions were entertained that the salutary movement of terror might take a new direction, and that the order of the day might be enforced against the government itself. At length, amidst the discontents of the people, who claimed aloud the free exercise of religious worship guaranteed to them by the Constitution, after many struggles and many unsuccessful evasions, slow, and reluctant, and ambiguous forth comes the repentance of the Convention ! Even in their repentance they still betray their affection for their crime, and their eager hope of renewing it under more propitious circumstances : They are compelled to tolerate religious worship, and to forbid the repetition of those violences which had been exercised to crush it in every part of the country ; but in the same decree they declare, that they do not mean " to furnish a pretext for the disturbance of patriots, or to check the aspiring flight of the public mind ; they invite citizens to abstain from all religious discussions, and to employ themselves wholly in the contemplation of the good of

their country." Upon farther reflection they add, "that they do not mean to dis-
approve of the measures taken by their Commissioners in the several departments,
to aid the people in the destruction of fanaticism." This last resolution sanctions
the imprisonment and proscription of the clergy, the shutting up and subsequent
profanation of churches of all religions, the arts and menaces employed to induce
Catholics and Protestants to abjure Christianity, the establishment of new forms of
burial, in which the existence of a future state is solemnly denied, and all the acts
of oppression and impiety which I have detailed to the House. Thus their very
repentance furnishes the most incontestable proof of the real scope of their original
design, of the extent to which it had been carried in practice, and of their future
intentions, if by time and assiduity they shall be able to eradicate from the public
mind that natural instinct which proved an insuperable obstacle to the success of
their first attempt. Having thus endeavoured to justify themselves in the eyes of
France, they felt that a government, which openly overturned the fundamental
principles of all religion, must become an object of alarm and abhorrence to every
foreign nation : their next step therefore was to endeavour to vindicate their conduct to all Europe ; and with that view Robespierre drew up an answer, (as he
styles it,) to the manifestoes of all kings, in which he refutes in the most triumphant
manner the charge of irreligion, which had been alledged against the revolutionary
government. He says, "We are accused of having declared war against Heaven
itself: But what people ever offered a more pure worship to the Supreme Being?
The death-warrant of tyrants lay dormant and forgotten in the timid breasts of
men ; we called it forth ; we executed it; to punish kings is to honour God."
Here, then, is their creed publicly proclaimed in the face of all Europe : in the
murder of their innocent king is comprized the whole principle and practice of
their religion, their sole profession of faith, and their established mode of worship
a profession of faith, and a mode of worship worthy only of those who have placed
the bust of Marat on the altar of God!

To return to the observations which have led me to this digression, I must remark, that while the detestable project of abolishing religion has failed of its proposed effect upon the minds of the people, it does not appear to have been much more
successful as a measure of revenue; there is every reason to believe that it has not
been productive of any considerable resource. Although the churches were plundered of all the articles of value which could be found in them, yet, when it is
recollected that many of the richest ornaments of the church had been sent into
the public treasury previous to the 10th of August 1792, under the name of
Patriotic Gifts, a large deduction must be made from what might have been supposed to be the amount of this resource. In addition to this circumstance Cambon
states, that little or none of the church plate had reached the public treasury,
having been pillaged by those whose zeal had been the most forward in promoting
the worship of reason, truth, *probity*, and the nation. In all probability the principal financial advantage of this measure is to be found in the reduction of the
salaries of the clergy.

I will now recapitulate the leading branches of the revenue of the revolutionary
government for the present year. The tax upon all yearly income below the value
of four hundred pounds, and the seizure of all yearly income above that sum, including a tax upon the funds, upon commercial capital of every description, upon
private debts, and upon all money not laid out at interest ; arbitrary local loans
levied upon the egotism of property, and the malevolence of wealth ; taxes raised
by incompetent authority; the confiscation of all concealed property ; and the
abolition of religion : To this list might be added the revenue arising from their
system of criminal justice, from their violations of personal freedom, and colla-

terally, from their regulations for the destruction of agriculture and commerce, and for the maintenance of their army : these will be more properly considered under their distinct heads.   Various accounts have been given of the sum in specie brought into the treasury by these exactions : it has been asserted to be fifteen millions sterling.   Even admitting the truth of such a rumour, when we compare this sum with a monthly expenditure of eighteen millions * sterling, it will appear inconsiderable ; and it must not be forgotten, that the means, which have been employed to procure it, are by the Convention itself admitted to be of a nature not to be renewed.†

I now come to mention the regulations of this government respecting agriculture, commerce, and internal trade, which are nearly connected both in principle and effect with their system of revenue : a few examples will be sufficient to give you an idea of the spirit of the whole.   The depreciation of assignats, and the general distress of the country having greatly raised the price of all the necessaries of life, the expence of maintaining the military force became so heavy, that the Government was compelled to resort to something beyond the extraordinary projects of revenue, which I have enumerated.   The price of the articles, which may be classed under the head of necessaries of life in France, was upon an average about two-thirds higher in the year 1793 than it had been in the year 1790 ; in many cases the encrease was infinitely greater ; ‡ the price of labour of every kind had risen in the same proportion.   On the 29th of September the Convention passed a decree to the following effect : "All articles enumerated § are to be sold at fixed prices, one-third above the current price in 1790.   All persons who shall buy or sell any of the articles enumerated at a price above the fixed price, shall pay double the value of the articles so bought or sold ; their names shall be inserted in the list of suspected persons, and they shall be treated accordingly.   All wages, salaries, and

---

* By an account laid before the Convention, on the 10th of January, 1794, it appears, that notwithstanding all the extortion, fraud, and outrage committed for the purpose of obtaining revenue, the deficiency between the receipt and expenditure of the month of Frimaire, ending the 20th of December 1793, was no less a sum than 275 millions of livres; a deficiency of eleven millions sterling between the receipt and expenditure of a single month !   Paper was actually created and issued in that one month to this enormous amount.

† The French Minister of Finance has boasted that his assignats were at par ; but the laws which have been passed for punishing with long imprisonment any person who takes, gives, or offers assignats under par, and the laws for preventing the circulation of specie, and compelling every man to declare the quantity in his possession sufficiently account for this circumstance.

‡ In the month of August last, woollens had risen about two-thirds ; linens, cent. per cent. leather and shoes about 80 per cent. soap and candles two-thirds ; sugar from 30 sols per lb. to 5 livres 10 sols, and in the provinces 10 livres.   In all the Provinces the distress was much greater than at Paris, which city under a particular law has been for some time past supplied by exactions from the neighbouring country.

§ Articles of which the price is fixed by the law of the Maximum : fresh meat, sweet oil, wine, cider, charcoal, salt meat and bacon, cattle, brandy, beer, coal, linen, butter, salt fish, vinegar, wood for fuel, woollens, pearl ashes, paper, brass, copper, woollen stuffs, cole and rape seed, train oil, sugar, leather, lead, hemp, kelp, tallow candles, salt, honey, iron, steel, flax ; all raw materials of manufacture; wooden shoes, leather shoes, snuff.

daily hire to labourers or mechanics, shall be fixed at the same rate as in the year
1790, with the addition of one-half of the current price at that time. The municipalities may put into a state of requisition, and punish according to the case with
three days imprisonment, any workman, mechanic, or labourer who shall refuse to
work at the reduced prices. All existing contracts for the public service are subjected to this law, and the contractors compelled to supply government at the
reduced prices notwithstanding the stipulations in their contracts; articles actually
delivered or despatched to the place of their destination, at the time of the decree,
alone excepted."

It is not difficult to conceive the effect of this law, which compelled every merchant, tradesman, and shopkeeper, who must have purchased the enumerated
articles at the high price of 1793, to sell them at the low price fixed by the Convention. The necessary and immediate consequence was the ruin of every person
on whom the law was executed; none could escape but those, who having goods
on hand not of a perishable nature, shut up their shops and warehouses in expectation of better times. In this state of things, a supplementary law was proposed
with two professed views which are singularly combined, to relieve the sufferers
under the former law, and to compel a more exact and rigorous execution of its
principle. It was introduced by a report from Barrere in the name of the Committee of Public Welfare which deserves particular notice, because it contains the
general maxims of agriculture and commerce, from which are derived all the decrees of
the National Convention relating to those important branches of political economy.

The report opens with a severe complaint in the name of liberty against agriculture and commerce :—" Liberty in establishing herself upon the French territory
reposed with pleasure in the arms of agriculture and of commerce.

"But what has agriculture done for liberty? Agriculture has only sought to
increase her own profits, to calculate her own advantages, and raise the price of all
the necessaries of life.

"What has commerce done for liberty? Commerce has wasted the sources of
internal circulation by clandestine exportations; commerce has neglected with a
a sort of counter-revolutionary peevishness every species of manufacture and useful
art. The avarice of commerce is become the accomplice of despotism. We might
be inclined to think that commerce is a monarchical slave unworthy of liberty, if
we did not know the cause of this misconduct; the mercantile Government of
England has raised against us the commercial interest of the whole world, and
among the rest, even the commercial interest of France." The report proceeds to
state that the law for fixing the price of the necessaries of life, or (as it is called)
the law of the maximum, had not been executed in many parts of the Republic, and
that the law itself was inadequate in its provisions.

"The law of the maximum ought to have embraced the whole system of commerce from the grower who furnishes the raw material, down to the retail merchant,
who sells the manufactured article to each citizen for his daily wants. The law of
the maximum ought to extend over the whole of the useful chain of growers,
labourers, manufacturers, mechanics, wholesale and retail merchants. The effect of
this would have been, to envelope commerce on all sides, to invest it (if such an
expression may be used) with the popular interests, by pursuing it from its very
source to its last and almost imperceptible ramification. This would have been the
true way to force commerce to become useful and beneficial. Commerce, in other
countries so useful, so beneficial, so necessary is become in this revolution of liberty
a sort of avaricious tyrant, whom, to render serviceable, we have been obliged to
enslave." The report concludes with an argument to prove, that the " Sans Culottes
alone, who had suffered under the operation of the law of the maximum, were

deserving of any relief, because the wholesale merchants had sufficient means of indemnifying themselves by stock-jobbing, and other similiar practices."

These opinions of the Committee of Public Welfare have no doubt astonished the House, accustomed to cherish the interests of agriculture and of commerce, as being essential to the happiness of the people, and to the opulence and strength of the empire. But let us examine the decree which followed this report, and see how far the practice of this Government surpasses its theory.

The decree allows five cent. profit to the wholesale dealer, and ten per cent. profit to the retailer of the articles enumerated in the former law over and above the price fixed by that law. It then proceeds to enact the two following regulations :

1. "The Convention, wishing to administer relief to the poorer class of the people, decrees that an indemnity shall be granted to those merchants or manufacturers, who can give satisfactory proof of their entire ruin under the operation of the law of the Maximum, or who shall be reduced to a fortune of less than 400l. capital.

2. "The manufacturers and wholesale dealers who, since the law of the maximum, have quitted or shall quit their manufactories or trade, shall be treated as suspected persons."

Thus then it is directly admitted, that the former law had already occasioned the ruin of many persons affected by it, although the interval between the passing of the two laws was little more than a month.* But the persons, to whom relief is to be given by the second law, are only those who can give *satisfactory proof of their entire ruin ;* or whose fortunes have been reduced to a republican level ; whatever may been the property of any merchant or manufacturer injured by the law of the Maximum, no indemnity is to be granted to any sufferer whose capital has not been reduced below the sum of 400l. By what scale the Revolutionary Government has measured the ruin of its subjects it is not very easy to understand. An opulent merchant or manufacturer in any other country, who by the sudden effect of a single law should find his commercial capital reduced to a sum of 400l. would be thought in a situation to *give satisfactory proof of his entire ruin.* But as in the law of the forced loan, the fundamental principle of the calculation was, that the income of every man in France should be reduced to one hundred and eighty pounds; so the law of the maximum seems to have pursued the same doctrine of equality and to have decided, that no individual should possess a commercial capital of more than four hundred pounds.

The second regulation is perhaps the most grievous act of injustice and oppression that ever was enforced against the interests of commerce. To compel subjects by an act of power to exercise any particular branch of trade, is always both unjust and impolitic : but it is reserved for the Revolutionary Government, first to render particular branches of trade ruinous to those who were actually engaged in them, and then to compel the same persons to pursue those ruinous branches of trade and to imprison every man who should endeavour to save his property from that destruction, of which he already felt the approaches.

The first effect of such violence would undoubtedly be, to transfer all the articles affected by the law into the hands of the Government, and to facilitate for a time the supply of Paris and of the armies : but it is evident that the reproduction of the same articles within the country would immediately receive a severe check, and that no man would purchase them from foreigners in order to sell them again at a

* The law of the maximum passed on the 29th of September, the Supplementary Law on the 1st of November.

considerable loss. The certain consequence of this measure must therefore be, to annihilate the stock of all the necessaries of life in France, and to hasten the moment when it will become impossible for the Government, either to subsist the people at home, or even to maintain an army upon the frontier.*

Previous to the passing of this law, the price of corn, grain, and flour had been fixed by a special decree; and I have already observed that the whole crop of every farmer under a fundamental article of the constitution of the Revolutionary Government was to be at the discretion of the Committee of Public Welfare, and of their agents in the several departments. This leads me to observe upon certain general rights with respect to the produce of the soil, and to articles of ordinary consumption claimed by the Government as arising out of the revolutionary state of the Republic.

The first is the right of pre-emption. Im the report upon the law of the maximum Barrere says, " that the law of pre-emption renders the government proprietor for the time of every thing which commerce, industry, or agriculture have produced from the soil, or imported into the territory of France." It is impossible to hear this doctrine without remarking the intimate connection between the principles of anarchy on which the Revolutionary Government was founded, and the principles of despotism by which it is maintained. From the sovereignty of the people and the natural equality of mankind the Government deduces its right to the produce of the whole soil of France, and to the whole property of every individual in the Republic : a right, which is the very essence of despotism, and which has hitherto been considered as the characteristic mark, by which arbitrary government was to be distinguished from limited power. Under this right so broadly laid down the Committee of Public Welfare affects to claim nothing more than a preference in the purchase of whatever articles may be required by their agents for public use; but I have shewn already, that by the law of the maximum they have exercised the power of fixing an arbitrary price upon all such articles.

The right of requisition is derived from that which I have last described ; under the right of requisition the officers of government are empowered to require from every man in the country not only whatever part of his property of any description they may choose to declare necessary for the public use, but also his manual labour, and his personal service ; and while this arbitrary requisition remains in force, no man can dispose either of his goods or of his labour to any other purchaser or or employer than the officers employed by the ruling faction. You have seen that by the law of the maximum, there is a power of imprisoning every workman or day labourer who shall attempt to evade this requisition. If any person shall make an incorrect declaration of property which has been put into a state of requisition, the Government derives from that circumstance a farther right, which is called the right of PREHENSION :† under this they immediately seize his goods, and sell them by auction to the profit of the public treasury. The vexations practised against

---

* In a letter published from Lyons are these words : " We have neither grain, coals, wood nor provisions of any kind. The tax called maximum was published on Saturday, which was in fact, to inform the peasants to bring nothing to market. The women rose up against them, and menaced them with the armed force. The peasants for six leagues round, kept back all eatables. They sound the tocsin when buyers approach them and treat them as monopolizers, rob and assassinate them."

† The right of prehension is explained by the following articles in a decree of the Convention, ordered, 1st. "That the Committee of Subsistence and Supply shall exercise the right of prehension in the course of the present day, and accordingly

farmers, who have not given in satisfactory accounts of their crop, or who have ventured to sell any part of it in compliance with the urgent demands of their neighbours are innumerable; and the same violence has been used against every person engaged in trade of any kind.

Out of these extraordinary rights arises as extraordinary a crime, which is called the *crime of monopoly*, and which is usually imputed to the class of merchants and wealthy farmers, or in general to those who are termed egotists, according to the definition which I have already given of that word.

A monopolist is the possessor of any quantity of the necessaries of life, beyond the exigency of his daily subsistance. Every man therefore, whose circumstances are above indigence, is liable to the charge of monopoly. Whoever happens to have laid up any quantity of the articles which the Government think fit to require for their service, is also deemed a monopolist: thus every farmer whose barns and granaries are are not empty, every merchant and tradesman whose warehouse or shop is not entirely unprovided with goods must be subject to the charge of monopoly.* This crime is punished differently according to the enormity of the case; in some instances the punishment is imprisonment attended with forfeiture of property, but it is much more frequently death.

With such theoretical maxims, and with such a practical system, the Convention might reasonably have expected to find both agriculture and commerce in that state of "counter-revolutionary peevishness," which should suspend every manufacture, every useful art of industry, and every honest pursuit of skill or labour. They need not have sought in the influence of the mercantile Government of England (as they term it) an effect, which is the natural and inevitable result of their own violence and oppression. But conclusions of more importance to our present deliberation may be drawn from this detail. I have shewn already, that by the forced loan, they have effectually checked the progressive increase of commercial capital ; by the law of the maximum with its supplement they have gone a step further, and have directly seized the whole commercial stock of the country for the service of the current year. I have shewn already, that according to their own statements and to the very nature of things their extraordinary expedients of finance cannot be renewed with any prospect of success. It is equally evident, that their regulations respecting agriculture and internal commerce cannot be continued without exhausting the country of the necessaries of life. The rapid operation of every part of this system may be seen in the effect of the law of the maximum, which had not passed more than a month, when (as Barrere states,) it had entirely ruined all those upon whom it had been effectually executed, and had

---

shall collect together all the shoes now lying or being in any magazine, warehouse, manufacture or shop whatsoever.

2nd. " All such shoes shall be sent within twenty four hours to the armies of the Republic.

3d. " The popular societies and the different sections are invited to *direct the generosity of the citizens towards civic gifts of shoes."*

* An idea of the nature of the crime of monopoly may be formed from a few particular instances : a wine merchant is denounced for having 2000 bottles of wine in his cellars : he is imprisoned, and they are put into a state of *prehension* for the public use; a female citizen is denounced for having a large stock of sugar and coffee in her possession; the agents of Government order it to be put into *circulation,* and accordingly it is sold by auction for the profit of the Treasury, and she is sent to the prison of Ste. Pelagie.

encreased the difficulty of procuring the very articles, the price of which it was intended to reduce.

With respect to foreign commerce it may be considered as nearly annihilated. The exportation of all the articles enumerated in the law of the Maximum (in which are included all the principal articles of the French export trade) is absolutely prohibited. Whatever foreign commerce now exists, is carried on exclusively by the Government for the purpose of supplying the armies, and of postponing that distress for the means of subsistence, which now threatens every part of France. When we recollect, that one third of the total collective income of the individuals of France is stated to arise from commerce, we may judge what a blow has been given to the resources of the Government by the entire destruction of the interests of commerce both internal and foreign.

Such is the system established upon the ruins of every right of property and of every foundation of general opulence, by which the Revolutionary Government have hitherto procured their revenue, and maintained and supplied their numerous armies.

It remains to be considered by what applications of terror this system has been enforced.

Among the most sacred rights of a free people and the most essential maxims of justice are the right of personal freedom, and the maxim, that no person should be punished without being heard. These rights were guaranteed to the people of France by the Constitution of the 10th of August 1793. In defiance however of this Constitution arbitrary imprisonment and punishment upon mere suspicion, the most vexatious and odious instruments of despotic power, have been employed by the Revolutionary Government with a violence surpassing all that is recorded of the most rigorous tyrannies that have ever afflicted mankind. They have formally and openly abolished every trace of personal liberty in France by a single law, which requires no other comment than the proceedings of the Convention itself. Barrere, in a Report from the Committee of Public Welfare, explains the principle and object of this law: he says, " The quality of mercy is the first sacrifice which a good republican owes to his country. In order to preserve the revolutionary vigour of the government, an institution terrible indeed, but necessary, an institution which has been the salvation of France, has been disseminated throughout all the sections and all the municipalities, I mean the law for the arrest of suspected persons. The keen and piercing eye of jealous liberty has been fixed upon every citizen, has penetrated into every family, and pervaded every habitation.

" Public opinion, which is formed upon the review of innumerable transactions of various kinds, which have passed at all the periods of the Revolution from its commencement down to the present time, public opinion has marked out the persons who ought to be suspected, and they have accordingly fallen under the severity of the law.

" Birth, prejudices of pride, and habits of aristocracy have branded every remnant of the *Gentry of France* as a just object of suspicion.

" The useless if not dangerous nature of their occupation, their illicit gains, their confidential concern in the pecuniary affairs of foreigners are sufficient grounds for the arrest of the *whole class of bankers.*

" Their cruel speculations, their contempt for assignats, their sordid attachment to their own interest have estranged *all merchants* from their fellow citizens; they therefore form another class of suspected persons:

" The relations of emigrants, those who have aided them in their escape, those whom nature and the ties of blood have made the necessary accomplices of all their sentiments of hatred or affection, all these are equally obnoxious to suspicion :

"*All the clergy* who have refused the Constitutional Oath, and who think that all is lost because *their trade is become useless*; all the *ancient magistrates*, all those who have been bred to the profession of the law, are destined by their hábits and interests to *people* the public prisons. These are the classes of society which are sentenced at once without being heard; these are the professions which carry their condemnation with them; these are the natural connections of parentage and affection which it is the duty of the law to strike without trial and without mercy. Let us banish all compassion from our bosoms! Oh what innumerable mischiefs may be produced by a false sentiment of pity! Shall not a few slaves of monarchy sacrifice some moments of their useless and inactive liberty for the salvation of the republic? They shall be taught to love liberty by suffering a long confinement. This is true humanity; for this is the only speedy and effectual method of finishing all our calamities, of completing the revolution, and of establishing the republic on an immoveable foundation. Thus this great and free republic shall draw new strength and vigour not only from the number of her defenders on the frontier, but from the number of her enemies imprisoned within her bosom; and the liberty of the people shall grow and flourish amidst crowded camps and overflowing jails."

I have quoted this passionate invective against mercy and justice, for the purpose of apprizing you of the general ideas of the legislators of France upon the subject of personal liberty; I will now read to you the law which passed on the 17th of September.

" 1. Immediately after the publication of the present decree all suspected persons, who shall be found within the territory of the Republic, and who are yet at large, shall be put into a state of arrest.

" Those shall be deemed suspected persons;

" 2. Who by their connections or relationship, by their discourses or writings, have shewn themselves to be partizans of tyranny and federalism, and enemies of liberty. 3. Who have no visible means of subsistence, or who cannot prove the discharge of their civic duties. 4. Those to whom certificates of civism have been refused. 5. Public officers dismissed or suspended by the Convention. 6. Such of the nobility, husbands, wives, fathers, mothers, sons and daughters, brothers or sisters, or agents of the emigrants, as have not constantly manifested their attachment to the Revolution. 7. Those who have emigrated between July 1st 1789 and the publication of the law of the 8th of April 1792, although they may have returned into France within or before the period prescribed by that law. 8. The Committees of Superintendance, or the Revolutionary Committees appointed in their stead by the Convention or by its Commissioners in the several departments are to make lists of all the suspected persons within the limits of their respective jurisdictions, to issue warrants of arrest, and to seal up their papers. 9. Arrested persons are to be permitted to take such part of their furniture into prison with them as may be of absolute necessity. 10. They are to defray the expence of their guard. 11. Civil and criminal tribunals may detain as suspected persons those whose indictments have been thrown out by the juries of accusation previous to trial, and those who shall have stood their trial and have been *acquitted*."

In addition to these precise definitions of suspected persons, by the fourth article of the law, all those, to whom certificates of civism shall have been refused, are included within that description. The certificates of civism are granted or refused at Paris at the discretion of the Municipality; and on the 10th of October 1793, " the procureur of the Commons of Paris reports to the Council General, the characteristic marks and signs by which the Council may recognize suspected persons, and those to whom Certificates of Civism ought to be refused." These characteristic marks and signs include so large a description of persons, that if a similar regulation were to be enforced in any country, or in any assembly; it is difficult to imagine any possible case which might not be brought under some one of the articles of this exposition of the law. For, Sir, you will observe that all persons are suspected and arrested,

" 1. Who check the energy of the people, and embarrass the proceedings of popular assemblies by artful speeches, turbulent cries, and menaces.

" 2. All those who with more prudence talk mysteriously of the calamities of the country, lament the condition of the people, and are always ready to spread bad news with an affectation of regret.

" 3. Those who change their language and conduct according to events.

" 4. Those who pity the greedy farmers and merchants, against whom the law is compelled to take effectual measures.

" 5. Those who talk of liberty, but visit the late nobility, the counter revolutionary clergy, the aristocracy, the Feuillants, and the Moderates, and appear to take an interest in their fate.

" 6. Those who have taken no active part in the Revolution, and who plead in their exculpation the payment of taxes, or of patriotic gifts, or the services either in person or by substitute in the national guard.

" 7* Those who have received the Republican Constitution with indifference, and have declared false apprehensions respecting its duration and establishment.

" 8. Those who have done nothing for or against liberty.

" 9. Those who neglect their attendance in the public assemblies under pretence of not being able to speak in public, or of being engaged in the care of their own affairs.

" 10. Those who speak with contempt of the established authorities, of the emblems of the law, of the popular assemblies, or of the defenders of liberty."†

All these, Sir, are suspected, committed to safe custody, and to be detained in prison until the peace.

By the last article of the law a class of persons is included, very inconsiderable indeed in number, but which one might suppose to be exempt from suspicion even under all the vigilance and jealousy of a Revolutionary Government; I mean those who have been acquitted by the previous Jury of Accusation, or who have been declared innocent after a regular and solemn trial. By reference to the daily lists which are published of criminals condemned or acquitted by the Revolutionary Tribunals I find, that far the greater proportion of the very few who have the fortune to escape death is detained in prison on grounds of suspicion at the mere requisition of the public accuser. This is the perfection of tyranny. It is not enough to deprive men of their liberty, without alledging any specific crime against them, or without admitting them to a hearing; but even after they have been heard and declared innocent, they are still subjected to penalties which belong only to convicted guilt.

By different laws and regulations several other classes have been added to the list of suspected persons; such as those who disobey the requisitions laid on their property; those labourers or workmen who disobey the requisitions laid on their

* The Constitution had actually been suspended when these resolutions passed.

† It appears that the virtue of civism has never been accurately defined, although the want of it subjects men to the loss of their liberty. One instance will serve to shew the manner in which certificates of civism are granted and refused at Paris; a certificate of civism was refused to Palissot, a dramatic author, for having ridiculed J. J. Rousseau in a comedy; it was granted to him some time after, on his proving that he had praised Rousseau in other works.

manual labour; those who have shut up their shops or warehouses on account of the reduced price of goods under the law of the Maximum; and, lastly, *those who keep the day heretofore called Sunday.* These laws were executed with such activity, that not only the prisons were soon crowded with suspected persons, but the churches and deserted palaces of the nobility and of the princes of the blood were converted to the same useful purpose. On the 15th of September previous to the passing of the law the total number of prisoners confined at Paris was 2020. At the latter end of December it was 5000, and notwithstanding the number of executions it is still rapidly increasing.* This unparalleled oppression has been extended with at least equal severity over all the provinces; the letters from the Commissioners of the Convention are filled with expressions of self-applause and of congratulation to the Convention upon the encreasing number of state prisoners in the several departments.

One of the Commissioners writes in the most triumphant tone from Rochefort: "The empire of liberty is established; the prisons begin to fill in every part of this neighbourhood."

Dumont, Commissioner from the Convention in the departments of La Somme and Pas de Calais, informs that assembly, "that he had harangued the people at Peronne with a dagger in one hand and a torch in the other, and had threatened to declare the whole town in a state of rebellion, if all the people did not aid him in the arrest of suspected persons; and that at Boulogne he had caused the suspected persons arrested in that town to be brought before him in *forty-four carts* on their way to their respective prisons." This letter furnishes us with some idea of the numbers who have been deprived of their liberty in the provinces. Camille Desmoulins, a person well acquainted with the secrets of the Revolutionary Government, calculates that the total number of suspected persons arrested all over France between the 17th of September 1793 and the beginning of January 1794 was not less than two hundred thousand; and his statement, which appears consistent with the general circumstances of the case, has never been contradicted, although he has since fallen into disgrace with his party, on account of the freedom of his animadversions upon their conduct.

The unfortunate persons thus confined receive such a treatment as might be expected from the despicable character of the Jacobin Faction. The tyranny exercised under the orders of Robespierre and his associates has uniformly been as minute and unmanly in every studious refinement of cruelty and vexation by which the sufferings of helpless individuals could be aggravated, as it has been audacious and violent in the subversion of all the most important rights and in the destruction of all the most valuable interests of the collective body of the people. A single circumstance will illustrate this observation;

On the 16th of November, Levasseur, a member of the Convention, enters that assembly in great heat; he says, "I am just returned from Chantilly, heretofore in times of slavery the palace of the family Condè, but now under the reign of liberty converted into a prison-house for the detention of suspected persons; I saw the kitchen of those arrested *gentlemen,* and I was scandalized at the preparations making for their entertainment. It would seem that those gentlemen, not expecting to live long, were determined to make the most of their time: all the eggs, butter, sugar, and coffee in the neighbourhood had been forestalled and monopolized for the use of those *gentlemen.* I immediately represented this enormous abuse to the Revolutionary Committee of the village; the whole committee shared

---

* Within the last month the encrease in the number of prisoners at Paris has been above eight hundred.

my just indignation, and we concerted measures together for a radical reform of this abominable luxury. We ordered that for the future the food of those *gentle-men* should be of the most ordinary kind; that no distinction of persons should be observed; and that all the prisoners, of whatever quality or description, should be put upon the same common and fraternal regimen." The Convention approves this Republican order, and decrees, "that the food of the persons detained in the different prison-houses shall be frugal, and the same for all, the rich paying for the poor." In consequence of this decree suspected persons are compelled to eat with their servants, and their property is indiscriminately applied to defray the common expences of the whole prison. On the 20th of December, when (to use the words of Barrere) the jealous eye of liberty had penetrated into every family, and pervaded every habitation, when the inflexible severity and the indefatigable activity of the delegates of freedom had "peopled" the dungeons of every prison, an humble petition was presented at the bar of the Convention by several women, the relations, the wives, the children, and the parents of persons confined upon suspicion, imploring that they might be brought to trial, if any crime could be imputed to their charge, or if not, that they might be restored to the enjoyment of liberty, the common right of all who have not transgressed the law. The petitioners were sharply reprimanded by the president, who told them, "that the Convention had been already too merciful, that it had departed from the ancient models of republican severity, for that in all the republics of antiquity suspected persons were not merely imprisoned, but put to death." However a new decree is proposed by Robespierre in a speech, in which he also animadverts upon the misconduct of these incivic women, who could listen to the voice of nature and to the cry of blood when the liberty of their country was at stake. The decree enacts, "that a secret commis sion consisting of two members of the Committees of Public Welfare and of General Safety shall be appointed to consider of the means of restoring to liberty any patriots, who by accident may have been imprisoned with the aristocrats. The Commissioners are to exercise their functions with all *necessary severity*, and are to be *peculiarly cautious not to enervate the energy of the revolutionary measures.* The names of these Commissioners are to be kept secret from the public, *in order to avoid the danger of solicitations;* and they are to discharge no person from prison without the authority of the two Committees of Public Welfare and of General Safety."

On the 26th of December, Barrere makes the humane report which I have already quoted to the House; and he moves in the name of the Committee of Public Welfare that five members in place of two should be appointed for the same purpose, should assemble twice every day, and should decide summarily on all cases of arrest, without reference to the Committees; in other respects Barrere's decree is perfectly conformable to the spirit of Robespierre's, neither the secrecy of the commission, nor the recommendation of severity being in any degree altered. But even this decree appears too mild not only to Robespierre, but to the majority of the Convention. Robespierre objects to it, as being of the most dangerous tendency, and quite contrary to the spirit of that which had already passed in consequence of his own motion. He says, "it would be a great prejudice to the state to absorb the energy of five members of the Convention, by employing them in deciding upon the innumerable complaints which they would receive from all parts of the Republic, where all the prisons were filled with persons arrested on grounds of suspicion. His own plan was more simple, and without any inconvenience; it did not require that so large a portion of the Convention should be exclusively occupied by the complaints of prisoners; two members *in their leisure moments whenever circumstances might happen to permit without exposing themselves to importunity* might have discovered the small number of patriots, who perhaps might be found in confinement with the aristocrats—by this plan the Committee of General Safety would not have wasted, in listening to the solicitations of bad citizens, *that time so precious to the cause of liberty.*" He adds, " that the new decree is dangerous, because, under favour of it, liberty might possibly be granted to *some* aristocrats." —What then was to be done between these contending motions ? The Convention is embarrassed ; they perceive at last that their embarrassment arises from an excess of mistaken clemency in their first proceeding; they immediately resume the severity of true republicans ; they repeal the decree of Robespierre, reject the motion of Barrere, and refer the unfortunate petitioners to those very committees of whose tyranny they complained.

Since this proceeding it appears that the Convention has endeavoured to draw a revenue from these arbitrary imprisonments.

A proposition has been referred to the Committee of Public Safety on the motion of Danton for the confiscation of the property of all suspected persons ; and the property of all parents of emigrants, under detention, has been confiscated provisionally, until they can give proof that they have done their utmost to prevent the emigration of their children.

If the people of France are animated by an enthusiastic zeal for liberty, what must be their temper of mind, when they constantly behold the miserable spectacle of 200,000 persons arrested upon no specific charge, condemned without trial, and deprived of the inestimable blessings of personal freedom upon the vague and equivocal suggestions of indefinite suspicion ? The specious title of a free, united, and indivisible Republic cannot deceive a great nation suffering under the weight of practical oppression, and distracted by the jealous policy of a few men, whose vigilant fears bear a just proportion to their conscious guilt. Unless we can agree with Barrere, that justice executed in mercy is incompatible with the vigour of a well-ordered state ; that the strength of a free government is in proportion to the number of state prisoners; and that to *people prisons* is to give the best pledge of popular liberty, we must conclude, that a large proportion of the people of France at this moment anxiously desires the destruction of the present government, as the only means of rescuing their relations and friends from the miseries of imprisonment, as well as of securing themselves against similar oppression.

But these violations of the liberty of the subject will appear as acts of clemency, when compared with the daily murders and massacres which compose that sanguinary and merciless system, entitled by the Revolutionary Government the administration of criminal justice.

When Robespierre and his faction began to gain ascendancy in the Convention, one of their first measures was, to erect an extraordinary tribunal for the trial of state crimes : a tribunal which might serve them in the first instance to acquire power by the murder of their adversaries, and eventually might enable them to maintain it by similar outrages. The first mention of this dreadful institution struck the Convention itself with consternation and horror. Prophecies were uttered, which have since been fulfilled, that this instrument of destruction would soon be turned against the representatives of the people ; and Vergniaux, who has since fallen a victim to that relentless tribunal, declared that he and his whole party would prefer death upon the spot, to any share in the formation of so formidable an engine of tyranny : but Danton decided the Convention; he contended, " that a Revolutionary Government could not subsist without some representative of the Supreme Tribunal of the vengeance of the people : that the institution proposed would be a proper substitute for those tribunals which the people had formed in a moment of their ungovernable fury : that the people would not have committed

d

the massacre of the 2d of September, if an extraordinary tribunal had then existed."
He concluded with these remarkable words : " We must employ great means to
accomplish dreadful ends ; we must establish an extraordinary criminal code, and
we must seek for its principles beyond the pale of civil society. Let us be terrible
ourselves, in order to save the people the necessity of being so." Thus was the
extraordinary tribunal created expressly to save the people the labour of massacre,
and to perpetuate by a legal institution and with the authority of the state those
scenes of blood, of which, even the principal actors in them have never yet ventured to speak openly without the affectation of regret. The favorite principle of
the sovereignty of the people (the source of every calamity which they are doomed
to suffer) affords an equal facility for the violation of liberty, and for the destruction
of life. In conformity to that pernicious doctrine criminal justice in France now
presents the image of the sovereign people employed in the exercise of the combined prerogatives of insurrection and massacre, and is assimilated both in form
and spirit to those tribunals of murder, which held their session in the prison of
the abbey on the memorable night of the 2d of September.

Under the decree constituting the extraordinary tribunal, the judges are named
by the authority of the Convention, and are removable at pleasure. A permanent
jury is named by the Convention for each division of the tribunal, and the commission of the jury is nearly of the same nature with that of the judge. The crimes
of which this Court is to take cognizance, are described by the original decree in
these general terms.

" Every Counter-Revolutionary enterprize, every attempt against liberty, equality,
the unity and indivisibility of the Republic, and the internal or external safety of the
state ; every conspiracy tending to restore monarchy, or to establish any other
authority dangerous to liberty, equality, and the sovereignty of the people." All
these indefinite crimes are punishable with death, and forfeiture of property.

The forms of proceeding are subjected to no restraint or rule. The Court is
empowered to found its judgments upon any evidence however vague, suspicious,
or even from its nature incompetent ; or to use the words of Lindet, (the person
who proposed the original motion) '' The Judges may satisfy themselves of the
guilt of the criminal by every possible means." The established practice is to
interrogate the prisoner both secretly and publicly, and to make use of his own
testimony against himself. From this Court there is no appeal, excepting the Convention should think fit by an arbitrary interposition to overrule its proceedings.

The founders of this tribunal have employed it for the accomplishment of two
objects ; first, as a party engine, to extinguish by violence the spirit of indignation
and abhorrence arising in every part of the Republic against their crimes ; and
secondly, as a source of revenue to procure money and goods by the murder of
opulent bankers and merchants, and by the confiscation of their property.

With the first view, numberless persons have been executed for incivic or counter-revolutionary words, and for discourses, or writings " tending to provoke" the
restoration either of monarchy or of any other authority in any degree dangerous
to the sovereignty of the people, or in other words, to the sovereignty of the
Jacobin faction : these executions have not been confined to the gentlemen, clergy,
or persons of property ; numbers in the inferior classes of the people have suffered
death for mere loose conversation: not only emigrants, but even the family or
friends of an emigrant who have aided and assisted him in escaping from a country,
in which he could no longer remain with safety, are punished with death. Many
parents, wives and children of emigrants have been executed, for having obeyed
the common dictates of nature by relieving the urgent dirstresses of their banished
relations ; and bankers have suffered the same punishment for having in the ordi-

nary course of their business permitted the money of emigrants to pass through their hands. To circulate false news, or to give any impediment by words, or otherwise to the recruiting of the army have been made capital crimes. Under various pretences of plots against the unity and indivisibility of the Republic, or of conspiracies for the establishment of some counter revolutionary authority, all those who had borne any distinguished part in the earlier periods of the Revolution, together with the whole party of Brissot, and most of the Executive Council appointed on the 10th of August 1793 have been publicly executed. In many cases, the Convention has passed against persons of this description acts of outlawry, under which, whenever they fall into the hands of any criminal tribunal, they are executed without even the form of a trial. Within the course of six or seven months from fifty to sixty general officers have been executed upon various loose and indefinite charges. Brissot says,—that if Turenne had commanded the armies of the Republic, he would certainly have been condemned by the extraordinary tribunal, for he was not always successful ; every defeat would have exposed him to the suspicion of treachery, and every victory to the imputation of dangerous ambition.

The purpose of obtaining revenue is scarcely attempted to be disguised in many of the sentences passed by these tribunals. By the original decree a power was given of condemning to the punishment of transportation any persons who should be convicted of crimes not previously defined by law, or to which no specific punishment had already been annexed ; and since that time a law has passed for the confiscation of the property of all persons under sentence of transportation. The tribunals also exercise a power of arbitrary fine and imprisonment.

In a letter from the Commissioners of the Convention at Strasburg are these words, "The Revolutionary Tribunal which we have established for the judgment of monopolists, stock-jobbers, and merchants who will not submit themselves to the price fixed on the necessaries of life has already made several useful examples ; many persons have been condemned to pay fines of fifty and an hundred thousand livres (of two or four thousand pounds) and to suffer some years of imprisonment. A few more sentences of this kind are wanting to destroy the desire of gain, which is carried to a scandalous excess in this commercial town, but the Tribunal spares nobody, and the cause of liberty will prosper."

From Bordeaux a regular account was transmitted to the Jacobin Club of the sums received for the State on account of persons executed, amounting to several millions of livres. The Mayor of Bordeaux was beheaded because his brilliant fortune enabled him to attempt to hold an even hand between the two contending factions in that city, and because he had seconded some resolutions of the popular society established there : his brilliant fortune, which was the essence of his crime, was seized for the use of the Government at Paris.

An account was given to the Jacobins that the execution of two jews of the name of Rabas at Libourne, had *produced* twenty-three millions of livres, (about a million sterling) to the Republic ; the charge against them was, that they had lent money which was to be employed in raising a force in the departments at the time when the lives of the majority of the Convention were threatened at Paris by Marat, Robespierre and the faction now exercising the powers of Government. innumerable instances of the same kind might be cited, in which persons have been condemned to death under various frivolous pretences, obviously for the purpose of seizing their property. The mere possession of a large property is considered as a crime, and is distinctly stated to be so by Robespierre himself on a remarkable occasion : I mean when he prefers an impeachment in the Jacobin Club against Anacharsis Clootz the orator of the human race. He charges Monsieur Clootz (as he styles him by way of disgrace on that occasion) with the atrocious crime of possessing five thousand pounds a year. Upon this Monsieur Clootz is expelled from the club, has since been expelled from the assembly, and will probably expiate the sin of being a man of property by the forfeiture both of his life and of his estate.

The stock in trade of merchants, as I have already observed in defining the crime of monopoly, is appropriated to the use of the Committee of Public Welfare, or in their own phrase, put into circulation by the same summary process. With what severity this law is executed we may judge by a remarkable instance in which the Convention graciously extended its mercy to a criminal convicted of monopoly, and was so elated with this distinguished act of clemency, as to express a desire that it might be published throughout all Europe, in order to confound the enemies of France, and to refute the calumnious charges which had been circulated against the justice, humanity, and mildness of the criminal courts instituted by the Revolutionary Government. Gaudon a wine merchant was accused of not having written over his door according to the directions of the law the quantity and quality of the wines contained in his cellars; he was condemned to death; but it appeared afterwards, that during his absence from his house, his son had by mistake omitted to place over his father's door the regular declaration of his stock in trade; and upon this the Convention pardoned the convict. By the very terms of the pardon it is evident, that every man, who wilfully omits to write over his door the exact amount of his stock in trade, is by law to suffer death.

I cannot attribute to the Revolutionary Government the merit of invention in this particular branch of their system. The idea of drawing revenue from fictitious crimes is taken from governments which do not seem to furnish the best models of imitation for a Republic founded on the natural rights of man; I mean the barbarous tyrannies on the coast of Africa, whose revenue is chiefly drawn from the sacrifice of the liberties and lives of their subjects under the pretence of crimes, imagined merely to serve the purpose of financial resource. Here, again, we may trace the near connexion between despotism and the sovereignty of the people. The sovereign people of France in their mad career of political liberty suffer their principles of revenue to be derived from the very spring and origin of the most odious civil slavery; and the national treasury under a republican and revolutionary administration exhibits a faithful copy of the slave markets of Dahomey and Whydah.

By adverting more particularly to the conduct of some remarkable trials and to other circumstances, I will endeavour to bring before you the true character of these tribunals, the sanguinary spirit of the judges, and their open violation of all the rules and principles of evidence which have been devised for the protection of innocence by the wisdom, justice, and humanity of free and civilized nations. Previous to the trial of Brissot and the impeached deputies of the Convention, Roussillon, one of the permanent jury of the Revolutionary Tribunal goes to the Jacobin Club, and having complained that he had not yet enjoyed the satisfaction of beholding those traitors at the feet of the Tribunal, assures the Club, that whenever they shall be brought to their trial, he will take care that they shall not escape; he is much applauded for the patriotic energy of this declaration. During the trial of the deputies a letter is received by the Convention from the judges of the extraordinary Tribunal to the following effect: "The deputies whom you have accused have now been five days upon their trial, and only nine witnesses have been examined; every witness delivers a long and substantial evidence; the prisoners cross-examine each witness, and afterwards make their observations upon the evidence; this produces a discussion, which is much protracted by the loquacity of the prisoners; this trial will be endless; we have already given you sufficient proofs of our activity and zeal to exempt us from any suspicion of negligence or delay; but our progress is obstructed by certain formalities, which will at once vanish before the authority of the Legislature. We all ask ourselves wherefore any witnesses? The convention and the whole people of France accuse the prisoners. The proofs of their crimes are evident : every man has in his heart the conviction of their guilt."

The embarrassment of the supreme and extraordinary criminal court will no doubt appear to a British House of Commons to be such as would require the immediate interference of the Legislature. One and twenty men on trial for their lives, and not a man but desires to be heard! Justice delayed, and in danger of being disappointed by her own vain and idle forms ! But the wisdom of the representatives of a free people came to the relief of these venerable judges; the Convention having consulted the Jacobin Club its approved counsellor in all difficulties and dangers, decreed, that "whenever any trial should have lasted three days, the judges should call on the jury to declare whether their consciences were sufficiently enlightened to enable them to give a verdict; if the jury should answer in the affirmative, whatever might be the stage of the proceeding, no farther testimony or argument should be admitted, and the Court should immediately give judgment, as if the prisoner had regularly closed his case. To this decree was added another, declaring that the extraordinary criminal tribunal should from that moment change its name and bear the honourable title of the Revolutionary Tribunal, and that in conformity to its new title it should judge all crimes of State by a *revolutionary process,*" or in other words, without formality and without evidence.

These laws were immediately dispatched to the Court then sitting in judgment on the deputies. The new regulations were instantly applied to the depending trial ; the evidence was suddenly interrupted ; the prisoners were silenced ; sentence of death was passed upon them ; and they were hurried unheard and undefended to the public scaffold.* The most just objects of the severity of the law, when denied the common privilege of a fair trial and of a free defence, will move the compassion of mankind, and will even in some degree excite the same sentiments, which naturally attend oppressed innocence. Guilty as most of these men were of the murder of their sovereign, guilty as they all were of that wicked conspiracy which contrived the massacre of the 10th of August, and which produced the massacre of the 2d of September, we yet forget the enormity of their crimes in the undisguised violence of their condemnation, and our indignation is (for a time at least) transferred from the suffering criminal to the murderous judge.

What then shall we say of the pretended trial of the Queen, where our attention is withdrawn from all the affecting circumstances of her unexampled situation by the flagrant iniquity of that unmanly exercise of lawless power? Her sex, her exalted dignity, her protracted and unequalled misfortunes are all forgotten in the outrageous perversion of the sacred forms and maxims of criminal jurisprudence. From her first imprisonment to the hour of her murder, while we trace her various sufferings we feel for the cause of justice itself, a cause inseparably united with the security and happiness of the lowest as well as of the highest ranks of civil society. The Convention, the Jacobin Club, and all the agents of the Government employ every means both of encouragement and of terror to exasperate the ferocity of the judges and juries in the discharge of their dreadful functions. The least delay of judgment against a rich or unpopular criminal produces a ferment in the regenerated popular societies, and among all the instruments of the prevailing faction ; while on the other hand every precipitate, corrupt, and sanguinary condemnation is extolled as the perfection of patriotic zeal, and the model of republican virtue. The desire of shedding human blood, is carried to such a passionate excess

---

* Inauditi, atque indefensi, tanquam innocentes periere.—*Tacitus.*

that in the letters of some of the Commissioners of the Convention, the office of common executioner is represented as an eminent distinction, and a primary object of honourable ambition. From Rochefort, Lequinio and Laignelot write a letter to the Convention in these words, "Behold another triumph of morality, not over presbyterian mummery, (for that exists no longer in this country) but over a prejudice as absurd and as deeply rooted in the minds of men! We have formed here a Revolutionary Tribunal upon the model of that at Paris ; we named of our own authority all the members of the Court, excepting *that member whose duty it is to close the proceedings, we mean the executioner ;* we wished to leave to the patriots of Rochefort the glory of shewing themselves the voluntary avengers of the Republic ; we signified *the vacancy in the tribunal* at a full meeting of the popular society ; the citizen Ance cried out with a noble enthusiasm, I am the man who aspires to the honour of beheading the assassins of the country. He had scarcely time to utter these words, when a crowd of other patriots pressed forward to offer themselves for the same office, and they all anxiously solicited to be at least indulged with the favour of being permitted to aid the fortunate candidate in the discharge of his duty. We made proclamation that the *patriot* Ance had been invested with the honourable office of common executioner, and we invited him to dinner, where we delivered into his hands his warrant of office, and poured a libation over it in honour of the Republic ; we think that in a few days the judges will put him in the way of giving *a practical proof of his patriotism.* To this patriot who has taken upon himself with so much generosity the trouble of executing the sentences of the Revolutionary Tribunal, we have given the title of *avenger of the people ;* and to the instrument which delivers us from traitors, that of *the justice of the people,* this title is inscribed upon the guillotine in large characters."

The zeal of some of these Commissioners has carried them even beyond the extravagance of this letter. With a strange mixture of ridiculous phrenzy, of wanton impiety, and of savage cruelty, after having profaned the established symbols of every religion, they have consecrated the instrument of ignominious death, and styling it in their public despatches, "Our Holy Mother the Guillotine," have thus attributed to it the combined character of parent and tutelary deity of the Republic.

The House will judge what must be the administration of criminal justice in France, when the commissioners of the legislature encourage contests, and hold public elections for the office of common executioner, admit the successful candidate to their table, join with him in toasting severity to the judges, and sanctify the axe itself as an object of filial affection and' of religious veneration. The spirit and practice of the Revolutionary Tribunal cannot be better summed up than in the words of Brissot, uttered a few days before his imprisonment. He says, "It is a tribunal arbitrary in its forms, absurd and partial in its proofs, iniquitous in its judgments, and fit to make one regret the bastiles of despotism."

The effusion of blood at Paris has been such, that not less than a thousand executions have taken place there within the course of six months. Yet the vengeance and avarice of the Government is so far from being satiated, that the Commissioners of Police have lately acquainted the Municipality of Paris, that the pit which had been appropriated for the burial of the unfortunate victims of the Revolutionary Tribunal was nearly full, and could not hold above "some sixty" more they therefore desire immediate authority to dig another in order to prevent any delay of justice. I cannot forbear to remark in this place, that during the whole period when all the power and authority of Government in France were exercised by that humane and benevolent prince, whose innocent blood was shed on the scaffold, not one instance is to be found of an execution for a state crime !

But the tribunal at Paris, although subdivided into four sections, could not cir-

culate the salutary movement of terror with sufficient promptitude and effect to
the extremities of the Republic. The guillotine had long been in a state of permanent activity at Paris; the ingenuity of zealous patriots was now exercised in de-
vising means for propagating the use of this favorite engine of liberty, and various
mechanical inventions were proposed with a view to provide portable axes, and
ambulatory scaffolds.

A new military force was raised at the expence of persons of property under the
title of a Revolutionary Army, for the express purpose of traversing every department of the Republic, and of suppressing every symptom of a counter-revolutionary spirit. To each regiment of this army is attached a corps of light armed
judges, and a flying guillotine. (I copy their own expressions; and if I appear to
treat too lightly proceedings calculated to inspire indignation and horror, you must
impute it to the peculiar genius and character of the men of whom I speak, to the
wild extravagance of their wickedness, and to the levity which is always mingled
with their most atrocious crimes.) But the Commissioners of the Convention in
the Western Departments have found that even the revolutionary laws were too
mild in their nature, and too slow in their execution to accomplish the great objects
which were proposed by the institution of the Revolutionary Army. Accordingly
they decreed, that the tribunal attached to their regiment should be both military
and revolutionary, and that its sentences should be of a mixed quality, partaking
of the principles of martial law, tempered by the mild spirit of that humane code,
which was substituted by Danton in place of the fury of the mob. To secure the
uniform activity of this amphibious court, it was given out in general orders, that
the judges, the public accuser, the clerk and other officers of the court should be
mounted upon the fleetest horses in the service, and should form a troop of Chas-
seurs, to be united to the establishment of the staff, and to take post near head-
quarters wherever the army might halt. Thus equipped, Laplanche, one of the
commissioners, informs the Convention that he has named his corps " the Infernal
Regiment," and that he parades the country " with justice and clemency at his left
hand, and the guillotine at his right;" an order of precedency perfectly consistent
with the etiquette of a Revolutionary Government.

It cannot be denied, that this army with its attendant tribunal, uniting all the
severity and vigour of civil and military despotism, is one of the most effectual expedients ever yet invented for extending the influence of tyranny to the remotest
parts of a great empire, and to every class and description of a numerous people.
It is applicable to every purpose of terror, of plunder, and of revenge; it has in
fact been applied to all of them in their turn, and has been the main engine of
government for some time past. Its principal duties in the course of its march
have been (as you may collect from the different reports made to the Convention)
to regenerate the municipalities, and to execute the former municipal officers; to
collect the revenue, and to superintend the ruin of agriculture and the abolition of
commerce; to compel the rich to " disgorge" their wealth; to compel the farmers
and tradesmen to sell their stock for one-third of its real value; and occasionally
to seize the stock itself, and to murder the proprietor; to lower the price of day
labour, and to force the labourer to work at the reduced price; to break open every
private house under pretence of searching for concealed treasure, and by the application of torture and the terror of death to extort the whole substance of every
opulent farmer, and of every industrious tradesman; to drag all suspected persons
to prison, and all declared adversaries of Government to the scaffold; to plunder
churches of every emblem of Christianity, and to suppress the worship of every
form and sect of religion; but amongst all the uses to which the Revolutionary
Army is applied, none is more important to the Government, none more vexatious

and oppressive in its effects on the happiness and welfare of the people, and none more ruinous to the internal prosperity of the country, than the duty of enforcing the levies for the army on the frontier. I have already endeavoured to explain the system of exaction and extortion practised for the purpose of procuring the means of paying the armies upon the frontier, I have described its destructive operation upon every species of property, and upon every permanent resource of revenue; I have also stated to you the violence and rapine employed in order to supply those armies with provisions, with cloathing, and with every necessary store; and I have traced the operation of those measures upon the internal trade and cultivation of the country. I shall now show that the evils which attend the raising of this immense military force highly aggravate those by which it is maintained; and that the mere levy of these armies is in itself an oppression of the most grievous nature, and productive of the most pernicious consequences to the interests both of agriculture and commerce.

The law for the requisition of the whole mass of the people, passed at the latter end of August. By this law every man in France from the age of eighteen to fifty is compelled to give his personal service in the army at the requisition of the National Commissioners. The rigour with which this law was executed, will appear from a resolution of the department of Herault sanctioned by the Convention, and since converted into a general law. "Every father and mother shall be bound to declare the place of abode of their children summoned by requisition for the service of the army; every citizen is forbidden to harbour or conceal any persons under requisition. The soldiers of the revolutionary armies are authorised to arrest all persons who shall appear to them to have been put into requisition, and to lodge them in jail if they endeavour to escape. The proper officers are to search every house twice a week, in order to discover any person who may attempt to elude the requisition." To enforce this severe military conscription a law was passed (to which I have already alluded) subjecting any person who shall impede the levy of the army by words or otherwise to the punishment of death. Not only no parent can venture even to advise his children to remain at home, but in most parts of the Republic *the executioner has been the recruiting serjeant,* and the unfortunate peasants and labourers in the provinces have been compelled to make their option between the perils of battle, and the unerring stroke of the guillotine. Many insurrections have happened in the several departments in consequence of this violence, and have been suppressed by the Revolutionary armies and their attendant tribunals.

The immediate effect of such a system must be to disturb the happiness of every private family, to involve all the inferior classes of the people in misery and ruin, to suspend every art of honest industry, and of useful labour, and to expose all who remain in the country to the complicated calamities of indigence and famine. To what degree these evils were expected to operate by the Convention itself, we may judge from the measures which have been taken to avert them. Towards the latter end of September a law passed to compel all farmers, manufacturers, or labourers remaining in France to cultivate the lands of those who were absent on the service of the army. This is the regular course of the revolutionary system, to endeavour to remedy the mischievous consequences of one act of oppression by committing another. Having torn five hundred thousand men from the bosom of their families, and from the cultivation of the earth, they attempt to supply that loss by the compulsory labour of those who have been rejected from the service of the army; they have recourse to the refuse of their own tyranny; and they rely for the subsistence of France on the miserable remnant of a depressed, impoverished, and dejected people. That an army, raised by such means, should be animated by the enthusiasm of liberty I cannot believe, until I can forget all the circumstances which I have just now described, as well as all the events which have happened in France since the accession of the Revolutionary Government. That so large a body of men collected together under military discipline, and opposed to an enemy, may feel a great degree of military enthusiasm, is a proposition which I do not mean to contest; but my object has been in whatever observations I have made on this part of the subject, to direct your attention to the internal state of France, as resulting immediately from the operation of these military levies. It is for the wisdom of the House to determine what must be the condition of that state whose army is raised by the suspension of agriculture, under the terror of death, and at the daily hazard of insurrection; paid by the destruction of the rights of property, and by the practice of public fraud; and supplied by the annihilation of trade, and at the risk of internal famine.

You have now before you the principal features both of the theory and practice of the Revolutionary Government. Reviewing this unexampled system in all its details, you will find special and effectual provision established for the indiscriminate misery and ruin of every rank and order of society. It contains a principle of impartial persecution, equally applicable (as the occasion may require) to the separate interests of every distinct class and description of the people, from the gentlemen of landed property, and the opulent bankers and merchants, down to the industrious manufacturer and the laborious peasant. Are these the arts of Government? Are these the means by which the discordant interests and the contending passions of mankind can be brought to act in concert, and can be directed to the welfare of the community, the end of all political society, and the only solid foundation of power? I speak to an assembly versed in all the great maxims of government, affectionately attached to the genuine principles of liberty, and accustomed to deliberate on whatever can affect the interests of a powerful state, and the happiness of a numerous people: in such an assembly I am persuaded that I should not be contradicted, if I were to contend without any further proof, that a tyranny so constituted and so exercised must of necessity be odious to the people, and consequently whatever might be its temporary efforts, must rest upon an insecure and uncertain foundation. But I need not rely on general topics, however justly drawn from the constitution of human affairs, and from the character of man in all situations, and in all ages. The people of France, (although hitherto unfortunate in the attempt) have not tamely submitted to the oppression of this mean and humiliating usurpation. In no less than forty of the departments, a spirit of indignation has broken out against the Government; in many, the people have taken up arms, and waged open war; in some, they have expressed their discontent by riots and insurrections, by opposing the levies for the army, and by refusing to submit to the confiscation of their incomes and to the plunder of their goods. This spirit has appeared with great strength in all the most opulent commercial towns; but it has not been confined to them; it has been diffused as widely as the oppression which excited it, and its symptoms (varying with opportunities, and with means of exertion) are to be traced in almost every town and village of France. They are to be traced in all those acts of arbitrary power by which the several municipalities have been regenerated, the popular societies purged and purified, and the sense of the people violently suppressed: they are to be traced in all the expeditions of those revolutionary armies and itinerant executioners, who have been embodied for the circulation of the movement of terror, and who traverse the country with express orders to stifle the rising flame of general revolt.

If we are to believe the testimony of the Convention, the object of all these commotions is uniformly the restoration of some species of monarchy; the Convention insists that the discontented spirits in France universally look up to some form of royal authority, as the only standard under which all the friends of order and law can re-assemble with safety, under which they may all forget their former animosities, reconcile their discordant opinions, and unite in a firm league for the destruction of that despotic anarchy which is their common enemy, and which cannot subsist without producing their common destruction. This spirit may have been oppressed for a time, but it is not extinct. After all the misfortunes which have fallen on those who had the courage to stand foremost in opposition to the plunderers of their country, after all the scenes of blood which have been acted under the authority of the Convention, the agents of their cruelty have been compelled to confess, that although they have gratified their revenge in the massacre of multitudes of their adversaries, they have not been able to subdue the unconquerable "incivism" of the survivors. At Bordeaux, when the Popular Society had been taken by storm, when the whole town had been disarmed, when three hundred rich merchants had been imprisoned, and when the Revolutionary Tribunal, seconded by the *patriotism* of the executioner, had destroyed every distinguished enemy of anarchy, a letter is written to the Municipality of Paris from one of their agents, lamenting, "that after having studied the temper of the public mind at Bordeaux, he must declare, that not one man in that city had yet reached the exalted level of the Revolution. The Commissioners of the Convention met regularly in the Temple of Reason on the last day of each decade, chaunted hymns in honour of liberty and sound philosophy, and preached sermons worthy of true Mountaineers; but they could scarcely collect a congregation."

In other accounts from Bordeaux it appears, that it had been found necessary to regenerate the whole company of actors at the theatre, to secure the performance of revolutionary plays : but even this measure failed of its effect; the actors were changed, but the audience remained the same ; the audience could not endure to hear a single revolutionary verse. To use the phrase of the afflicted patriot who reports this transaction, "they hissed all the passages which were most conformable to the order of the day;" and the new mayor (the successor of him who had been regenerated by the guillotine) was obliged to interpose, and to compel by force the free and sovereign people to receive without indignation the homage offered to their sovereignty, and to listen with patience to the panegyric of their freedom.

Although the Convention has repeatedly boasted that the seat of the war in the north-western departments presented nothing to the view but a heap of ashes bedewed with the blood of the insurgents, although we have often heard of the total extirpation of the army of the Royalists, that army has as often risen again, and opposed a vigorous resistance to every force which has yet been employed against it.

Even at Lyons, notwithstanding all the feasts and orgies of murder (for so they were styled by those who celebrated them) the sentiments of the citizens remain unaltered, and even undisguised. After having sequestrated the property of all who were engaged in the insurrection, and having levied a forced loan upon all who were not, for the express purpose of "defraying the expences of the necessary demolitions," after the actual demolition of all the most beautiful buildings, the execution of the principal citizens, and (according to their own words) "the complete enfranchisement of the city," the Commissioners of the Convention were "astonished at the insensibility of the inhabitants. A sullen silence accompanied every period of the salutary work of regeneration; not one expression of joy was heard for the return of liberty ; not one address of thanks or congratulation was presented on an occasion which seemed naturally to call forth every sentiment of gratitude and satisfaction."

The Commissioners, however, were not discouraged, they proceeded with encreased vigour; concluding that the effusion of human blood had not yet been sufficient to inspire the people with the enthusiasm of true liberty, they now rejected the use of their favourite engine of death, as being wholly inadequate to the prodigious magnitude of their extensive designs. Mixing the instruments of war with the perverted forms of criminal justice, and blending the solemnity of a public execution with the tumult and slaughter of battle, they accomplished a project of massacre such as never before had been attempted, or even conceived by the most inventive genius in the arts of cruelty.* This effort also disappointed their expectations; and they complain, that "the traitors, whom they had punished, persisted in their treason even to the hour of their execution."

Death in its most formidable shape, attended with every accumulated circumstance of terror, could not shake the constancy of these brave men. In the face of the executioner, in the very mouths of the cannon pointed against them, they maintained their principles, they avowed their attachments, and in their dying agonies, mingled the expressions of veneration for the memory of their murdered sovereign and of loyalty to his surviving issue with their last prayers to their insulted God.

The effects of this unprecedented barbarity were not more favourable on the minds of the spectators. Some time after the commencement of the new system of execution, the General of a division of the Revolutionary Army declares, that "when he entered the city of Lyons, although the inhabitants paid him the compliment of shutting up their houses and shops as he marched before their doors, they demonstrated by the most unequivocal gestures their obstinate adherence to the crimes of those whose punishment they had beheld." He says, "he met several women dispersed through the streets, and in every face he perceived the expressions of rage and resentment, rather than those of repentance or fear." The Commissioners of the Convention appear at length absolutely to despair of the complete regeneration of this enfranchised city, in one of their last reports they acknowledge, "that among an hundred and forty thousand inhabitants, they have as yet discovered not more than fifteen hundred exempt from the guilt of rebellion; and they recommend as the last expedient, that all the inhabitants should be banished from Lyons in bodies of twenty or thirty thousand, and settled in some remote part of France; they express a hope that these colonies, when transplanted into a better soil, may bear the fruits of liberty." But where is that happy soil to be found, in which they shall learn to forget the indignities which they have suffered, and the cruelties which they have beheld?

It is observed by a French author,† that the Jacobin faction has encreased the number of its enemies by the very means employed to exterminate them. Massacre will not extinguish popular discontent. Every victim of injustice and cruelty bequeaths his revenge to his connections, to his friends, and to his relations: or (if all these should be involved in the same common fate with himself) every such execution raises detestation and abhorrence even in the breast of ordinary spectators, and unites the public opinion against a Government which exists only by the daily practice of robbery and murder.

---

* The suspected persons at Lyons were drawn out in a very numerous body in chains in one of the squares of that city; a park of artillery was drawn out opposite to them; and the cannon, loaded with grape and chain shot, were discharged upon the prisoners.—[ED.]

† Camille Desmoulins.

From this disgusting scene, let us turn our eyes to our own situation ; here the contrast is striking in all its parts—" Here (to use the eloquent language of a distinguished Member of this House) we see nothing of the character and genius of arbitrary finance ; none of the bold frauds of bankrupt power ; none of the wild struggles and plunges of despotism in distress ; no lopping off from the capital of debt ; no suspension of interest ; no robbery under the name of loan ; no raising the value, no debasing the substance of the coin."*

Here we behold public credit of every description flourishing under all the disadvantages of a general war ; an ample revenue, flowing freely and copiously from the opulence of a contented people, from the encreasing sources of agriculture not only unimpaired, but actually improved even in the midst of hostilities ; from a commerce, not engaged in a hostile contest with the Supreme Power of the State, not " enslaved and invested on all sides" by arbitrary restraints, not reproached, suspected, and punished for its accumulating profits, but protected in its gains, unrestrained in its enterprizes, supported in difficulty, and relieved from danger by the vigilant care of a wise and provident legislature. We behold armies not levied by compulsory requisitions, not torn from the plough and the loom by the hands of the executioner, not paid and supplied by prehensions and seizures of private property, but proceeding from the spontaneous effort of a brave nation, maintained without difficulty and without oppression, and assisted under all the hardships of war, by the voluntary generosity of their fellow subjects. Instead of the proscription of honest industry, and the confiscation of all private fortunes, instead of peopled prisons and crowded scaffolds, instead of persecuted Christianity, and established atheism, we see property respected, justice allied with mercy and liberty with law, an inviolable regard for the rights of personal freedom, and a sacred reverence for the principles of religion ; and in the public mind we find a due sense and value of all these blessings, a general conviction that they are all involved in the issue of the present contest, and a firm determination to prosecute it with vigour, as the only means of securing their continuance.

The result of this view both of the condition of our enemy and of our own leads to a variety of deductions, all of which are essentially connected with the subject of our present deliberation : it proves, that the whole fabric of the government now prevailing in France is unsound in every part ; that the measures by which the efforts of that government have been maintained in the last campaign, are at this moment exhausting the resources of the country, not slowly and gradually, not according to the regular progress of ordinary evils in the administration of States, but with a rapidity and violence which at once dissolve the very elements of the system of political economy, and preclude the possibility of recurring even to the same destructive projects in the event of any new exigency ; it proves, that these measures are not only temporary and occasional in their very nature, but are expressly admitted to be so by the persons who proposed them ; all the most important operations of finance are of this description ; and Barrère himself felt the levy of the mass of the people to be a project of such danger, that when he introduced it into the Convention, he justified it upon this single argument, "that it would bring the war to a termination in the course of the campaign," meaning that campaign which has just now been closed.

It proves, that such having been the true causes of whatever difficulties we have already experienced, we may entertain a reasonable expectation, that causes so unnatural, together with their monstrous effects, must ultimately yield to a steady and unremitting exertion of our natural and genuine strength, confirmed by the

* Vide Mr. Burke's Speech on the Economical Reform of the King's Household.

co-operation of our numerous allies; it proves farther, that the same measures which have enabled the ruling faction to resist our attacks, have been so odious to the feelings, and so ruinous to the interests of every class and description of persons in France, as to have entirely alienated a large proportion of the people from the Government; and this circumstance becomes a strong additional reason for perse-verance in our efforts, as it must tend to facilitate the success of any impression which we may hereafter be enabled to make.

Such are the reasons on which I ground my hopes of our final success in the present war. The necessity of our perseverance is to be deduced from the same considerations. For it appears, in the first place, from the detail which I have laid before you, that the destructive doctrines and the false principles of Government, of which you dreaded the extension even in their infancy, have now attained full maturity and vigour, and have produced enormities infinitely surpassing whatever you had apprehended from their progressive malignancy, and from their active powers of mischief. It appears that these enormities have been formally digested into a code, and embodied in a regular system, from which has sprung a tyranny so atrocious in form, in substance, in principle, and in practice, that as every man of common humanity must desire to see it destroyed in France for the sake of the people who suffer under it, so every member of civil society would willingly en-counter the calamities of the most protracted war, rather than incur the risk of subjecting his own country to the pernicious effects of such an evil. The question, therefore, which remains to be considered is, whether we can effectually secure ourselves against the inroad of that evil, by any other means than the continuance of our present exertions.

From the facts which I have already enumerated, it is incontestible, that in pro-portion as this tyranny consumes the property of France, it must entertain projects of ambition and aggrandizement; it must endeavour to repair its disordered finances by preying upon its neighbours, and to supply the exhausted resource of domestic confiscation by foreign plunder. It is equally evident, on the same general grounds, that it must be the immediate interest of a Government, founded on principles wholly contradictory to the received maxims of all surrounding nations, to propagate the doctrines abroad, by which it subsists at home, to assimi-late every neighbouring state to its own system, and to subvert every constitution which can form a disadvantageous contrast with its own absurdities; such a Go-vernment must, therefore, from its nature, be hostile to all regular Governments of whatever form, but above all to those which are most strongly contrasted with its own vicious structure, and which afford to their subjects the best securities for the maintenance of order, liberty, justice, and religion.

Engaged in a contest with enemies of such a character, nothing can secure us against the danger of their future violence, but an effectual reduction of their pre-sent power. A peace founded on any other principle would not only be illusory, but must inevitably produce the most fatal consequences to all our most valuable interests. But the Government of France neither can nor will accede to terms of peace in any degree conformable to this principle so indispensably necessary to our security.

By an article of the Constitution of the 10th of August, 1793, it is positively declared as a fundamental maxim of the foreign policy of France that she will not conclude peace with an enemy who occupies any part of her territory; this article was not suspended by the institution of the Revolutionary Government; it was acted upon by the agents of the Convention in the island of Corsica during the course of the last campaign, and their proceedings have since been deliberately approved by the Convention.

Under this article it is obvious, that no peace can be concluded with France, unless we previously surrender into her hands all the acquisitions which we have made from her territory in the course of the present campaign; and here the importance of those acquisitions will perhaps be felt even by those who have hitherto undervalued them. We must surrender not only Valenciennes, Condé, and Quesnoy; but our conquests at Newfoundland and in the East and West Indies; and having thus abandoned all means of indemnity, we are to rely upon the good will of the Convention for such security as they may vouchsafe to grant us.

But this humiliating and dangerous concession is far short of the extent of the indignity and hazard to which we must subject ourselves even in the preliminary steps towards a Treaty of Peace in the present moment.

It has been supposed by some persons, that in the month of April the obnoxious decree of the 19th of November, 1792, was repealed; and arguments have been drawn from that circumstance to prove that the Jacobin Faction have wholly abandoned their system of ambition and of interference in the internal affairs of other countries. But the fact is, that the decree of the 19th of November, 1792, has never been formally repealed. On the 13th of April, 1793, a period in which it may naturally be supposed that the failure of their designs against Holland, and the expulsion of their army from the Netherlands had depressed the spirits of the Convention, a decree was proposed and passed at the suggestion of Robespierre and Danton, for the express purpose of throwing difficulties in the way of any negociation with the belligerent powers. In introducing this decree, Danton uses the following expressions:

" The principle of my motion is, that the penalties of death shall be inflicted on any man who shall propose to the Republic to treat with any enemy, who has not as a preliminary recognized the sovereignty of the people; in a moment of enthusiasm, we made a grant of universal fraternity, by which we seem to be bound to succour any patriot who may chuse to make a revolution in China; but our first care ought to be the foundation of the power of France; when the Republic shall be securely established, our energy and our new lights will attract every people on earth; let us therefore declare, that we will not interfere in the affairs of other States, but let us also determine to condemn to death any person, who shall propose a negociation; which has not for its basis the principles of our liberty."

After this speech a decree was passed, in the first article of which the Convention declares, " that it will not interfere in the internal government of other powers." The next article enacts the penalties of death against " whoever shall propose to negociate or treat with any power at war with the Republic, unless such power shall have previously made a solemn recognition of the independance of the French nation, and of the sovereignty, indivisibility, and unity of the Republic founded upon liberty and equality." I pass over the observations which might be made upon that part of this decree which requires the previous and unconditional acknowledgement of a new power in Europe, as the preliminary to a negociation for peace. But it is necessary to understand distinctly what is meant by the acknowledgement of the " unity and indivisibility of the Republic." This expression is clearly explained by subsequent circumstances.

On the 25th of August, a report is made by Herault Schelles, in the name of the Committee of Public Welfare to the following effect: " The people of Savoy are apprehensive that France is disposed to abandon that department united to the Republic by the ties of liberty. It is essential to counteract a rumour so fatal to the interests of Savoy, and so injurious to the honour of France. On the 13th of April you passed a decree, by which you entered into a formal engagement with the people of the re-united countries, that you would never consent to abandon them. You are bound by the laws of nature, which have traced the limits of the French empire on the extreme verge of Savoy, you are bound by every consideration of interest and of duty to remove the apprehensions of the people of Savoy, by repeating and confirming the declaration which you made in the month of April; a declaration, which placed under your guardianship all the nations situated between the confines of liberty and of slavery."

" In consequence of this report, a decree was passed, declaring, that the Convention considers itself bound to afford equal protection to all parts of the Republic one and indivisible against all tyrants and their slaves." And accordingly Commissioners were named to take proper measures for delivering Savoy from the incursion of the Piedmontese troops. In the debate upon this decree, it is maintained " that Savoy is an integral part of the Republic, and must be so considered, even if it should appear that the Constitution had been accepted there only by a minority of the inhabitants." Barrere closes the debate, and says, " England has bound herself by a treaty with Russia not to conclude peace with France, until France shall have restored her conquests to their original possessors, but Savoy is not a conquest, nature and the wish of its inhabitants, have united it to France." The whole of this debate, and the decree by which it is terminated, refer immediately to the decree of the 13th of April, and furnish a clear exposition of its true sense and effect. It is evident, that notwithstanding the ostentatious renunciation of the principle of fraternity, France still maintains her claim to all those territories united to her dominion by the influence of corruption and of fear, so forcibly described in the confessions of Brissot. This decree of counter-fraternity is therefore in reality a fresh instance of her rooted principles of aggrandizement and ambition, and it is the more remarkable as it was passed in the hour of adversity, in a period of domestic division, and of foreign misfortune. If any doubt can remain respecting the true intent of this decree, it is entirely removed by the events which happened during the solemnity of the 10th of August, 1793. On that day, the representatives of " *eighty-six*" departments appeared at Paris, for the purpose of acknowledging the acceptance of the new Constitution, and the President of the Convention, in a magnificent speech pronounced at the feet of the altar of the country, declared, that the Constitution had been accepted by the " *eighty-six*" departments of France, a number which includes all the re-unions.

The first step therefore towards the negociation of peace must necessarily be, to acknowledge the right of France to the Dutchy of Savoy, and to surrender the Netherlands and the principality of Liege into her hands. Who is the Statesman that shall advise us either to insult our allies, by proposing to them a concession equally incompatible with their interest, and degrading to their dignity, or to renounce every obligation of public faith, and every sentiment of honour, by commencing a separate negociation for peace on such terms without their previous concurrence? They* who have frequently argued in this House, that national honour is the most if not the only justifiable cause of war, will not (I presume) contend that national disgrace can be a solid foundation of peace.

If it were possible to imagine that we could be disposed to commit an act of such flagrant perfidy, the sense of our own immediate interest would be sufficiently strong to restrain us. We must indeed have forgotten the original cause of this war, the nature of that necessity which compelled us to embark in it, together with every circumstance which has attended its progress, before we can consent to confirm to France the command of the frontier of Italy, to reinstate her armies in their former position on the frontier of Holland, to sacrifice every advantage which

---

* Mr. Fox.

we have gained, to repair every loss which she has suffered, to abandon all the resources of the Netherlands to the immediate effects of her rapine, and to leave the wealth and power of Holland at her discretion. After having thus weakened our own barrier, and given new strength to the enemy, after having submitted to such preliminaries, what new indignity might we not expect in the definitive treaty of peace? A further preliminary concession required by this decree may serve to apprize us what might hereafter be exacted from this country as a separate article, whenever France should be in a situation to enforce such a demand. It is required that we should acknowledge the sovereignty of the Republic founded upon liberty and equality. To repeat the words of Danton "the principles of French liberty are to form the basis of the negociation." We must therefore sanction and ratify by a formal act of recognition all those pernicious doctrines from which the calamities of France have flowed, we must abjure the fundamental maxims of our own limited monarchy, we must renounce the elementary principles of every branch of the British Constitution, and all this, in order to put ourselves into a situation, in which the National Convention will deign 'to admit us to treat for peace. If it should be argued that the Constitution and the law of France do indeed present all these obstacles to the negociation of peace, but that the Constitution and the law may be disregarded in this instance, as they have been in others, by the ruling faction : I answer, first, that no man in France can even propose an infraction of this law, without immediately incurring the penalties of death. Secondly, if it were probable that any existing power in France could have the boldness to brave this danger, and the influence to obtain permission for Great Britain to open a negociation on less disgraceful terms, the whole transaction would on the first favourable occasion be imputed as a crime to those who had conducted it, the stipulations of a treaty commenced in open defiance of the law would be easily annulled, and we should discover too late our fatal error in having relaxed our efforts precisely at the most critical period of the war, for the prospect of negociating with a Government utterly unable to fulfil its engagements.

But after some attention to the subject, I cannot discover any such symptoms of a pacific disposition in the Jacobin faction, as to justify a rational hope, that they would incur the slightest risk for the sake of giving peace to Europe, and least of all, for the sake of giving a separate peace to England. I have already had occasion to make some allusion to the general character of their system of foreign politics. They were the most zealous promoters of the famous decree of fraternity ; a decree which was passed by acclamation and with an excess of frantic enthusiasm occasioned in great measure by their violence. Danton himself moved the re-union of the Netherlands, and upon that occasion first broached the extravagant doctrine, that the limits of France were marked by nature in four points, the Ocean, the Rhine, the Alps, and the Pyrenees, and that peace must never be made until the dominion of France has reached these four natural boundaries. Danton was afterwards one of the Commissioners who fraternized with the Flemish people by seizing their wealth, by arresting their persons, by subverting their laws, and by profaning their religion. Cambon moved the re-union of Nice, and was the author of the fraudulent decree of the 15th of December, 1792, by which the property of all the re-united nations was placed under the "safeguard and protection" of the French Republic, and converted accordingly to the use of the French treasury, and by which, war was declared against every people who should dare to preserve their loyalty to their prince, or to tolerate any distinction of ranks and orders of society. Robespierre was loud in his complaints against Dumourier for not having more rigorously executed this very decree, and for not having invaded Holland immediately upon the first conquest of the Netherlands in the month of December, 1792. Barrere was that president of the Convention, who in the true spirit of fraternity received the ambassadors of sedition and treason from this country, and joined with them in a fervent prayer for the subversion of the British Constitution. His principles were known to be so ardent, that at the moment of the declaration of war he was appointed together with Thomas Paine to draw up an address to the people of England for the purpose of alienating their affections from their lawful sovereign and from the constitution of Parliament. The dangerous spirit which unquestionably prevailed among the Jacobin faction at the breaking out of the war, has not been mitigated by the course of subsequent events. It breaks forth in various shapes, according to the difference of occasions, tempers, and situations. The Jacobin society, the parent of the existing Government in France, and the fountain head of all political doctrines in that country, so lately as the month of October last printed and circulated through all the affiliated societies of anarchy, and through all the regular official channels provided for such purposes a very curious treatise entitled "Revolutionary Diplomatics, by Anacharsis Clootz Orator of the Human Race." In this work the Orator of the Human Race addresses himself to the Sans Culottes of Holland, and exhorts them to take consolation under their present oppressions. He says, "the principal Members of the National Convention and of the popular societies are still convinced of the importance of uniting the mouths of the Rhine with the mouths of the Rhone, and of restoring to France the natural limits of ancient Gaul. The geographical position of France is not changed since last year; France cannot be confined within the factitious limits fixed by the folly of her kings; public opinion has already condemned those, who would patch up a peace by sacrificing to the Cabinet of St. James's the interests of Savoy, Nice, Liege, and the Netherlands. The extension of the territory of France is equally essential to her own domestic happiness, and to the establishment of the rights of man in every part of the world." Towards the conclusion of this new essay on the law of nations, it is announced, " that the day is approaching when the people of England shall rise, and demand the convocation of an assembly, where there shall be no question either of My Lords or Gentleman." It is true that Mr. Clootz, having been detected in the crime of enjoying a considerable property, has been lately expelled from the Jacobin Club; but it does not appear that these enlarged doctrines of universal fraternity, inculcated on the minds of the people of France by order of the Jacobins, have been since withdrawn from general circulation; and we have no more reason to conclude from the expulsion of Mr. Clootz, that his Revolutionary diplomatics have been involved in the fate of their author, than that the Convention in expelling Thomas Paine intended to renounce the rights of man. Robespierre, in terms somewhat more measured, has expressed sentiments of the same mischievous tendency in his report of the 17th of November, 1793, upon the political situation of the Republic, a report made in the name of the Committee of Public Welfare, which had before that time been invested with the whole powers of Government.

" The Brissotins while they left our soldiers without arms, our fortresses without provisions, and our armies in the hands of traitors, urged us to go and plant the standard of the Republic on the extremities of the world; with the stroke of a pen they overturned all thrones, and added Europe to the French empire. The sincere friends of the Republic had a different plan: before they attempted to break the chains of the universe, they wished to secure the liberty of their own country; before they carried war into the countries of foreign despots, they wished to direct it against the tyrant who betrayed them at home; convinced that a King was but a bad guide to conduct a people to the conquest of universal liberty."

You may understand from this passage, with what view Robespierre and his

e

party urged the murder of their unfortunate sovereign; it was (according to the avowal of the Committee of Public Welfare in this report) for the purpose of establishing a government, under which the people of France might be more readily conducted to the *conquest of universal liberty*; a phrase which now requires no comment. On the 5th of December Robespierre reported his celebrated answer to the manifestoes of all Kings. In this extraordinary composition is contained a more scandalous libel against every Prince in Europe, and a more virulent invective against monarchy itself, than any which has yet appeared, even in France. He calls all Kings " slaves in a state of insurrection against the sovereignty of the people." He says, " that royalty is the master-piece of human corruption." He maintains (as I have already stated) "that regicide is an act of the purest piety; but he declares, that he has no further intention, than to enlighten the minds of mankind with regard to the crimes of their respective Governments." He concludes with an argument to prove that " the British Government must be a despotism, because there is an opposition in Parliament; and he calls the British people, a vile and insolent race, which has the presumption to talk of the rights of freedom, and of the duties of morality."

These expressions bring before your view not only the general hostility professed by the Jacobins against all regular Government, but their particular animosity against the united people of these happy kingdoms, and against the whole frame of the British Constitution. Similar expressions of fixed and inveterate hatred are to be found in every important act of the Government; I will quote a few instances, all taken from the reports made by different persons to the Convention, in the name of the Committee of Public Welfare.

On the 16th of October 1793, Saint Just proposes a decree for the arrest of all Englishmen remaining in France, and for the seizure of their property: he concludes his report with these words, " we will give our friendly assistance to the people of England, in order to enable them to rid themselves of kings."

Upon the evacuation of Toulon, Barrere says, in a triumphant tone, " the day is not distant, when the people of England shall recollect that they were once Republicans, and that it was an usurpation which reduced them again to the calamitous conditions of subjects living under monarchy."

The same person on the 21st of September, 1793, proposing an act of navigation for the express purpose of destroying the commerce and naval power of Great Britain, uses these words ; " Carthage was the torment of Italy, Carthage was destroyed by Rome; London is the torment of Europe; London is an ulcer which wastes the strength of the Continent : London is a political excrescence which liberty is bound to destroy; may England be ruined! May England be annihilated! Such ought to be the concluding article of every *revolutionary* decree of the National Convention of France !"

I cannot dispute the wisdom and policy of this sentiment; I must agree with Barrere, that the ruin and annihilation of England would be, in the technical sense of the phrase, a *revolutionary* measure. Every motive of interest or of passion, which could engage the Jacobin faction to disturb the peace of any independent state, must operate with redoubled force against Great Britain : enemies not to the tyranny but to the order of absolute monarchy, enemies to the principle of order itself, their animosity must be most peculiarly exasperated against a frame of Government, in which that principle appears in its most perfect and beautiful form. This is so consistent with the genuine character of anarchy, that the very same sentiment is attributed by Milton to the " old anarch" Chaos himself. He is introduced complaining to his guest Satan of the various encroachments which have been made upon the ancient empire of confusion and discord ; he first complains even of the order established in the infernal regions, but he is incensed to the utmost height of indignation against the beautiful order of the creation. Since the completion of that work he declares, that he is compelled to keep perpetual watch upon his frontier, endeavouring if he can to preserve the remnants of his anarchy from invasion. When he is informed that Satan is upon his passage to Paradise in the character of a missionary from the rebellious spirits for the express purpose of disturbing the peace of mankind; he receives him with great cordiality, directs his course, and wishes him a prosperous voyage; Satan repays this hospitality by a promise that he will use his utmost efforts to disorganise the world, he says,

> " Direct my course;
> Directed, no mean recompense it brings
> To your behoof, if I that region lost,
> All usurpation thence expelled, reduce
> To her original darkness, and your sway,
> (Which is my present journey) and once more
> Erect the standard there of ancient night;
> Yours be th' advantage all, mine the revenge."

All the scenes of fraternity which have been acted by the modern Anarchs, all their libellous speeches and virulent reports seem to have been modelled from this precedent. Their general view has uniformly been, and still continues to be the subversion of all regular Government of whatever description, but their primary object is, and must be to abolish every trace and vestige of a Government, which furnishes a practical lesson to mankind, that a just gradation of ranks and orders of society connected with the principles of a limited monarchy affords the best protection for the liberty and happiness of individuals, as well as the most permanent basis of national union and political strength.

Such being the passions and interests of the Revolutionary Government, and such being the nature of the system established under their influence, while that system shall exist either under their administration, or, without changing its character, shall pass into the hands of any other faction, we cannot attempt even the preliminary steps towards a negotiation for peace, without relinquishing all hope of indemnity for the hazard and expence of the war, and without renouncing all prospect of security against the designs of France. We must augment her resources, we must aggrandize her dominion, we must recognize and confirm her principles of Government, we must abandon our allies to her mercy, we must let her loose to prey at discretion upon the whole continent of Europe; and after having by this unconditional grant furnished her with the most formidable means of universal aggression, we are to confide in the words of a treaty for our sole protection against the common danger; then might be applied to our weakness and infatuation the words of a sacred writer, once before applied to a nation under the influence of a similar delusion.

" Ye have said, we have made a covenant with death, and with the grave are we at agreement; when the overflowing plague shall pass through, it shall not come unto us.

" But your covenant with death shall be disannulled, and your agreement with the grave shall not stand, when the overflowing plague shall pass through, then ye shall be trodden down by it." And trodden down we shall be, if we shrink from our duty on this day: for how can we indulge the visionary hope, that in the general plunder of property, in the destruction of order and government, in the wreck of civil society, the British empire alone shall be spared? How can we delude ourselves with the vain imagination that France in the plenitude of her power and in the full career of her success will respect that nation alone, which is the avowed and peculiar object of her hatred, which offers the strongest temptation to her insatiable avarice, and opposes the most effectual obstacle to her licentious ambition?

Thus, Sir, I have endeavoured to prove, that the original justice and necessity of this war have been strongly confirmed by subsequent events; that the general result of the last campaign both upon our own situation and upon that of the enemy affords a reasonable expectation of ultimate success; and that not only the characters, the interests, and the dispositions of those who now exercise the powers of Government in France, but the very nature of that system which they have established render a treaty of peace upon safe or honourable terms impracticable in the present moment, and consequently require a vigorous and unremitting prosecution of the war.

Hitherto, I have addressed my arguments to the whole House; in what I shall now urge, I must declare, that I do not mean to address myself to those few among us who did not share the common sentiment of the House and of the Public in that period of general alarm, which immediately preceded this war. But I appeal to those, who previous to the commencement of the war felt in common with the great body of the people a well-grounded apprehension for the safety of our happy Constitution, and the general interests of civil society; do they now feel the same degree of anxiety? Even in the midst of hostilities, in the very heat of the contest, and after a campaign which, although greatly successful in its general result, has neither been exempt from difficulty, nor from the ordinary vicissitudes of a state of war, do they not now feel in their own breasts, and perceive in the public mind such a degree of confidence in the security of all that can be dear and valuable to British subjects, as they would have gladly purchased before the war, even by surrendering a part of those interests, the whole of which was menaced in that gloomy period of general consternation?

What change of circumstances, what happy combination of events has calmed the anxiety, and revived the depressed spirits of the nation?

Is it the decree of counter-fraternity declaring, that France will no longer interfere in the internal affairs of independent states, but reserving to her—the sovereignty of all those countries which were overrun by her arms in the first career of her inordinate ambition? Is it the reply of Robespierre to the manifestoes of all the Princes of Europe, in which he pronounces Kings to be the master-piece of human corruption, in which he libels every monarch in Europe, but protests that France has no intention to disturb monarchy, if the subjects of Kings are still weak enough to submit to such an institution? Is it the murder of Brissot and his associates? Is it the disgrace and imprisonment of Anacharsis Clootz the author of the Revolutionary Diplomatics, or of Thomas Paine the author of the Rights of Man? Is it any profession, assurance, or act of the Revolutionary Government of France? You all know it is not. The confidence of a wise people could never be rested on such weak and unsubstantial foundations. The real cause of our present sense of security is to be found in our own exertions combined with those of our allies. By those exertions we were enabled to withstand and repel the first assault of the arms and principles of France; and the continuance of the same effort now forms our only barrier against the return of the same danger. Who then shall venture to persuade you to cast away the defence which has afforded you protection against all the objects of your former apprehension, to subvert the foundations of your present confidence, and to resort for your future safety to the inconsistent decrees, to the contradictory declarations, and to the vague assurances of a guilty, desperate, and distracted faction, which offers no possible ground of security either in the principles of its policy, or in the stability of its power? All the circumstances of your situation are now before you. You are now to make your option; you are now to decide, whether it best becomes the dignity, the wisdom, and the spirit of a great nation to rely for her existence on the arbitrary will of a restless and implacable enemy, or on her own sword: you are now to decide, whether you will entrust to the valour and skill of British fleets and British armies, to the approved faith and united strength of your numerous and powerful allies the defence of the limited monarchy of these realms, of the constitution of Parliament, of all the established ranks and orders of society among us, of the sacred rights of property, and of the whole frame of our laws, our liberties and our religion; or whether you will deliver over the guardianship of all these blessings—to the justice of Cambon, the plunderer of the Netherlands, who to sustain the baseless fabric of his depreciated assignats, defrauds whole nations of their rights of property, and mortgages the aggregate wealth of Europe;—to the moderation of Danton, who first promulgated that unknown law of nature which ordains, that the Alps, the Pyrenees, the Ocean, and the Rhine should be the only boundaries of the French dominion;—to the religion of Robespierre, whose practice of piety is the murder of his own sovereign, who exhorts all mankind to embrace the same faith, and to assassinate their kings for the honour of God;—to the friendship of Barrere,—who avows in the face of all Europe, that the fundamental article of the Revolutionary Government of France is the ruin and annihilation of the British Empire; or finally, to whatever may be the accidental caprice of any new band of malefactors, who, in the last convulsions of their exhausted country, may be destined to drag the present tyrants to their own scaffolds, to seize their lawless power, to emulate the depravity of their example, and to rival the enormity of their crimes.

ERRATA.

p. 10, l. 34—*for* his approbation *read* the approbation.
  12, l. 29—*after* the *read* mission of.
  — l. 30—*for* 16th *read* 10th.
  17, l. 34—*for* Jones *read* Torres.
  18, l. 19—*for* latter *read* later.
  20, l. 4—*for* Sacra *read* Sierra.
  26, l. 10—*for* No *read* The.
  36, l. 18—*for* 25th *read* 15th.
  42, l. 10—*for* remove to *read* remain in.
  52, l. 32—*for* 18th *read* 12th.
  55, l. 17—*for* an *read* our.
  57, l. 21—*for* non-limitation *read* more limitation.
  85, l. 8—*for* My Lord *read* Sir.
  88, l. 15—*for* implicit *read* implied.
 112, l. 21—*for* 1802 *read* 1809.
 115, l. 11—*for* on *read* or.
 119, l. 26—*for* No. XXXI. *read* No. XLI.

CONTENTS.

ii

CONTENTS.

APPENDIX.

The Despatches, Minutes and Correspondence of the Marquess Wellesley, K. G. during his Administration in India.—Edited by Mr. Montgomery Martin. In 5 vols. 8vo. with Portrait, Maps, Plans, &c.

" This is a publication of extraordinary interest in many points of view. The whole of the brilliant policy which ended in crushing the great enemy of our Indian Empire among the native powers, in restoring our political influence with the other courts, and in extinguishing that of France in the East, is here laid before before our eyes in every part of its progress : we have the whole history of the events given with a degree of authority and particularity of which there is no other example. We have access to the plan in its first conception ; we see it struggle with various difficulties previous to the execution ; we can trace its progress to maturity ; and have the means of ascertaining how those difficulties were overcome, and lesser minds were made to yield a compliance, sometimes reluctant—more frequently cheerful, while the instruments were always able as well as hearty, because they were the selection of the framer of the design, who hardly ever was disappointed in any one chosen by him for civil or military service. In short the whole springs and wheels of the machine are exposed to our view ; and we doubt, if any continuous history could arrest the attention, or occupy the mind of any discerning reader more entirely than this mere series of state papers and demi-official letters is calculated to do. The consummate ability—the truly statesman-like-views—the admirable combination of temper and firmness—the rare union of patience with despatch, of vigour with perseverance, by which the formation of Lord Wellesley's plans were characterized, and by which their uniform and complete success have never been questioned by any one at all acquainted with the sub-ject. His confidence in his own resources, and his determination to carry through his own measures were tempered on all occasions by the greatest urbanity and kindness, and the best and most appropriate monument of his Lordship's fame, and the marvellous exhibition of capacity and vigour which we have been surveying, is the record which this volume contains of his actions."—[*Edinburgh Review, No. 128, July* 1836.]

" We have received this first Vol. and perused it with delight : The despatches may truly be called national records of which England may justly be proud, and the very best materials for History, if it be not History itself. Not only do those documents throw almost in every page new lights upon imperfectly known subjects, but they give us fresh facts with all the multiplicity of their remote causes. They tend to uphold the English character and do infinite honor to the Noble Marquess whose wise government they so well illustrate. This is the best field to study the oriental character,—how little it is to be depended upon ; how loose is the hold that moral restraints have upon it is verified in almost every transaction. These papers relate to so far back as when regenerating France attempted to excite the native powers to rebel against us, and by their unwearied, and we must add skilful machinations, placed the Marquess Wellesley in a very delicate position from which nothing but British honor, British wisdom and British courage could have extricated us. All these plottings and intrigues led ultimately to the storming and capture of Seringapatam. No invasion was more just or more necessary than this which we brought to a conclusion so triumphant. * * * * * As to the labours of the Editor we know not whether they have been light or onerous, but the name of Mr. Martin is a guarantee that what he undertakes will assuredly be well done. We are therefore not surprized that in the getting up of this Volume there remains nothing to be wished for. * * * * Indeed the volume is complete and will not only give satisfaction but just pride to the British public."— *Metropolitan Magazine, No.* 61.]

" A work which displays the comprehensive mind and high statesman-like qualifications of the Noble Marquess in a remarkable manner. The greatness of his general policy—the profoundness of his views, and the skill with which he conducted every affair of difficulty and peril, with powerful and threatening opposing interest are here demonstrated throughout. The work possesses that high standard value which must make it the inmate of every public and private library."—[*Literary Gazettes, of 2nd and 9th April* 1836.]

The Despatches of the Marquess Wellesley embrace the most important period in the history of British India. His Lordship had to encounter difficulties which would have baffled a less able statesman ; but the Despatches shew us the sound judgement with which his Lordship directed the combined movements of the British powers."—[*Athenæum, No.* 442, *April 6th* 1836.]

" This work cannot fail to command attention. The space which the noble Marquess long filled in the political world, the prominent positions he maintained—the great objects he atchieved—the wisdom and foresight which he displayed for so many years, in the most important and varied characters all give weight to this publication, in the pages of which will be traced the workings of a master mind, through a period of the greatest interest to the British nation."—[*John Bull, April 10th,* 1836.]

" It is now generally admitted, that had not the splendid talents of the Marquess Wellesley been called into active exercise at the critical conjuncture of his Lordship's assuming the government, the necessity for discussing Indian affairs would long since have ceased. The issue of the contest with Tippoo Sultaun was a triumphant proof of the political sagacity, energy, and above all, the moral courage (his peculiar characteristic) of Lord Wellesley's highly gifted mind."—[*Asiatic Journal for June,* 1837.]

" The despatches of the Marquess Wellesley are a fine course of political science, detailed in the language of an orator. The letters and papers of the Marquess are of the Wellesleyan stamp ; they are masterly."—[*New Monthly Magazine for June,* 1837.]

" To the diplomatist the despatches of the Marquess Wellesley will be a necessary Work. In a popular sense, the third volume is the best of the series. By far the most striking point of view of the second volume, is the insight it furnishes into the diplomacy and general skill of the Indian diplomates."—[*Spectator, Sept. 17th,* 1836, *and March 5th,* 1337.]

" With the exception of a promised Supplement, the volume before us completes the celebrated publication to which it belongs, a publication which is destined to continue a standard contribution to English history, in that most wonderful department of the Empire's relations, which has Hindostan for its theatre."—[*Monthly Review for July* 1837, *p.* 446.]

" In common with the periodical press, we hailed the appearance of the first volume of these despatches with that tribute of commendation due to their utility, and the able manner in which they were compiled by the Editor. Perhaps this second volume which is now before the public, deserves a still greater meed of praise. It certainly equals its predecessor in interest, and places many most important subjects in new and true lights."— *Metropolitan Magazine.*]

" This most valuable publication will long be consulted, not only for the clear historical light it throws upon the important affairs of the East, during an epoch of intense interest, but as a manual for diplomatists and statesmen. It exhibits the Marquess of Wellesley in strong colours, as a man well and wisely chosen to fill the high station, and meet the vast responsibilities of Governor of India; and while our admiration rises as we read every new proof of his acuteness, sagacity, and talent, we breathe a prayer that the welfare of England may never be perilled by the administration of her affairs being intrusted to incompetent hands."—[*Literary Gazette.*]

" This, perhaps the most interesting volume of the series hitherto published, comprises the period from January 1804, to August 1805, in which latter month Lord Wellesley closed his brilliant administration of the Government of India, and embarked for Europe. The despatches of Lord Wellesley are elegant compositions, and the collection is not only valuable as affording the best materials for Indian history, but it is an excellent guide and authority for military officers and civilians who may be employed in the East. The work shews the warm paternal affection of the Marquess Wellesley for his gallant brother, to whom whilst in India as well as in Spain and Portugal, his Lordship afforded all the aid of his splendid talents and political influence. The volumes are edited with great care, and do credit to Mr. Martin."—[*Naval and Military Gazette, 1st and 8th of July* 1837.]

" The present volume contains the chronological series of the Marquess Wellesley's despatches from January 1804 to August 1805. Our conviction of the great importance of these valuable papers has been confirmed by every volume we have examined. High as we have always esteemed the statesman-like qualities of Lord Wellesley, we never till reading this collection of his Indian despatches had so distinct a notion of the consummate ability and admirable sagacity with which he applied the science of politics to the very peculiar exigencies of British India at the period of his administration.
We are not surprized at the high testimony borne by the Court of Directors of the honourable East India Company to this work, which we repeat is not only a rich treasury of historical facts, but also a mine of political wisdom."—[*Asiatic Journal for August*, 1837.]

" Possessing all the high characteristics we have noticed as belonging to the preceding volumes, the present volume embraces the important epoch of 1804-5, where our contests with Scindiah, the Rajah of Berar, Holkar and the Bhurtpore Rajah (all memorable in Indian history) and their results are fully and clearly expounded. The whole work is a valuable, sterling and lasting contribution to the History of England, and especially as connected with one of the most extraordinary colonies that the world ever saw."—[*Literary Gazette, June 24th,* 1837.]

" The despatches and correspondence in the present volume extend over the busy years of 1804-5, and contain a mass of official documents and information that will be serviceable to the future historian of British India, and in many respects exceedingly useful to the present sojourners in that country, whether employed in the civil or military branches of government, or occupied in commercial pursuits. The despatches are honourable proofs of the ability and industry of the noble Marquess, as also of the liberal and humane spirit in which he governed the country and endeavoured to raise the moral condition and physical well-being of the many millions of natives placed under his rule."—[*Metropolitan Magazine for August,* 1837.]

" The two preceding volumes (i. and ii.) embrace events of unquestionable interest, and display the Marquess Wellesley's talents in an eminent degree, but it was reserved for these subsequent volumes (iii. and iv.) to demonstrate the extent of those powers of mind which, under Providence, contributed to place our Empire in India, in a position of security and dignity it had never before attained. The course pursued by Lord Wellesley was that of a high and generous spirit, and his straightforward and manly course affords a gratifying contrast to the treachery, falsehood and low arts practised by those Asiatic chiefs. There is no period of our Indian history so remarkable as Lord Wellesley's has been for the uniform success attending his administration,—an administration crowded with transactions of the highest importance, and involving interests of the most complicated character. Wherever danger appeared to menace our power his sagacity perceived its approach, and with prompt decision repelled it, on every occasion which the constant vicissitudes of Indian politics presented for improving and consolidating our power : the means of accomplishing that object were always selected with judgment, and applied with vigour and despatch to their destined purposes. In selecting the instruments for carrying his masterly plans into effect his Lordship's tact in discriminating character was eminently conspicuous. Among the number of those who were employed by his Lordship in high political and military trusts, not one ever disappointed his expectations; almost all who were honoured with his confidence have since become distinguished in public life, and amply confirmed the accuracy of that judgment which first perceived and appreciated their talents. It is no wonder then, that with such hands, and the wisdom, energy and moral courage which animated and directed them, the splendid results recorded should have been effected. It must be a proud triumph to his Lordship,—one of the highest indeed to which an honourable mind is susceptible, that the ardent and undeviating devotion with which he applied his great talents to the true interests of his country has been justly appreciated. Time, the securest and the only true test of merit, has also established the wisdom of his policy on a basis which never can be shaken. Great praise is due to Mr. Montgomery Martin for the manner in which he has presented these volumes to the world."—[*Asiatic Journal for September,* 1837.]

DESPATCHES

AND CORRESPONDENCE,

&c. &c. &c.

SPAIN.

No. I.

The Marquess Wellesley to the Right Honourable George Canning, &c.

Sir,   Seville, August 11th 1809.

1. I have the honour to acknowledge the receipt of his Majesty's commands* contained in your several despatches, of which I enclose a list.

2. On the 24th of July I embarked at Porstmouth on board his Majesty's ship *Donegal*, and arrived off Cadiz on the 31st in the evening; I immediately despatched the messenger Basset with the packets which you had entrusted to my care for Mr. Frere, and with a letter to him apprizing him of my arrival, and requesting him to notify it to the Supreme Junta in the most respectful manner. By the same convey-

---

* The Marquess Wellesley was appointed ambassador to Spain in April, 1809, but a sudden and severe illness prevented his leaving England until the 24th of July. The reasons for the appointment of the Marquess Wellesley to the Court of Spain are stated by Mr. Canning in a letter to Mr. Frere of the 1st of May, 1809, of which the following is an extract :—

Mr. Secretary Canning to the Right Honourable J. H. Frere.

SIR,   Foreign Office, May 1, 1809.

" In my despatch No. 21, written after the arrival in this country of Don Pedro Cevallos as Ambassador Extraordinary from his Catholic Majesty and in his royal name, from the Supreme and Central Junta of Spain and the Indies, I stated to you, by his Majesty's command, that his

ance I also addressed a letter to Sir Arthur Wellesley, expressing my desire to receive from him such communications as he might think it proper to make to me upon the public service.*

3. In the morning of the 1st. of August as I was preparing to land, I received verbally from Lieut.-Colonel Doyle intelligence of the actions which had taken place at Talavera de la Reyna on the 27th and 28th of July, and of the glorious success of his Majesty's troops under the command of Sir A. Wellesley on that memorable occasion. No official advices of those events having reached me, and being satisfied that the most accurate and early intelligence of the operations of the British and Spanish armies must already have been transmitted to England by Sir Arthur Wellesley and Mr. Frere, I did not attempt to forward any despatch to you with the imperfect statements, alone at that time in my possession.

4. I was received at Cadiz with every demonstration of public honour, and with the most cordial and enthusiastic expressions of veneration for his Majesty's person and respect for his government, of zealous attachment to the British

---

Majesty had not then determined whether this mission might or might not require a correspondent mission on his Majesty's part, of a minister invested with a similar diplomatic character.

" The continued stay of Don Pedro Cevallos in this country, induces the supposition that the Junta may possibly expect a return to the compliment which they have paid to his Majesty; and the probability that other powers of Europe, particularly Austria, may send a person of ambassadorial rank to Seville, appears to render it expedient that the British mission at that residence should be placed forthwith on the highest footing, both in respect to personal rank and diplomatic character.

" From these considerations, his Majesty has been graciously pleased to appoint the Marquess Wellesley to proceed to Seville, with the character of his Majesty's Ambassador Extraordinary and Plenipotentiary; and I am commanded by his Majesty to direct you to announce to the Junta the appointment of this nobleman, and to inform them, that he has received his Majesty's commands to repair to his post with the least possible delay."

I am, &c.

GEORGE CANNING.

The despatches referred to in the first paragraph of the text will be found in the Appendix.

* The whole purport of these two letters which were but a few lines each, are given above.—[ED.]

alliance, and of affectionate gratitude for the benefits already derived by the Spanish nation from the generosity of his Majesty's councils, and from the persevering activity, valour and skill of his officers and troops.

5. The difficulty of obtaining a house at Seville detained me for several days at Cadiz, during which time I had the satisfaction to receive continual and distinguished marks of attention and respect towards his Majesty's embassy from every description of the public authorities, civil, military, and ecclesiastical, and from every class of the nobility, gentry, and people.

6. The same happy disposition and temper were displayed in every part of the country through which I passed on my road to Seville, and in my reception at the residence of the Supreme Government of Spain, on this day.

7. The manifestations of this spirit of friendship and union, have been so general and so evidently sincere, that I feel myself bound to submit this detail to his Majesty's gracious notice: and I discharge a grateful duty in assuring you, that the sentiments which have been uniformly declared in my presence by all ranks of the. Spanish nation towards his Majesty are scarcely surpassed by their acknowledged loyalty and affection for the person of their own sovereign.

8. During my residence at Cadiz I endeavoured to obtain information on several points of the orders which I have had the honour to receive from you. I shall take an early opportunity of submitting to your judgment my sentiments and proceedings on those important branches of my instructions.

9. Immediately after my arrival at this place I sent the enclosed note to Don Martin de Garay* (to whom I had addressed a private note from Cadiz) he has returned a verbal answer, signifying his intention of visiting me at my house in the course of this evening.

I have the honour to be,
with great truth and respect, Sir,
your most obedient and faithful servant,
Wellesley.

---

* The note was as follows :—

Sir,—I have the honour to inform your Excellency of my arrival at this Residency : I request your Excellency's permission to pay my personal respects to you as soon as may be suitable to your convenience.

I have the honour to be, &c.
Wellesley.

No. II.

The Marquess Wellesley to Don Martin de Garay.

Seville, August 12th, 1809.

The undersigned, Ambassador Extraordinary and Plenipotentiary from his Britannic Majesty, has the honour to represent to his Excellency the Secretary of State, the indispensable necessity of adopting immediate measures for the aid of the operations of the British Army, in the present crisis.

1st. It is absolutely necessary to bring into action, without delay, the corps of the Marquis of Romana, of the Duque del Parque, and any force which can be moved in the north of Spain, or in the vicinity of Madrid, for the purpose of compelling the enemy to reduce his strength in Estremadura, and of enabling the allied armies to resume offensive operations. The undersigned requests that immediate and effectual orders be issued for this purpose.

2dly. The British troops cannot maintain even a defensive position, unless the supply of provisions and the means of transport be regularly established. The undersigned therefore requests, that magazines of provisions be immediately formed at such places in the rear of the allied armies as he shall point out; and that supplies of biscuit, sheep and oxen, and also of barley, be regularly conveyed to those magazines, according to the plan which he shall furnish.

3dly. The undersigned further requests, that measures be taken, without delay, to supply the British Army with means of transport, as well for the purpose of moving the magazines, as of enabling the army to communicate with them, and to send to any part of the country for supplies of provision or forage. For these objects, the undersigned requests, that immediate orders be given for supplying to the British Army a number of mules to the amount of 1,500, and of Valencian or Catalonian carts to the amount of 100, according to such a plan as the undersigned shall suggest.

The undersigned avails himself of this occasion to offer the assurances of his high consideration to his Excellency Don Martin de Garay.

WELLESLEY.

No. III.

Don Martin de Garay to the Marquess Wellesley.

Sir,   Seville, 12th August, 1809.

I have presented to the Supreme Central Junta, of which I have the honour to be secretary and member, the note which your Excellency did me the honour to transmit with the date of to-day, relative to various points, respecting which I will reply to your Excellency with the brevity which the time and circumstances require.

Notwithstanding that by an express sent yesterday for this purpose, an order had been given to the General Commandant of Gallicia and the Asturias, and the Duque del Parque, that, putting themselves in motion, they should come down towards Castille, and taking the direction of the Capital, should compel the French to diminish their forces, to attend to this diversion, and allow the combined armies to act on the offensive; the Junta has thought it peculiarly its duty to repeat these same orders; and, communicating them by the corresponding minister, to direct them to your Excellency: this I now do, in order that your Excellency may use them as you please. In them it is repeated to the aforesaid Commandants, that they are to act without delay, as I communicate, and as your Excellency desires.

Before this period all the necessary arrangements had been made, that nothing might be wanting to the British troops; however, these same orders are now renewed; commissaries and persons of entire confidence are sent, who will take care that nothing shall be wanting to the said army, establishing magazines where it may be advantageous, and where your Excellency thinks convenient; the said commissaries go with ample powers and funds to provide and prepare all the succours that are necessary, and which the scarcity of the country may permit, which, desolated by the enemy, sacked by the soldiers, having suffered the weight of war for eight months, and not being moreover of the most fruitful, is not in a state to supply all that might be desirable. The efforts of the commissaries and the zeal of those who are employed, will supply the want of means. In the same manner the commissaries are on the point of immediate departure, in order to be able to facilitate the competent number of mules and carriages for the armies, although the difficulty of assembling as many as are desired is known. The rapacity of the enemy, and his care in removing animals of draft, render the collection more difficult; it will be endeavoured to effect it by means of purchases at proper prices, for which purpose commissioners depart to-morrow, as also the number of carts which your Excellency requires, which can only be of this country, where it is considered to construct them in the Catalonian or Valencian manner would cause infinite delay in the operations of the army. Finally, the Junta, convinced of the urgent necessity of repelling and removing the common enemy, will not spare means, diligence or expense, to contribute on their part to the enabling the armies of both powers to act on the offensive.

Your Excellency will be convinced of the good faith of the Junta, of the efforts of the nation, and of the necessity, now greater than ever, of re-union for the purpose of driving the enemy from this part of Spain.

The Junta is persuaded that your Excellency will interest yourself with General Wellesley, in order that he may co-operate in desires so just, convinced as your Excellency must be, how prejudicial it would prove for the enemy, in these circumstances, to obtain advantages in Estremadura and the Andalusias.

The Junta requests your Excellency to communicate these orders to General Beresford, that he, with the troops under his command, may assist in furthering this enterprize.

I seize this opportunity of manifesting to your Excellency, &c.

MARTIN DE GARAY.

No. IV.

The Marquess Wellesley to Sir Arthur Wellesley.

Sir,   Seville, 13th August, 1809, 4 P. M.

Brigadier General Doyle and Major Armstrong will leave Seville in the course of the approaching night, with such communications from me as the short period of my residence at this place has enabled me to prepare. In the meanwhile, I have the honour to forward to you by an express courier, an order for the Duque del Parque, which you will use as you think most expedient.

I have the honour to be, &c.

WELLESLEY.

(Enclosure.)

Translation of a Letter from M. Cornel to the Duque del Parque.

Sir,   Royal Castle of Seville, 12th August, 1809.

Notwithstanding the Royal order, which I communicated to you in the night of yesterday, that combining your arrangements with the Marshal General Beresford, and expediting another order to the General Commandant of the army of Gallicia, who ought already to have entered into your district, all the troops should make a rapid movement on the Puerto de Baños, which appears the most practicable point for distracting the attention of our enemies, who are harrassing the Anglo-Spanish army. His Majesty desires, that having overcome all the difficulties which may present themselves, you should regulate with the aforesaid Marhal General a prompt march, and should repeat to the aforesaid General Commandant of the army of Gallicia the order to the same effect, indicating to him the nearest point at which the forces can be united.

I make it known to your Excellency by the Royal order, that you may fulfil it, &c. &c. &c.

CORNEL.

No. V.

The Marquess Wellesley to Sir Arthur Wellesley.

Sir,   Seville, 13th August, 1809.

1. I have the honour to acknowledge the receipt of your several despatches noted in the margin; and Mr. Frere's correspondence with me, including copies of your letters addressed to him, has afforded me the necessary information respecting the general situation of affairs in Spain, and the operations and conditions of the British and Spanish Armies.

2. Immediately after my arrival at this place, and even before I had been admitted to an audience by the Supreme Junta, I employed every endeavour to induce the Government to adopt the measures and arrangements suggested in your letter of the 8th of August.

3. For this purpose I yesterday presented a note to the Secretary of State, of which the enclosed is a copy; and last night I received an answer, of which I also enclose a copy for your information.*

---

* See pp. 4 and 5.

4. The orders to the Duque del Parque were transmitted to you by an express courier this evening, and I am inclined to believe that this Government is disposed to make every effort compatible with its powers, with the state of the country, and with the inveterate defects of the military department in Spain.

5. You are, however, sufficiently aware of the impossibility of relying upon such efforts, unless a regular system can be established under such authorities as may secure its efficiency and seasonable operation; and although you may be assured that I will omit no endeavour to contribute to the establishment of such a system, I cannot entertain a confident expectation of success.

6. It is evident, that in order to secure to your army the articles which you require, supplies must be drawn from remote sources, to such points as may be properly calculated for the establishment of magazines; and that your means of transport and of movement cannot now be furnished from the countries in which your army is acting. I have, therefore, advised this Government to call forth every resource of the southern provinces of Spain, and to convey the requisite articles in the first instance to Santa Elalia, a place in the rear of Monartino, where I understand a magazine might be formed with advantage.

7. From this magazine you might draw forward your supplies to any other points which you might think fit to indicate; but the efficiency of the whole arrangement must depend in a great degree upon the proper selection and control of the agents for the collection and conveyance of the several articles required for your use.

8. Under a serious and painful impression of the difficulties of your situation, and of the sufferings of your army, I feel the indispensable necessity of communicating with you on the most minute details of the subject of your distress; and I therefore forward this despatch to you under the care of Brigadier General Doyle and of Major Armstrong, to whom I request you to state all the circumstances of your situation, and every point connected with the means of relieving your wants, and of securing you against similar inconvenience, if you should think it practicable or advisable to remain in Spain.

9. As soon as these officers shall be fully apprised of your wishes and intentions, I request that you will direct them

to return to me with your despatches. In the meanwhile I shall not fail to use every exertion to accelerate the efforts of this Government for your relief.

10. You may be assured that I shall take a proper opportunity of representing to this Government the defects of the Spanish army, which you describe in your despatch of the 8th of August.

11. I shall also recommend to this Government the defensive plan of operations which you advise for the future conduct of the Spanish armies.

12. I have informed Don Martin de Garay of the absolute necessity of communicating solely and exclusively with the British Ambassador, and he has assured me that he will hereafter adhere, without deviation to the rule established in that respect by His Majesty's commands. I have already acquainted you with the representation which I have addressed to this Government on the subject of the distress of your army, and of the answer which I have received.

13. Under the discretionary power which you were pleased to leave to me, I have sent your second letter,* on the subject

---

* *Sir Arthur Wellesley to the Marquess Wellesley.*

MY LORD, Deleytosa, August 8th, 1809.

I have the honour to enclose a letter which I have received from Don Martin de Garay, conveying to me the approbation of the Junta of the conduct of the British troops on the actions of the 27th and 28th of July, and the information, that the Junta had been pleased to appoint me a Captain-General of the Spanish army.

I conceive that I cannot with propriety accept this commission without the consent of his Majesty ; and I have accordingly written a letter to Don Martin de Garay, by which I have made the acceptance of the commission conditional upon his Majesty's pleasure. This, however, may be considered offensive to the Junta, or your Excellency may have reasons, unknown to me, which might induce you to wish that I should not decline the acceptance till his Majesty's pleasure should be known, although it is necessary that the office should be considered as referable to his Majesty : I have therefore written a second letter, and I beg your Excellency to decide which of them you will send to Don Martin de Garay.

I likewise enclose a third letter to Don Martin de Garay, in which I have accepted the horses presented me by the Junta in the name of King Ferdinand the Seventh ; but I have declined to accept the pay of a Captain-of the rank of Captain-General in the Spanish army to Don Martin de Garay. If it should be His Majesty's pleasure that you should not permanently hold that rank, the mode which you have adopted in that letter affords a sufficient opportunity for the operation of His Majesty's commands; and I am satisfied that this course of proceeding will be more agreeable to this Government than that which was proposed in your first letter. I have forwarded to Don M. de Garay your letter respecting the horses, presented to you by the Junta, and also concerning the pay of Captain-General.

14. I have received with great concern the description contained in these letters of the distress of your army, and of the perverse conduct of General Cuesta. This Government is disposed to remove General Cuesta from his command, whenever it shall have received from you, or from the British Ambassador, a regular and detailed statement of his misconduct. It is my intention to present to the Secretary of State a recital of the several facts stated in your despatches res-

---

General. I shall be obliged to your Excellency if you will send this letter also to Don Martin de Garay.

I have the honour to be, &c.

ARTHUR WELLESLEY.

Sir Arthur Wellesley to Don Martin de Garay.

SIR,   Deleytosa, 8th August, 1809.

I have had the honour of receiving the letter which your Excellency did me the honour of writing to me on the 30th of July, in which you have expressed the approbation of the Central Junta of the conduct of the British army under my command, in the action of the 28th of July.

I am very sensible of the approbation of the Central Junta, and I beg that you will convey to them my respectful acknowledgments. I am particularly flattered by the confidence they have reposed in me, in appointing me one of the Captains-General in the Spanish army, and I have this day written to his Majesty's principal Secretary of State, to request him to lay before his Majesty this testimony of his approbation and confidence of the Central Junta; and to request his Majesty's permission for me to accept the commission in the Spanish army with which the government are pleased to honour me.

Until his Majesty's answer will be received, I shall be happy to render the government every service that may be in my power.

I have the honour to be, &c.

ARTHUR WELLESLEY.

pecting General Cuesta; but, in my judgment, it would not appear to me, to be proper that I should directly insist upon his removal. As far as I can collect your sentiments upon this point they appear to coincide with mine. It is not to be supposed that this Government will continue to employ General Cuesta in the chief command of the army, after having received full notice of the several facts which you have stated; and I am satisfied that his removal would be made with more cheerfulness and alacrity, and with less danger of unpopularity, if it should appear to be rather the necessary consequence of his own conduct than the result of the interference of the British Ambassador.

I have the honour to be, &c.

WELLESLEY.

No. VI.

Sir Arthur Wellesley to the Marquess Wellesley.

MY LORD,   Jaraicejo, August, 13th, 1809.

I have the honour to enclose an answer which I have received from General Cuesta to the letter which I addressed to him on the 11th instant, with my reply of this date.* The plan which he proposes, of dividing between the two armies, in proportion to their numbers, all the provisions received at Truxillo, however specious in appearance, would be fallacious in practice, and would probably starve the British army.

It would not be difficult to forbid the convoys of provisions coming from Seville, from going to Truxillo; and it is probable that the supplies of provisions from Seville do not amount to one fourth of the consumption of both armies; the remainder being supplied by the country, in which of course the Spanish army has the preference. An arrangement of this description is impracticable of execution, even if the commissaries of the two armies would act fairly by each other; but this is not to be expected: every commissary will do the best he can for the troops to which he is attached; and many articles must be procured in the country, which will not be brought to account in the magazine of Truxillo.

---

* See pp. 12 and 13.

In short, my Lord, it comes to this; either the British
army must be fed with the necessaries which it requires, or
I will march it back into Portugal, whether that kingdom is
invaded or not by the French corps which have moved
within these few days towards Placencia. I have received
Mr. Frere's private letter of the 10th, in which he encloses
the copy of a correspondence which he had had with Don
Martin de Garay on the subject of General Cuesta's evacuation of Talavera. I observe from these papers that General
Cuesta had given the Junta reason to believe, that when I
marched from Arzobispo on the 5th, I intended to return
to Portugal; and that he prevailed upon me to take up the
position of Almaraz, by a message by General O'Donoghue
and Lord Macduffe.

I beg to inform your Lordship, that although General
O'Donoghue and Lord Macduffe did come to me at Peraleda
de Gavin on the morning of the 6th, General Cuesta knew
on the 4th my opinion respecting our future operations, and
my determination to secure, as soon as possible, the important
points of the Mesa d'Ibor and Campillos; which if the
enemy had seized, on his arrival at Almaraz, the combined
armies could not have extricated themselves from the mountains.

I have also another observation to make upon this correspondence:* my letters to Mr. Frere of the 3d and 4th, were
given to the General to be sent from Arzobispo on the 4th;
yet it appears, that they were not transmitted till after the
General had written on the 6th his account of the supposed
success of the General O'Donoghue and Lord Macduffe;
and Mr. Frere did not receive them till the 16th.

I have the honour to be, &c,

ARTHUR WELLESLEY.

P. S. I beg to mention to your Excellency that the troops
have received, this day and yesterday, only half an allowance
of bread; and the cavalry no forage except what they can
pick up in the fields. The troops suffer considerably for
the want of salt; and neither officers or soldiers have had
any wine for the last fortnight. In case I should move, I
must leave behind me two thirds of the small quantity of

---

* See Appendix.

ammunition I have got; having been obliged to give all the Portuguese carts (which had carried the ammunition hitherto) to move the wounded; and not having been able to procure means of transport for any thing in this country.

Surely, my Lord, the Junta have had time since the 19th of last month, to supply the wants of the army, with which they were then made acquainted?

[1st Enclosure]

General Cuesta to Sir Arthur Wellesley.

SIR,   August 11th, 1809.

I have received by Colonel Joseph O'Lawlor the letter which your Excellency is pleased to address to me with the date of this day, on the subject of the supplies and provisions, and on the transport of them from one army to the other. It has been my duty to credit the corresponding accounts, which have been presented to me officially by all the Commissioners of the Spanish provisions, and many other individual officers, up to the moment at which your Excellency is pleased to declare to me, that no provisions addressed to the Spanish army have been detained by the British;—the which assertion I prefer before every other testimony: however, by enquiring into the origin of this difference, I suspect that it consists in the little order and agreement which prevail amongst the respective Commissioners.

Those of this army shew me the original letters of the persons who transmit these provisions for the Spanish troops; and, on the other hand, Colonel O'Lawlor assures me that the Intendant, Don Juan Lozano de Torres, directs those provisions from Truxillo with the destination of the English army; on which account each of the said armies considers itself to have a right to them.

Being then desirous that both should enjoy, in just proportion, all the provisions which can be obtained, I have conceived that it would be convenient, that all should have their magazines in Truxillo without distinction; and that the supplies which arrive, should be distributed to both armies, in proportion to their numbers, by the Spanish Commissary and by one authorised by your Excellency, with union and agreement; since, when the number of daily rations which each army requires is known, the division would easily be made by the respective Commissioners. On the other hand, I will repeat my orders, that no Spanish party or Commissioner may detain or receive any article which does not belong to the said magazine, with the approbation of the respective Commissioners; and I will punish with rigour those who disobey, as I am now doing, with respect to the sergeant of the King's regiment of cavalry, Joseph Gonzalez; whose receipt your Excellency encloses.

I am far from thinking that all the provisions which the country produces, or which come from Seville, are for the Spanish army alone; I do not admit this unreasonable notion; but that in the arrangement which the Commissaries have endeavoured to follow, up to this moment, each army should have a right to those provisions which it collected for itself; and even in this case, I have charged them at all times to prefer the English army in its necessities, according to the means they possess.

I do not know whether any magazines of provisions have yet been formed and destined to the army; but it is clear to me that the Government is making the most active arrangements for the corresponding supply of both armies; and I hope they will not be long in taking effect.

With respect to your Excellency's withdrawing your troops from the bridge of Almaraz, I confess that it would be very painful to me, on account of the great injury it would at this moment bring on the public cause, and to the defence of the provinces of Estremadura, Andalusia, and the kingdom of Portugal; in as much as our actual position is the only one which can secure those countries: since at no other point more in the interior could we make front to the enemy with so much advantage; and therefore I beg your Excellency to take this subject into your consideration before you form any resolution.

I have the honour to repeat to your Excellency my particular esteem, and remain your most attentive and faithful servant,

GREGORIO DE LA CUESTA.

P. S. After writing the above, I have received your Excellency's letter, including that of the Junta of Placencia, concerning the entry of 4000 troops into that city.

[2nd Enclosure.]

Sir Arthur Wellesley to General Cuesta.

SIR,   Jaraicejo, August 13, 1809.

I have had the honour of receiving your Excellency's letter of the 11th.

The plan which your Excellency proposes, of placing all the supplies in a magazine to be formed at Truxillo, and to divide them between the two armies, in proportion to the strength of each, would answer perfectly if it were practicable: but your Excellency must be aware that many articles of provision are received by your Excellency's army, which do not pass through Truxillo, and could not be brought there without great inconvenience and delay; and would never appear in the accounts of the magazine; and that other supplies can easily be turned off from Truxillo without my having any knowledge of the fact. The British army receives no provisions of which M. Logano de Torres has not a knowledge; and your Excellency has it in your power to give him such orders as you may think proper, both as to the formation of the magazine and the share which the British troops shall have of it.

When the British army entered Spain I had reason to expect, and I expected that a great effort would be made to afford us at least subsistence for payment, and those means of transport and other aids, without which, your Excellency is well aware, nothing can keep the field. Your Excellency also knows how these expectations have been fulfilled. Since I joined your army, the troops have not received upon an average half a ration; and on some days nothing at all; and the cavalry no forage or grain, excepting what they could pick up in the fields, of an unwholesome description, by the use of which hundreds of horses have died. I can procure no means of transport, and your Excellency knows that I have been obliged to leave some ammunition in the mountains, of which you have possession; and if I should now move, I must leave behind me two-thirds of the small quantity of ammunition I have got, having been obliged to allot the Portuguese carts, (which have moved it hitherto) to the purpose of removing the wounded soldiers.

The fire of the enemy, and the badness and scarcity of food, have destroyed many of my artillery horses; and I have asked, but in vain, for some assistance of this description. The consequence is, that I shall be obliged to destroy many guns, when I shall move from hence.

I have not received even an answer to the request I made, to have a remount for the cavalry, of only 100 mares, which would be entirely useless to the Spanish cavalry.

Under all these circumstances, your Excellency cannot be surprised that I should think that the British army have been neglected and ill treated; or at the determination which I now communicate to you, that whatever may be the consequences to the valuable interests to which you refer in your letter, I will march them back into Portugal, if they are not more regularly and more plentifully supplied with provisions and forage, and with the means of transport and other aids which they require.

I have to observe, that whether I put this determination into execution or not, the evil consequences which you apprehend to the valuable interests to which you refer, will equally follow; as the army will be unable and unfit to perform any operation, if the privations which it has suffered are to continue.

I request your Excellency to give orders to the troops you have sent to Truxillo, not to prevent the officers and soldiers of the British army from buying what they want there. The troops have had no salt, or other necessary articles, for some time; and it is desirable that they and their officers should be allowed to buy at Truxillo what that place can afford.

I have the honour to be, &c.

ARTHUR WELLESLEY.

No. VII.

Sir Arthur Wellesley to the Marquess Wellesley.

MY LORD,   Jaraicejo, August 14th, 1809.

I received yesterday from General Cuesta the letter of which I enclose your Excellency a copy, in which he informs me that he has resigned the command of the army on account of his increasing infirmities. It appears that he had a paralytic stroke on the night of the 11th which deprived him of the use of his left leg, and he cannot now walk.

I likewise enclose the copy of a letter which I have received from, and my answer to General Eguia, the present Commanding Officer of the army.

The letter to which he refers, as having been written by me, is that addressed to General Cuesta, of which I transmitted a copy to your Excellency yesterday.

I have not yet heard that the enemy have made any alteration in their position at Placentia. It appears that they have thrown their posts forward towards Baños by some accounts, as well as towards Corice and Gallatia.

I have the honour to be, &c.

ARTHUR WELLESLEY.

(Enclosure No. 1.)

General Cuesta to Sir Arthur Wellesley.

SIR,   Miza de Ibor, August 12th, 1809.

My disorder having encreased to such a degree as to incapacitate me for discharging the duties of the command of this army, I have delivered it to-day into the hands of the second in chief, Lieut.-General Don Francisco de Eguia; and I depart for Truxillo to-morrow to take some remedies, and to wait for the decision of the Central governing Junta of the kingdom. I make it known to your Excellency for his information, and that he may consider me, in whatever situation, his most attached and humble servant.

GREG. DE LA CUESTA.

(Enclosure No. 2.)

General Eguia to Sir Arthur Wellesley.

SIR,   Miza de Ibor, August 13th, 1809.

I have the honour to inform your Excellency that the Captain General Don Gregorio de la Cuesta delivered into my hands the command of the army yesterday, who was incapacitated from commanding in the same by his disorders, and he took this morning the direction towards Truxillo. On this account I have received the despatch which your Excellency has been pleased to address to that General on the arrangement of provisions, or rather on the present scarcity of them, which the British army under your command unfortunately feels. And being desirous to contribute by every possible means to remedy an evil of consequences so fatal, and which has undoubtedly been produced by the sad situation in which the places invaded by the enemy have been left, I entreat your Excellency to depute an officer in your confidence who with another of my appointment may regulate this department in such a manner, that no doubt can remain of the sincerity of my expressions, and of my constant desire that the English army should be attended to with an absolute preference to that which I have the honour to command ad interim.

The national gratitude towards valorous soldiers who have known how to prove with their blood in the fields of Talavera, the good will with which they have fought for our liberty demands every kind of sacrifice, and the first should be to deprive ourselves of all that may be possible, in order that that brave army may have no want. But your Excellency knows that it is of small use to make efforts if the effects do not answer the ends for which they were made, and this will inevitably happen unless there be a permanent method in the distribution, and an absolute confidence that this distribution is made with good faith, and with the preference which I propose. I make known to your Excellency my sentiments with frankness, in which you will never find an alteration ; and I shall take a very particular pleasure if your Excellency will admit them for trial.

The Commissioner whom your Excellency will send if you are pleased to approve of my plan, in order to treat on the subject in question, will be able to regulate those which remained previously in discussion, and upon which I have as yet come to no agreement.

FRANCISCO D'EGUIA.

(Enclosure No. 3.)

Sir Arthur Wellesley to General Eguia.

SIR,   Jaraicejo, August 14th, 1809.

I have had the honour of receiving your Excellency's letter of the 13th, and I beg leave to congratulate you upon succeeding to the command of the Spanish army.

I assure your Excellency that I have every desire to adopt any arrangement which can tend to facilitate the procuring and distribution of supplies to the combined armies ; and I am fully convinced of your Excellency's desire to relieve the wants and remove the inconveniences which the British army has already suffered during its operations in Spain.

I must observe to your Excellency, however, that with every confidence in the good faith with which an arrangement made by you will be carried into execution on your parts, I am apprehensive, that from the nature of the proposed arrangement, it is impracticable of execution ; but at your Excellency's desire, I have sent Lieut.-Colonel Waters, of the Staff, and Mr. Venyss, of the Commissary General's department, to Truxillo, where they will meet any officers who will be appointed by you, and in concert with Mr. Loyno de Jones, the Intendant employed by Government with the British army, will settle such an arrangement as may be practicable.

These officers will likewise be charged to communicate to them, who you will appoint, the particulars of the other wants of the British army.

I have the honour to be, &c.
ARTHUR WELLESLEY.

No. VIII.

Sir Arthur Wellesley to the Marquess Wellesley.

MY LORD,   Jaraicejo, August 15th, 1809.

I received from Marshal Beresford this morning a letter, stating that the enemy's corps which had gone to Placentia, had on the 12th attacked and carried the Puerto de Baños. This point was defended by Sir Robert Wilson's corps, and I believe a detachment from the garrison of Ciudad Rodrigo. Sir Robert Wilson has retired from the neighbourhood of Talavera, by the hills of the Vera de Placentia; and had arrived at the Puerto de Baños on the 11th. He writes from Colmenar on the 12th at night.

I do not understand that the enemy had made any movement from Placentia since the 12th; his patroles were yesterday on the Tagus, in the neighbourhood of Talavera, and of the Puente de Cardenal. Marshal Beresford was yesterday between Moraleja and Zarca la Mayor.

I have the honour to enclose the copy of a letter which I received yesterday from General Eguia, and the copy of my answer this day.*

I have just received your Excellency's despatch of the 13th instant; † your Excellency will observe from my letter to General Eguia, that the Marquis de la Romana was still at Corunna on the 3rd of August, and probably even at a latter period. There is no chance therefore of a diversion being made by his army in favour of the operations of the troops in Estremadura; and your Excellency will observe, that the attempt of the Duque del Parque, to hold only the Puerto de Baños, although aided by Sir Robert Wilson's corps, the assistance of which he had no reason to expect, has entirely failed.

I consider the answer of the Junta to the note of your Excellency, in respect to supplies of provisions for the army and to the means of transport required, to be entirely unsatisfactory. The army cannot exist in the shape of an army, unless these supplies and means are provided; and the Junta has already been informed by me, that if Spain, or rather that part of Spain which is under their government, which in fact now comprizes the whole kingdom, excepting that part of Estremadura and of Castile and Arragon occupied by the enemy's troops, cannot, or is unwilling to make the exertion which is necessary in order to provide the supplies and means, Spain must do without the British army.

In respect to Marshal Beresford's corps, which the Junta

---

* See pp. 19 and 20.   † See p. 7.

was so desirous should be brought forward, I have to observe, that the Marshal has great reason with myself to complain of the deficiency of supplies of provisions and other assistance since he has been in Spain. But this army is the only disposable corps of Portuguese troops which exists, and is all that Portugal has to depend upon for its defence. It is not in a very efficient state for offensive operations, as it wants cavalry, is newly raised, and but imperfectly trained and disciplined. The object in collecting it upon the frontiers, was to train and discipline it, and at the same time to defend the frontiers of Portugal, and to give an *appui* to my left flank; and the Government of Portugal willingly consented in its quitting the frontiers for these objects; but I doubt whether the Government of Portugal would consent, or that I could recommend that they should consent, to the employment of this corps in an operation in Castile, giving up the defence of their own frontier, which is menaced with an attack, at the call of the Government of Spain, who do not appear willing or capable of making any exertion for themselves. Accordingly your Excellency will observe in the different letters which I have written, in which I have recommended movements towards Madrid, I have not mentioned Marshal Beresford's corps, knowing that its service could not be at present spared at a distance from the Portuguese frontier, and that the Portuguese Government would not allow it to move to any distance.

I have the honour to be, &c.

ARTHUR WELLESLEY.

[1st Enclosure.]

General Eguia to Sir Arthur Wellesley.

SIR,   Miza de Ibor, August 14th, 1809.

Although it does not appear, from the accounts of the movement which the enemy's forces are making on Placentia, and of the routes which they are taking to Galisteo, that they have at present any settled plan of continuing this route with the intention of attacking us, since the movement may alone have been made for the sake of taking up a strong and convenient position, from whence it would be easy for the enemy to collect those provisions of which he stands in need; nevertheless it appears to me to be requisite, in consequence of these accounts, that some precautionary measures should be taken, which may be effected by a general movement of the combined army. The combined army might either act upon the defensive, in a position which may appear to be the best, or by a forward movement to menace Victor and Sebastiani if they join, as they have done once, or otherwise; General Vanegas, having detached a division to the Passes of the Sacra Merina, in order to strengthen the force which he has left there, might unite his troops to ours, and thus with the addition of 20,000 men, at the least, to the force upon which we may reckon, we might arrange a plan of operations in which the Generals Beresford, Romana, and Parque, should take an active and expeditious part. Our present situation amongst the mountains without any immediate resources, is the destruction of our army, and overcomes us so much, that we are no longer able to bear what we suffer; and I am of opinion, should you think it an advisable measure, that we should agree upon some regular plan, whether it be to act on the defensive in the position which we now occupy, or whether it be to pass the Tagus, and menace the Vera de Placentia, where it seems the enemy now is, or whether we should determine to await a more favourable state of things.

The wish I entertain of acting in concert with your Excellency in all points, and of not taking a single step which may not be by mutual agreement, induces me to address your Excellency, in the hopes that you will have the goodness to let me know what is your opinion with regard to the above-mentioned subjects; and in this I am actuated by my desire of frankly explaining to your Excellency what is the state of my own opinion.

Last night I had the honour of informing your Excellency what was my opinion with regard to the provisions; and although we did not treat upon the means of transport, this will be arranged in the same manner.

The energetic measures taken by the Government will put us into the situation of being without a want in a few days, and in the meantime your Excellency may rely upon your receiving the benefit of all the assistance which comes to the army of which I have the command, as I had the honour of making the offer to your Excellency yesterday.

I repeat to your Excellency my affection and attachment to your person, and I pray God that your Excellency may live many years.

[2nd Enclosure.]

Sir Arthur Wellesley to General Eguia.

SIR,   Jaraicejo, August 15th, 1809.

I have had the honour of receiving your letter of the 14th instant, relative to our future operations.

The last accounts which I have received of the enemy, state, on the 12th they attacked the Puerto de Baños with a large corps of cavalry, artillery, and infantry; where they were opposed by Sir Robert Wilson's corps, which had retreated from Talavera by the hills, and had arrived at Baños on the 11th. The enemy carried the Puerto after an obstinate resistance, which lasted the whole day; and Sir Robert writes from Colmenar on the 12th at night.

My opinion is, that notwithstanding the strength of his reinforcements, the enemy is not strong enough yet to undertake any offensive operations, but that if he should undertake any against the right of the combined armies (I mean the Spanish corps under General Vanegas) the French corps at Placentia, supposing it to remain there, will be well situated to impede any operations which we in this quarter might undertake in order to make a diversion in his favour.

The first object of our attention should be to get provisions for the horses and men of the army. The horses of the British army are now so much reduced for want of food, that they are scarcely able to march the distance which it is necessary they should march in order to relieve the out-posts; much less to undertake any hostile or forward movement, while the arrangements for procuring food and collecting magazines are making. I have already stated to General Cuesta, in a letter of the 10th instant, which I understand has been communicated to you, the defensive positions which, in my opinion, the army ought to occupy in this quarter.

When they will be prepared to carry on more active operations, my opinion is, that they ought to be directed in the right of the enemy at Placentia, and it might be possible to bring the corps of Marshal Beresford to co-operate in this plan ; but I fear that nothing can be expected from the Duque del Parque, who is too weak, or from the Marquis de la Romana, who appears to have been at Corunna still on the 3rd of this month.

ARTHUR WELLESLEY.

No. IX.

The Marquess Wellesley to the Right Honourable G. Canning.

SIR,　　　　　　　　　　　　　　　　　　Seville, August 15th, 1809.

1. M. de Garay visited me in the evening of the 11th instant according to the intimation, which I had received from him. The conference commenced with mutual expressions of solicitude to cultivate harmony and good intelligence for the purpose of facilitating the despatch of public business, and of promoting the objects of the alliance, and the prosperity of the common cause.

2. I availed myself of this occasion to state the general tenor of my instructions; I particularly explained my disposition, according to the spirit of His Majesty's commands, to regulate the extent of my communications on matters of internal concern and administration, within such limits as might be agreeable to the Government of Spain, professing at the same time my readiness to state to the Supreme Central Junta without reserve my sentiments on every point of whatever description, connected with the reciprocal interests of our respective Sovereigns and Nations, whenever such a

freedom of communication might appear to be necessary or acceptable.

3. This declaration was received with apparent satisfaction and the course of conversation immediately turned to the state of the campaign in Spain, and especially to the condition of the British Army.

4. My attention had been fixed on this painful subject even by the earliest intelligence of the success of our arms at Talavera. The first rumours which had reached me of the splendid achievements of Sir Arthur Wellesley and his Majesty's gallant troops were accompanied by such alarms respecting the state of their supplies and means of movement as mixed a considerable degree of concern and solicitude with the sentiments naturally inspired by the extraordinary and glorious circumstances of that brilliant victory.

5. My anxiety was further encreased by the despatches which Mr. Frere had been so attentive as to address to me during my detention at Cadiz, and on the journey to Seville; and the reply of Sir Arthur Wellesley to my letter of the 31st of July exhibited the most afflicting view of the condition of the British Army in Spain.

6. Mr. Frere informs me that he has transmitted in duplicate to you the copies of the despatches which he addressed to me. I have therefore thought it sufficient to refer to their dates in the margin of this despatch.*

7. I enclose copies of Sir Arthur Wellesley's despatches from the 8th to the 12th of August inclusive,† with a copy

---

* Mr. Frere to the Marquess Wellesley, 8th August 9 enclosures. Do. 9th do. 9 enclosures. These letters enter into details as to the distressed state of the British army and the correspondence with General Cuesta and others on the subject. See appendix. [Ed.]

† These letters refer also to the distressed condition of the army and the conduct of the Spanish Chiefs : they are published in vol. 5 of the Duke of Wellington's despatches. The following may however be here inserted, as affording a true picture of the state of Spain when Lord Wellessley arrived there. [Ed.]

Lieut.-General the Hon. Sir A. Wellesley, K. B., to his Excellency the Marquess Wellesley, K. P.

'MY DEAR WELLESLEY,   'Deleytosa, 8th August, 1809.

'The public despatches which I transmit with this letter will give you a full and faithful picture of the state of affairs here. You have under-

of a letter which I forwarded to that officer by a courier on the 13th instant, and of another forwarded under the care of Lieut.-Colonel Doyle and Major Armstrong. I shall have occasion to request your attention to many parts of this correspondence, but its most important and prominent feature is the severe distress of the British Army arising from the defect of its supplies and means of movement.

8. Sir Arthur Wellesley's first letter of the 8th instant, reached me on the 11th in the morning, as I approached to the city of Seville; and although M. de Garay informed me that the Supreme Junta could not grant me an audience during that night, and had formally fixed the 13th instant, for the delivery of my letters of Credence, the urgency of the occasion appeared to me to require an immediate application to the Government. Under this impression I entered fully into the discussion of the situation and wants of the army in my conference with M. de Garay on the night of the 11th. On the 12th, I presented the Official Note of which I have the honour to enclose a copy, and on the same night I received the answer of which a translation is also enclosed.*

9. The despatches which you will receive from Mr. Frere will apprise you of the circumstances which compelled the

---

taken an Herculean task; and God knows that the chances of success are infinitely against you, particularly since the unfortunate turn which affairs have taken in Austria.

'I wish I could see you, or could send somebody to you; but we are in such a situation, that I cannot go to you myself, and I cannot spare the only one or two people, to converse with whom would be of any use to you. I think therefore, that the best thing you can do is to send somebody to me as soon as you can; that is to say if I remain in Spain, which I declare I believe to be almost impossible, notwithstanding that I see all the consequences of withdrawing. But a starving army is actually worse than none. The soldiers lose their discipline and their spirit. They plunder even in the presence of their officers. The officers are discontented, and are almost as bad as the men; and with the army which a fortnight ago beat double their numbers, I should now hesitate to meet a French corps of half their strength.

'Send somebody, however, by the road of Merida and Truxillo, at both of which places he must hear of me.

Believe me, &c.

ARTHUR WELLESLEY.

* See p. 4.

British Army to retire to a defensive position behind the Tagus; Sir Arthur Wellesley in his letter to me of the 8th instant, (No 1.) refers to his despatch addressed to Lord Castlereagh under date the 8th August for a full explanation of that movement.* He then proceeds to state the necessity that the Spanish Forces stationed in the northern provinces of Spain should be brought into action for the purpose of drawing the attention of the enemy to that quarter and of relieving Estremadura from the pressure of the concentrated French army which had been brought into combination against the allied forces of his Majesty and of Spain on the banks of the Tagus. In the same letter Sir Arthur Wellesley represents in the strongest terms the necessity of forming magazines of provisions and forage in the rear of the armies, and also of providing mules and other means of transport for the purpose of securing the supply and movement of the troops. This letter also recommends several improvements of a less pressing nature for the regulation of the Spanish troops, and states the outline of a defensive system of war for the adoption of the Spanish Government.

10. The matters of most pressing exigency contained in this letter formed the substance of my note of the 11th inst. to M. de Garay, and from the answer you will perceive with satisfaction that immediate attention was paid to my representation. I have reason to believe that great exertion has since been made by this government for the purpose of giving speedy effect to the plan which I proposed, and that I shall be permitted to superintend the completion of the several details necessary to the commencement of an improved system of supply and movement for the troops in the field. But the impoverished state of the country, the weakness of the government and the inveterate defects of the military department in Spain render any speedy improvement impracticable, and induce me to apprehend great difficulty even in the ultimate success of any plan, which can now be suggested.

11. In Sir Arthur Wellesley's letter (No. 2) of the same date, received also on the 11th, the description of the distress of the army occasioned by the want of provisions is

---

* See the despatches of the Duke of Wellington, vol. 5.

in the highest degree afflicting. Sir Arthur Wellesley concludes this letter by stating that he must render justice to
Mr. Frere in declaring that he does not conceive this deficiency of supplies for the army to be at all imputable to
any neglect or omission on the part of Mr. Frere ; Sir Arthur
Wellesley imputes this calamity to the poverty and exhausted
state of the country, to the indolence and timidity of the
magistrates, to the insubordination and disobedience of the
people, and to the want of authority in the government and
its officers.

12. To the causes which have produced and augmented
the sufferings of the army, must be added the perverse and
intractable disposition of General Cuesta the Commander-in-
Chief of the Spanish troops acting with Sir Arthur Wellesley. Of this disposition you will find innumerable proofs
in Sir Arthur Wellesley's letters, expecially in (No. 4, 5, and
6,) of the 9th, 10th and 12th of August.

13. These unhappy circumstances have contributed to
produce an unfavourable result in the state of the campaign.

14. In the letter dated the 9th, Sir Arthur Wellesley
forwards a despatch from Lieut.-Colonel Roche written on
the preceding day from Paraleda de Garvin, stating that the
enemy had attacked the bridge of Arzobispo on the Tagus,
having previously passed that river at a ford immediately
above the bridge; and that preparations were making by
General Cuesta to retire to La Mesa D'Ibor. This was the
first intimation that Sir Arthur Wellesley had received of
the removal of General Cuesta's head-quarters from the
bridge of Arzobispo. The Duque of Alburquerque who
arrived at Deleytosa the same evening, gave an account to
Sir Arthur Wellesley of the operations by which the enemy
had gained possession of the bridge and of the cannon
destined to defend it, together with five pieces of artillery
belonging to the Duque's division, and stated it as his opinion that the French were that morning at Paraleda de Garvin,
where General Cuesta's head-quarters had been the preceding evening; an aide-de-camp of General Cuesta and
Colonel Roche came in soon after and from the account
which they gave of the Spanish army, Sir Arthur Wellesley
was apprehensive that they must lose the greater part of
their artillery; he wrote immediately to General O'Donohue

pointing out the steps which should be taken to save it, and strongly urged the necessity of withdrawing the heavy artillery behind the·passes of the mountains.

15. The letter of the 10th (No. 5) was written after having visited General Cuesta's head-quarters. The whole of the Spanish artillery and waggons had then crossed the river Ibor, and about half of them had been drawn up the mountain to a place of security.

16. The last letter from Sir Arthur Wellesley is dated on the morning of the 12th from Jaraicejo. No French troops had then re-crossed the Tagus, excepting those which remained immediately at the bridge of Arzobispo. On the 9th, 10th and 11th, large columns of the French were seen in motion towards Placencia, from which movement Sir Arthur Wellesley concluded that the enemy was apprehensive either of the Duque del Parque's troops, or those of General Beresford in the mountains of Baños and Perales, or that the enemy intended to invade Portugal. Sir Arthur Wellesley expected to ascertain their position in the course of the 12th inst. and if they should have moved towards the frontier of Portugal, he states his intention to follow them. This letter concludes in the following words. " The experience of every day shews the absolute necessity that the British army should withdraw from this country. It is useless to complain; but we are certainly not treated as friends, much less as the only prop on which the cause of Spain can depend. But besides this want of good will, (which can easily be traced to the temper and disposition of the general commanding the Spanish army, and which ought to be borne with patience if there was any hope of doing good,) there is such a want of resource in the country and such little exertion in bringing forward what is to be found, that if the army were to remain here much longer, it would become totally useless. The daily and encreasing loss of horses in the cavalry and the artillery, from a deficiency and the badness of their food is really alarming; and the Spanish cavalry having begun to interrupt the small supplies of food for horses which we could find, this evil must encrease."

17. From the tenor of these letters I cannot form any reasonable expectation that the system which I have attempted to pursue for the relief of the wants of the army can pro-

duce any salutary effect in sufficient time to enable Sir
Arthur Wellesley to resume offensive operations, or even to
maintain a defensive position in Spain at any early period of
the season.

18. In the meanwhile the greatest alarm has been excited
by the rumour of the proposed return of the British army
into Portugal. This government appears not only to contemplate the probability of that event with terror and despair, but to consider it as the symptom of a disposition to
abandon the cause of Spain, and to relinquish the obligations of our alliance.

19. M. de Garay and a deputation from the Junta have
urged me in the most pressing manner to use my influence
for the purpose of detaining Sir Arthur Wellesley's army in
Spain, and of averting the destructive consequences which
must ensue, if the French arms should be turned into Andalusia, and the southern provinces of Spain. But although
I am deeply sensible of the urgency of this crisis, I cannot
attempt any other mode of averting the calamity than the
active employment of the Spanish troops in the northern
provinces of Spain, and the establishment of such regulations, as may ultimately render the subsistence of a British
army in Spain practicable and secure. The Government of
Spain cannot reasonably complain of the natural and necessary result of its own defective management, nor does
any obligation of the alliance require that the British army
should be sacrificed to the erroneous policy of a weak
administration, or to the capricious and impracticable temper
of its officers: the reduced state of the resources of the
country is perhaps to be ascribed to a variety of causes,
many of which are of remote origin, and of long operation.
But it is not just to expect that the British troops should
be exposed to the destructive effects of such a state of things,
because the poverty of the country is not the crime of its
present government.

20. I am not yet fully acquainted with the original motives and objects of Sir Arthur Wellesley's expedition into
Spain, nor have I been able to ascertain what arrangements
were made by the Spanish Government to provide for the
movement or supply of his army; it is sufficient to know
that the means of both have entirely failed, that they cannot

be provided under the present system and that no consideration inferior to absolute necessity could have checked such
an army under such a general in the full career of success,
and in the moment of decisive victory. Under such circumstances it would be fruitless, if not disingenuous to engage
to recommend to Sir Arthur Wellesley a plan, which I know,
and which he has declared, to be impracticable.

21. I trust therefore that his Majesty will graciously approve my conduct in having abstained from offering any
positive pledge to this government respecting the continuance
of our army in Spain, and in having limited my efforts to
the improvement of the disposition of the Spanish army in
the north of Spain, and of the means absolutely necessary
to enable our troops to move or even to subsist.

22. In the meanwhile I am confident, that if any favourable
change of circumstances should diminish the pressure of distress which now impedes the active exertions of the army.
Sir Arthur Wellesley will either resume offensive operations,
or occupy such a position in Spain as may be deemed most
effectual for the protection of the southern provinces.

23. Among the measures which might be suggested for
relieving the sufferings of our army, the removal of General
Cuesta from the command of the Spanish forces might certainly promise considerable advantage. In every quality
necessary for an extensive military command, General Cuesta
is said to be absolutely deficient, with the exception of personal courage. His impracticable temper renders him peculiarly unfit for the command of any force destined to act
with an allied army, and it is scarcely possible that another
officer could be found in the Spanish service with equal dis-
qualifications. Notwithstanding my conviction of General
Cuesta's defects, I have not thought it necessary or expedient to demand or insist upon his removal. This government is under some apprehension of General Cuesta's influence, which is said to be extensive and dangerous; although it rests merely on the precarious foundation of un-
merited popularity. But I have found no symptoms of
a disposition to support General Cuesta by obstinacy, or
by artifice, or to sacrifice any interest of the alliance to his
views or temper. The Junta is well disposed to remove
General Cuesta from his command in such a manner and by

such means as they deem decorous and safe. If he should tender his resignation it will be accepted with satisfaction and gratitude, and at all events the Junta is prepared to receive a regular and detailed statement of General Cuesta's misconduct from me, and to act upon that statement. It is my intention (unless I should be anticipated by General Cuesta's seasonable resignation) to present to the Secretary of State a recital of all the facts respecting General Cuesta which have been stated in Sir Arthur Wellesley's despatches. I am satisfied that the immediate result of such a representation will be the removal of General Cuesta.

24. In the meanwhile, I have limited my interference on this occasion to a strong expression of my sense of General Cuesta's misconduct, and of the impossibility of conducting military operations with any spirit of concord or union, while he shall continue in the command. The tenor of His Majesty's instructions of the 29th of June,* especially of the 8th paragraph, would require me to pursue this course of moderation and caution in a matter of such delicacy, if the ordinary principles of prudence had not recommended a strict observance of the same policy in discharging every part of the important trust which His Majesty has been pleased to confide to me.

25. I am satisfied that the removal of General Cuesta will be made with more cheerfulness and alacrity, and with less danger of unpopularity, if it should appear to be the necessary consequence of his own conduct, rather than the result of the direct interference of the British Ambassador.

26. The unexpected state of the campaign in Spain and the exigencies which affect the condition of the British army have compelled me to fix my attention on those points, which constitute the principal topics of this despatch, and to reserve the consideration of many important circumstances for a future opportunity.

I have the honour to be, &c.

WELLESLEY.

P. S. Soon after the battle of Talavera, the Junta appointed Sir Arthur Wellesley to the rank and pay of Captain

---

* See Appendix.

General in the Spanish army. They also presented some horses to that officer in the name of King Ferdinand the VIIth., as a testimony of gratitude and respect. The rank of Captain General in the Spanish army is nearly similar to that of Field Marshal in the British service; and does not necessarily include the chief command of the Spanish army. I therefore was induced to conceive that the orders stated in your despatch (No. 15, July the 18th) were not applicable to this proposition from the Junta.

I have the honour to refer you to Sir Arthur Wellesley's despatch (No. 3,) under date the 8th of August, by which you will perceive that he left me a discretionary power of forwarding to M. de Garay either of two letters, which he had enclosed to me; and in my despatch under date the 13th of August, addressed to Sir A. Wellesley, you will find, that I selected that letter which appeared to me to be the most respectful to the Junta, while it afforded a sufficient opportunity for the operation of his Majesty's commands, if it should be his Majesty's pleasure, that Sir Arthur Wellesley should not continue to hold the rank of Captain General in the Spanish army.

Sir Arthur Wellesley has accepted the present of horses, tendered by the Junta, but has declined receiving the pay of Captain General; in both instances, I trust, that his conduct will meet his Majesty's gracious approbation.

No. X.

Don Martin de Garay to the Marquess Wellesley.

MY LORD,   Seville, 15th August, 1809.

I have the honour to communicate to your Excellency the information I have this moment received.

The Duque del Parque, Captain-General of Old Castile, sends advices of the 14th of this month, that Sir Robert Wilson informed him of the enemy having forced the pass of the Puerto de Baños after an obstinate resistance, in which one of our battalions, under the orders of the Lieutenant Don Carlos de España, exerted itself with valour; that on the same day of the 12th General Beresford, *Mariscal de Campo* was in motion towards Marcelaga; and that il Marques de Castelfuata informed him from Salamanca, that the enemy to the number of 4,000, with artillery and cavalry, was directing his march towards that city, having already entered Santa Pedro de Razados at four leagues distance from Salamanca.

Under these circumstances, the Section of War conceive it to be most urgently necessary that the combined army should move, because the forces which Victor can present is diminished; and in consequence suitable communications have been made to Lieut.-General Francisco D'Eguia for the object which has been pointed out, if he should agree upon it with Sir Arthur Wellesley.

I transmit this for the information of your Excellency, in order that you may be pleased to make known your opinion to Sir Arthur Wellesley, and may decide on the measures which will be most useful to the common cause with attention to the circumstances.

I have the honour to be, &c.

MARTIN DE GARAY.

No. XI.

Don Martin de Garay to the Marquess Wellesley.

MY LORD,　　　　　　　　　　　　Seville, 17th August, 1809.

I have just received from the Secretary of the War Office an official paper of the following tenor. For the information of the ambassador of his Britannic Majesty, the supreme governing junta of the kingdom gives me notice, that on the 14th of this month the Captain General Don Gregorio de la Cuesta was informed, that by accounts communicated by the Duque del Parque of the 11th, it was known that Marshal Beresford had put in motion his army, comprised of 26,080 men armed in every manner, by the Puerto de Perales and Gata, with the direction of Corici, in order to assist the Anglo-Spanish army in their operations; that on this account it appeared expedient and necessary to combine an operation on the offensive, and that on this view he should consult and agree with Sir Arthur Wellesley. That Lieut.-General Don

Francisco de Eguia was informed of the same on the 15th, and that on the 16th it was repeated to him in consequence of information, that the English General had received accounts of the entry of the enemy in considerable numbers into Placentia, and that there were in Corici 30,000 men, which can be no other but the 26,080 of Beresford, although there may be a difference in the number (in which, however, it was very easy for the person who gave the account to be mistaken). But it appeared that there ought to remain no hesitation in recrossing the Tagus ; and with more reason, since it was known that there were very few troops of the enemy at the Puerto del Arzobispo ; that it could not but be expedient that Marshal Beresford, by retiring towards Perales and Gata, should call away the attention of Soult in order that Victor being diminished in number by the absence of these troops, the Anglo-Spanish army might attack him. The time having been calculated which it would require to pass the river and to attack Victor before Soult could return, and that he should make these observations to Sir Arthur Wellesley for his approbation. By the despatches received to-day from Eguia, it is confirmed that the enemy has very few troops in the Puerto del Arzobispo, although they had some cantoned in the neighbouring towns ; it was made known that our army was moved on the 15th to Deleytosa, both on account of the great scarcity of water at the Misa d'Ibor, and of the closer vicinity to the English army, in order to have the power of combining operations with its General.

The Section of War conceives it to be very expedient that your Excellency should be urgent with the ambassador of his Britannic Majesty in order that this movement may take place ; since, besides the advantages which may be gained over the enemy the more the armies advance, the more easy will be the means of subsistence ; and it would be equally expedient to advise Marshal Beresford, that in case of Soult's falling back to the aid of Victor (if it should prove that he has followed the Marshal) he should return with all possible celerity to succour the Anglo-Spanish army.

All which I transmit to your Excellency by the order of the Supreme Central Junta for your information ; and his Majesty hopes that your Excellency will be pleased to make the communications which you may conceive to be expedient, in order that these operations proposed by the Section of War may be carried into effect.

With this motive,

I have the honour to be, &c.

MARTIN DE GARAY,

No. XII.

Sir Arthur Wellesley to the Marquess Wellesley.

MY LORD,   Jaraicejo, 18th August, 1809.

I have the honour to enclose different reports, which I received yesterday, of the measures taken by the Spanish officers and troops to prevent the British army from foraging. The foraging parties, to which the reports relate, were necessarily obliged to go to a distance of four or five leagues (from sixteen to twenty miles) in order to procure the forage they required; which, with the distance they would have to to return, appears to be sufficient work for the parties and their horses. But, when having performed this work, they are deprived of the forage by the Spanish cavalry, it must be obvious that the equipments of the army must be ruined. I understand that similar outrages were committed on the foraging parties yesterday; but I have not yet had the official reports of them.

General Eguia did me the honour of calling on me yesterday, when I communicated to him these reports, and he promised that the evils complained of should be redressed. I desired him, however, to prepare to occupy, in the course of this night, the posts in the neighbourhood of the bridge of Almaraz, as it was impossible for me to remain any longer in this part of the country, suffering, as the army does, wants of every description.

In my last letter I apprized your Excellency of the wants of the cavalry, and of my having been obliged to remove them to the neighbourhood of Caceres to look for food. In my conversation with General Eguia yesterday, I found that the Spanish cavalry had on every day received some barley although not an entire ration. The enclosed reports will shew your Excellency in what manner this same cavalry, which occupies every village in the neigbourhood of this army, supplies itself with straw. The British army has no bread for this day; the troops receiving in lieu of that necessary, half a pound of flour, or one-third of their ration for each man; notwithstanding that General Eguia told me yesterday, that on this day, and always in future, provision would be made to supply both infantry and cavalry with their full rations of provisions and forage.

More than a month has now elapsed since I informed General Cuesta, that if the British army were not supplied with means of transport and with provisions, not only I would not co-operate in any forward movement beyond the Alberché, but that I could not remain at all in Spain; and the General informed me that he sent a copy of my letter to the Supreme Central Junta; and indeed I sent a copy of it to Mr. Frere. In the course of this month, if proper measures, or indeed if any measures had been adopted, supplies might have been forwarded to us from the most distant parts of Andalusia; but instead of that, we have not received a mule or a cart, or an article of provision of any description, under any order given or arrangement made by the Government: so that when I shall march, I shall be obliged to leave behind me my ammunition, and six, and probably twelve pieces of cannon; and I assure your Excellency most solemnly, that since the 22d of last month the horses of the cavalry and artillery have not received three deliveries of barley, and the infantry have not received ten days bread.

Under these circumstances, I can remain in Spain no longer; and I request you to give notice to the Government that I am about to withdraw into Portugal. I have no doubt that the Government have given orders that we should be provided as we ought to be ; but orders, I have to observe, are not sufficient. In order to carry on the contest with France to any good purpose, the labour and services of every man, and of every beast in the country, should be employed in the support of the armies ; and these should be so classed and arranged, as not only to secure obedience to the orders of the Government, but regularity and efficiency in the performance of the services required from them.

Magazines might then with ease be formed and transported wherever circumstances might require that armies should be stationed. But as we are now situated, 50,000 men are collected upon a spot which cannot afford subsistence for 10,000 men, and there are no means of sending to a distance to make good the deficiency. The Junta have issued their orders to supply the deficiencies of means of transport as well as of provision; but for want of arrangement, there are no persons to obey these orders, and this army would perish here, if I would remain, before the supplies would arrive.

I hope your Excellency and the Government will believe, that I have not determined to go till it has become absolutely necessary. I assure you that there is not a general officer of this army who is not convinced of the necessity of my immediate departure.

I have the honour to be, &c.

A. WELLESLEY.

[1st Enclosure.]

Captain Aceives to Major Hartman.

SIR,   Camp, near Truxillo, August 17, 1809.

I have the honour to report, that on the 16th instant, in the morning I ordered a foraging party, consisting of two gunners, one corporal, and and five men of the 29th regiment, armed, with four wains, to supply the horses belonging to the park of reserve.

The party went to a field on the left of Truxillo.

On their way home towards the camp, a Spanish piquet of cavalry, commanded by an officer, stopped them, made them go a mile back, compelled them to unload, telling the corporal that he wanted the forage for himself.

I have the honour to be, &c.

ANDREW ACEIVES,

Captain Royal German Artillery.

[2nd Enclosure.]

General Hill to Sir Arthur Wellesley.

SIR,   Camp, August 17, 1809.

I beg leave to report to you that the parties sent out by the officers of my division yesterday to procure forage, were in more instances than one opposed by the Spaniards.

The following circumstances have been made known to me, and I take the liberty of repeating them for your Excellency's information.

My servants were sent about three leagues on the Truxillo road, in order to get forage for me, and after gathering three mule loads, a party of Spanish soldiers, consisting of five or six, came up to them with their swords drawn, and obliged them to leave the corn they had collected. My servants told me that the same party fired two shots towards other British men employed in getting forage. The Assistant Commissary of my division likewise states to me, that the men he sent out for forage were fired at by the Spaniards.

I have the honour to be, &c.

R. HILL,
Major-General.

No. XIII.

Don Martin de Garay to the Marquess Wellesley.

MY LORD,   Seville, 18th August, 1809.

The Secretary of the War-Office sends me the following information under the date of yesterday:

Lieut.-General Don Francisco de Eguia writes from Deleytosa, with the date of the 25th of this month, that by the recent account which he had received, the head quarters of the French army were in Placentia; and that in the places which lie in the vicinity of the Puerto del Arzobispo the enemy had no more than 1,500 men. He adds, that General Sir Arthur Wellesley informed him, that on the 12th the enemy attacked Sir Robert Wilson at the Puerto de Baños, and that the attack lasted the whole day; at length, however, he was compelled to retire to Colmenar. That in consequence I have instructed Don Francisco de Eguia by the courier of to-night, that as the reasons for an operation on the offensive have been confirmed, he should agree with Sir Arthur Wellesley on the most expedient determination.

In consequence of having received the said note I shall expedite on this very night the suitable order for the immediate approach of the commissioner for the purchase of mares, in order that he may purchase the 300 which are required; and the Ministers of Finance will give an account of all that has been performed respecting the mules and carts.

I make this communication to your Excellency by the royal order,* that you may make it known to the Ambassador of his Britannic Majesty.

---

* Meaning the order of the Supreme Junta.—[*Ed.*]

I transmit the whole to your Excellency for your due information, and for the use which you may suppose convenient; and I include the note above-mentioned.

I have the honour to be, &c.

M. DE GARAY.

No. XIV.

Marquess Wellesley to Don Martin de Garay.

SIR,   Seville, August 19th, 1809.

In all my recent conferences with your Excellency, I have stated to you my sincere regret to find that great embarrassments have been felt by Sir Arthur Wellesley and the British Army in consequence of the conduct of the officer holding the chief command of the Spanish troops. Having fully explained all the facts stated by Sir Arthur Wellesley on this painful subject, I assured your Excellency that I relied entirely on the Government of Spain to provide an adequate remedy for an evil which menaced the glory and even the security of the allied armies.

In a matter of such delicacy as the removal of a General distinguished by the favour of the Government of Spain, I wished to abstain from interference, unless the absolute necessity of the case, or the positive desire of your Excellency, should require me to express my sentiments.

Innumerable events have proved that it is impossible to hope for any system of united exertion in the allied armies, for any degree of concert or co-operation, or even for any aid from the troops of Spain to the British army, if the chief command of the Spanish army should be in the hands of General Cuesta. Your Excellency also has earnestly desired that I should express my opinion on this point with the freedom which becomes the Ambassador of a King whose cause is the same with that of your Sovereign and of the Spanish nation.

To such considerations it is a public duty to postpone all motives of delicacy, and all sentiments of regret for the officer whose name has been mentioned; without reserve, therefore, I request your Excellency to acquaint the Supreme Government, that in answer to your Excellency's enquiries I think it necessary to declare that I shall applaud the wisdom and public spirit of the Government of Spain, if it shall proceed without delay to make an arrangement for the chief command of the Spanish army which may afford a more favourable prospect of union, cordiality, and energy in the prosecution of the war.

I am, &c.

WELLESLEY.

No. XV.

Don Martin de Garay to the Marquess Wellesley.

MY LORD,   Seville, 21st August, 1809.

I have given an account to the Supreme Central and Governing Junta of the kingdom, of the contents of the official note which your Excellency was pleased to address to me under date of the 19th instant, in which your Excellency pointed out the necessity that existed of altering the command of the Spanish army of Estremadura, now in the hands of the General Don Gregorio de la Cuesta ; and his Majesty* being acquainted with the motives which your Excellency explains as requiring this alteration, commands me to answer your Excellency as follows :

" On this day permission was granted to the said General to go and take the baths in the kingdom of Grenada, as your Excellency will perceive from the enclosed copy, which I transmit for that purpose.   Consequently the cause no longer exists which might have caused the delays and dissentions which have unfortunately taken place with the General Sir Arthur Wellesley ; and that with regard to proceeding immediately to form an arrangement for the command in chief of that army which might give a more favourable prospect of union, cordiality, and energy in the prosecution of the war, the Supreme Junta could desire nothing with more zeal and satisfaction than to accomplish this point, in agreement with your Excellency or with General Wellesley ; since the results which would be obtained would be the advantages proposed by your Excellency, which are the same that the Junta de-

* This title (Majesty) was assumed by the Supreme Junta.—[*Ed.*]

sires with the greatest ardour, and of which it has given so many proofs ; but as it is manifest from the letter which the General Sir Arthur Wellesley has written to your Excellency, and of which your Excellency has been pleased to transmit to me the original, that it is his decided resolution to retire into Portugal ; it appears, that in order to determine a question of so much importance, it would be equally necessary to suspend the execution of that design ; for if the reverse should happen, no arrangement, however adapted it may be to the interest and views of the two nations, could be carried into execution, or could cause the effects we so much desire, and which are so much to the advantage of both powers."

The Supreme Junta hopes that your Excellency will take these reflections into your consideration ; and that, with your well-known integrity and zeal for the just cause we are engaged in defending, you will make the arrangements which your prudence dictates and which you conceive most conducive to the attainment of the object to which our respective Sovereigns so ardently aspire ; as you will be firmly convinced that the want of provisions for the English army, and of other articles of which its General has complained, is in a course of expeditious remedy as far as the country and the circumstances allow, since the most precise and efficient orders to this effect have been expedited to the various departments. Your Excellency is not ignorant of the enthusiasm and joy which pervaded the whole Spanish nation when it beheld the British army approach to co-operate in its defence, and to deliver it from the tyrant who attempts to despoil it of its independence ; and for the same reason your Excellency will be able to imagine to yourself with ease what would be the desolation of that nation should they behold the retreat of that same army on which they had fixed all their hopes for the attainment of their liberty ; for they would conceive that other motives must have produced the departure of an ally on which they had reposed their whole confidence.

I have the honour to lay before your Excellency these observations for your consideration, in consequence of a royal order ; and I repeat on this occasion,

&c. &c. &c.

MARTIN DE GARAY.

[Enclosure.]

General Cuesta to Don Antonio Cornel.

SIR,   Truxillo, August 8th, 1809.

I have received, with the highest respect and gratitude, the royal order which your Excellency is pleased to make known to me, dated the 15th of this month, with the permission which his Majesty has deigned to grant me to take the baths of Alhama; I shall depart for that place by the straight road through the *Pedroches of Cordova* on the day after to-morrow, for not even the repose of these last days has produced any alleviation of my disorder; this would not impede my wishes to remain in the command at any price, unless I considered it impossible for me to discharge its duties, since I count for nothing, in balance with the service of your Majesty, a life as often exposed as it could be useful; but I think, on the other hand, that it would cause nothing but delay in the affairs and arrangements, with injury to the State. I shall not succeed in expressing my gratitude for the high estimation which your Excellency is pleased to entertain of my confined services, unless by declaring my lively wishes for the recovery of my health, in order solely to enable me to continue them.

GREGORIO DE CUESTA.

No. XVI.

The Marquess Wellesley to Don Martin de Garay.

SIR,   Seville, August 21, 1809.

Since I had the honour of addressing your Excellency on the 12th instant* relative to the defective condition of the supplies and means of transport of the British army under Sir Arthur Wellesley, I have continually received the most afflicting intelligence of the increasing distress of those brave and meritorious troops.

Without attempting to doubt the exertions of this government, I am deeply concerned to inform your Excellency that they have hitherto proved entirely fruitless.

On the 18th instant, Sir Arthur Wellesley informs me that the British army was without bread for that day; the cavalry was also without forage: which defect, I am grieved to inform your Excellency, was in a great degree to be ascribed to the interception, by the Spanish cavalry, of the supplies of forage provided under Sir Arthur Wellesley's orders for the British troops.

Sir Arthur Wellesley further informs me, that more than

* See p. 4.

a month has now elapsed since he declared, in a letter to General Cuesta, that if the British army was not supplied with the means of transport, and with provisions, not only it could not co-operate in any forward movement beyond the river Alberché, but that it could not remain in Spain; and General Cuesta assured Sir Arthur Wellesley that he despatched a copy of that letter to the Supreme Central Junta. In the course of that month, if proper measures had been adopted, supplies might certainly have been forwarded to the British army from the most distant parts of Andalusia; but Sir Arthur Wellesley declares, that he has not received a mule, or a cart, or an article of provision of any description, under any order given, or arrangement made by the government; and Sir Arthur Wellesley most solemnly assures me, that since the 22d of July, the horses of the cavalry and of the artillery have not received three regular deliveries of barley, and the infantry have not received ten days bread. Under these circumstances, Sir Arthur Wellesley states that the British army cannot remain in Spain; and he has requested me to give notice to the Spanish Government that he is about to withdraw the British army into Portugal.

I had the honour of communicating to your Excellency Sir Arthur Wellesley's letter on this painful subject last night, immediately after I had received it; and I am satisfied that your Excellency will do me the justice to admit, that I have not failed to make the most unreserved communications to your Excellency, respecting the condition of the army, since the moment of my arrival at Seville.

It is further my duty to represent to your Excellency, that Sir Arthur Wellesley expresses no doubt that the government has given orders that his army shall be properly provided; but, he observes, " that mere orders are not sufficient; that with a view to bring the contest with France to a favourable result, the labour and services of every man, and of every beast in the country, should be employed in the support of the army; and that they should be so classed and arranged, as not only to secure obedience to the orders of the government, but regularity and efficiency in the performance of the services required from them.

" Magazines might then with ease be formed, and transported wherever circumstances might require that armies should be stationed. But as we are now situated, 50,000 men are collected upon a spot, which cannot afford subsistence for 10,000 men, and no means exist of sending to a distance to supply the local deficiency." Sir Arthur Wellesley further remarks, that the Supreme Central Junta has also issued orders to supply the deficiencies of the means of transport, as well as of provisions; but from inadequate arrangement, no persons obey these orders; and if the British army had attempted to remove to the position which it lately occupied, it must have perished before the proposed supplies could have reached it.

Under all these circumstances, I trust your Excellency will perceive that Sir Arthur Wellesley did not determine to fall back on his supplies in Portugal until the necessity of his situation became absolutely irresistible.

Your Excellency will observe, that the British general has stated without reserve his sentiments respecting the defective arrangement of the military resources of Spain, which has occasioned this severe calamity to the interests of the alliance. In the spirit of friendship, and for the common benefit of the great cause in which we are engaged, I submit Sir Arthur Wellesley's remarks to the serious consideration of the Spanish Government. Availing myself of this occasion to repeat my sentiments of high respect and esteem,

I have the honour to be, Sir,

your Excellency's most faithful

and obedient servant,

WELLESLEY.

No. XVII.

The Marquess Wellesley to Don Martin de Garay.

SIR,   Seville, August 21, 1809.

I have the honour to enclose for your Excellency's consideration, the suggestions which have occurred to me for the improvement of the system of movement and supply of the British army employed in Spain.

The principles on which this plan is founded are equally applicable to the condition of the Spanish armies, and the same principles will apply at any time to any positions which the armies may occupy, either in the event of their retiring upon a system of defence, or of their advancing for active operations.

I take the liberty, at your Excellency's repeated solicita-tion, of earnestly recommending the immediate and active adoption of this plan.

I have added a paper, containing some propositions for occupying a new defensive position, upon the banks of the Guadiana.

It is impossible for me positively to enforce, or even to assure your Excellency, that Sir Arthur Wellesley will adopt the propositions contained in that paper; but the acknow-ledged zeal of that distinguished officer for the success of the Spanish cause, and his transcendent exertions in the defence of the independence of Spain, leave no doubt that he will readily accept any proposition, which can provide for the safety of Spain, without exposing the British army to the horrors of famine and disease.

If therefore it should be agreeable to the Supreme Central Junta, to adopt without delay the plans enclosed in this letter, and commence the execution of these plans with ac-tivity and vigour, I will despatch an express to Sir Arthur Wellesley to-morrow with these papers; and I will recom-mend the whole plan to his favourable consideration; pro-vided he shall be of opinion that my suggestions do not en-danger the existence of the British army; for which im-portant object it is my duty to provide; and I am satisfied that it never can be the inclination of the Spanish Govern-ment to expose the British army to destruction, without any prospect of honour or advantage to the common cause.

I have the honour to be, &c.

WELLESLEY.

[Enclosure No. 1, marked A.]

Plan to enable the British Army to procure the Means of Movement.

To enable the English army to recommence offensive operations, it is absolutely necessary that it should possess effective and ready means of movement.

The means of subsisting an army in the field depend on the means of transport. If the power of movement should fail, all offensive operations must of necessity cease, and it becomes difficult even to maintain a defensive position.

To an army of 25,000 men in this country, should be attached a thousand mules and a hundred carts. This will provide for the transport of the hospital stores, military chest, and five days rations of biscuit, rice, and bacon. But these means of transport are not to be considered as forming part of the train necessarily employed in conducting the supplies of grain, biscuit, wine, brandy, &c. from the magazine to the army.

In the present position of the British and Spanish armies in Estremadura, two lines of magazines might be formed. The depôts nearest the army should be collected at Villa Nova de la Serena, Dom Benito, Almendralijo, Asauchal. They should be formed of flour, biscuit, rice, bacon, barley, oats, wine, and brandy.

The part of the country in which these places are situated is equal to supply the magazines. The means of transport also might be collected in that province, without difficulty, partly in mules, and partly in carts.

The second depôts might be formed at Monasterio, Santa Olalla ; and should be entirely supplied, both in provisions and means of transport, from Seville and its vicinity.

The town of Seville is famous for its biscuit. It might therefore be convenient to make Monasterio and Santa Olalla the principal depôts for biscuit, as well as for wine and brandy.

But it will be in vain to establish magazines, and procure the means of conveying supplies to the army, if the convoys of provisions be not placed under the direction of military officers, who shall be made answerable for their regular and punctual delivery.

A military officer, to be named by the British general, assisted by six or eight commissaries, should be at the head of each line of depôts.

The mules and carts employed in the transport of provisions, should be divided into brigades, and each brigade should be escorted by an officer, and by a sufficient number of men to protect it from insult.

These officers and men should of course be under the command of the officer at the head of the magazines.

In the town of Almendralijo, and in the neighbourhood, there are considerable quantities of wheat and barley. It is absolutely necessary that this supply should be secured for the use of the army, and conveyed within the line of the position which it is likely to occupy.

Immediate means should be taken for purchasing this grain, under a requisition which should compel its delivery at proper prices. The money should be paid immediately on delivery of the grain.

Returns should be collected of all articles of provision existing in Estremadura, with a view to purchase and bring within the same line whatever may be necessary for the use of the army.

Bread, rice, and barley, are the articles of which the army are at present in most need.

Money must be sent forward to make the necessary purchases.

Seville, and even Cadiz, might furnish means of transport, and for this purpose, every sacrifice of private convenience must be required.

The horses, mules, and carriages of all individuals, should be considered to belong to the war department, until they should have performed a certain number of journies to the army.

This demand, however, should be exclusive of the supply required for attaching to the army brigades of carts and mules.

The whole plan might then be connected in the following manner.

At Cadiz, all the articles both of provision and of transport which could be collected from that vicinity, and even from Africa if necessary, should be placed under the direction of a proper officer, to be approved by the British ambassador.

Cadiz should furnish the means of conveying these articles to Seville.

At Seville a similar arrangement should be made for collecting and distributing the provision ; and Seville should furnish the means of moving these articles to Santa Olalla and Monasterio, where the magazines nearest to Seville will be established. These magazines also must be furnished with their separate means of transport from this line to Asauchal, Almendralijo, &c. where a similar establishment is to be made, with separate means of conveyance.

The line of communication with the army being once determined, regular halting places should be fixed for the convoys ; and provision should be made at each of these halting places for the men and beasts employed in the convoys.

Regular daily returns should be made to the British general, and to the government of Seville, of the state of each magazine and of each convoy.

These returns should contain a list of the nature and quantity of each article conveyed, and of the time of departure and arrival of each convoy, together with the name of the officer commanding the escort, who should be rendered responsible for the due delivery of the articles to be conveyed.

A proper system of rewards should be established under the direction of the British general, for those persons who should distinguish themselves in the collection of the articles required for the magazines, and in the safe conveyance of them to their several points of destination. The rewards should be given on the spot, and should not be deferred to any remote period of time, or rendered liable to any contingency.

If this plan should be approved, lists can be made out immediately of the whole establishment necessary for carrying it into effect.

WELLESLEY.

[Enclosure No. 2, marked B.]

Plan for the British Army taking up a Position upon the Left Bank of the Guadiana.

If the Spanish and British armies should retire from the positions which they at present occupy, they might take up a position on the left bank of the Guadiana, from Villa nueva de la Serena, nearly to Badajoz.

If the British army occupied Merida as an advanced post, and stationed their right at Almendralijo, extending their left towards Badajoz, perhaps Portugal would be as effectually covered by that position, as by the occupation of Elvas ; at the same time that, by occupying this position, Seville would be protected, and a firm point d'appui would be given to the left of the Spanish army, which should, in that case, be cantoned in the towns of Medellin, Don Benito, and Villa nueva de la Serena.

This position of the armies would immediately facilitate their means of subsistence, under the plan proposed ; as the country which they would occupy is abundant, and consequently the distances of transport short.

Before the armies can have consumed the existing produce of the country, it is to be hoped the magazines at Monasterio and Santa Olalla, according to the plan proposed, will be in a state amply to supply all the wants of both armies.

Another advantage to be derived from the positions proposed would be, that the right of the English, and the left of the Spanish army, would be too far separated to allow of any dissentions respecting forage, or supplies of any kind.

But in order to give full effect to every part of this plan, the general commanding the Spanish army should be positively ordered to conform, in every respect, to such instructions as he might receive from Sir Arthur Wellesley, and should be directed to occupy such positions, and to pursue such a plan, either of offence or defence, as Sir Arthur Wellesley may propose.

WELLESLEY.

No. XVIII.

The Marquess Wellesley to Don Martin de Garay.

SIR,   Seville, August 21, 1809.

In my note of the 12th instant, I submitted to your Excellency my desire to be permitted to state to you the plan which it might be necessary to adopt for providing the British army in Spain with the means of supply and of movement.

Before I could attempt to suggest such a plan, it was requisite that I should know, with some degree of precision, the arrangements which had already been made by the government of Spain for these important objects, and the result of those arrangements. This knowledge alone could enable me to determine the measures from which success might be expected, or those from which failure was to be apprehended.

The documents which I have received this day from your Excellency, compared with Sir Arthur Wellesley's letters, have afforded me a clear view of the real causes of distress, which has checked the operations of the British army in the

* See p. 4.

full career of its glory, and has at length compelled it to fall back on the supplies provided in Portugal.

From these papers it appears, that the government, at considerable intervals of time, has issued orders to different officers and public authorities to provide supplies for the army: but it does not appear that the necessary means have been employed to enforce and to secure the execution of those orders, or to ascertain, in due season, to what extent they had been executed, in what respects they had failed, or what were the causes either of their total failure or of their partial success.

No magazines or regular depôts of provisions have been established, under persons properly qualified to superintend the collection and distribution of provisions, and to make regular returns of their proceedings to their British general, as well as to the Spanish Government. No regular and stated means of transport and movement have been attached to the army or to magazines, for the purpose of moving supplies from place to place; nor have any persons been regularly appointed to conduct and superintend convoys, under the direction of the general commanding the army.

No system of sufficient efficiency has been adopted for drawing forth from the rich and abundant provinces the resources which might have been applied, by a connected chain of magazines under due regulation, to relieve the local deficiency of those countries in which the army might be compelled to act.

Accordingly, the result of the well-intentioned but inefficient zeal of the officers of government has been totally inadequate to the exigencies of the occasion.

The supply of the various articles enumerated in the returns, which your Excellency has done me the honour to communicate to me, is very unequal to the wants of the army, especially in those articles which include the means of movement.

But I must observe to your Excellency, that even these inadequate supplies have not reached the object of their stated destination; and that the British army in point of fact has derived no benefit whatever from any of the orders described in the papers which I have had the honour of receiving from your Excellency. The failure of these orders, issued with so sincere a desire of aiding the efforts of the British army in the general cause, precludes all rational hope of better success under the same defective system.

Your Excellency will therefore understand the considerarations which prevented Sir Arthur Wellesley from confiding the safety of his gallant troops to the result of measures, which however amicable and sincere in their principle, had been proved, by fatal experience, to be entirely fruitless in their consequences, and therefore utterly insufficient to secure to his army the means of continuing beyond the reach of those supplies which he had provided in Portugal.

I have the honour, &c.

WELLESLEY.

No. XIX.

The Marquess Wellesley to Mr. Secretary Canning.

SIR,   Seville, August 21, 1809.

1. In consequence of the discussions which took place between M. de Garay and me respecting General Cuesta, M. de Garay at length requested me to state in a note my desire, that the Spanish Government should take the necessary measures for placing the command of the army in the hands of a more competent and tractable officer than General Cuesta appeared to be by his conduct in the last campaign.

2. This request of M. de Garay was the natural result of the course which I had pursued, in throwing upon the government of Spain the responsibility of leaving the command in Estremadura in such hands.

3. Being now relieved by M. de Garay's express solicitation from any difficulty, I addressed the enclosed note to him, to which he has returned the answer, of which a translation is enclosed.*

4. You will observe that General Cuesta's health had required him to desire to be relieved from the command in Estremadura, and that his resignation had been accepted by the government.

5. The government avails itself of this occasion to urge

---

* See pp. 37 and 38.

the continuance of the British army in Spain, and insinuates that some assurance from me to that effect would be required previously to the selection of a successor to General Cuesta: I have not thought this insinuation of sufficient importance to justify any particular notice. In the meanwhile, the command in Estremadura has devolved on General Eguia, an officer whose local knowledge of Spain is said to be considerable, but who is described to be otherwise quite incapable of holding such a command.

6. The most proper person for the command in Estremadura, would be the Duke of Albuquerque, who has been distinguished by several acts of gallantry and spirit in the last campaign. He is however an object of jealousy to the Junta, and if he should be appointed to the command in Estremadura, attempts will certainly be made to reduce the strength of that division of the Spanish army.

I have the honour to be,
with great truth and respect,
Sir,
your most obedient and faithful servant,
WELLESLEY.

No. XX.

Sir Arthur Wellesley to the Marquess Wellesley.

MY LORD, Truxillo, August 21st, 1809.

I did not march from Jaraicejo, till yesterday, not being able to arrange till that moment for the carriage of the sick of the army, to remove whom has taken every carriage and every mule we had to carry the remnant of our reserve ammunition, and the stores in the Commissariat; and I have given over the ammunition to the Spanish general. We have not received any assistance of any description from the country, or from the agents of the Spanish Government.

I have the honour to enclose to your Excellency copies of letters which I have received from General Eguia, and copies of my answers: your Excellency will observe in General Eguia's letter to me of the 19th instant, a very injurious, improper, and unfounded assertion; that I made use of the want of provisions as a pretext for withdrawing from Spain,

and that it was a false one, for that there was plenty of provisions for the army; while I assured your Excellency that
on that very day, the troops in my camp at Jaraicejo received
only three quarters of a pound of flour, and the cavalry and
other horses of the army no forage excepting what they
could pick up.

Until this insulting assertion was withdrawn, it was impossible for me to continue my correspondence with General
Eguia, after I should have replied to his letter I hope with
the temper which became my situation and character. Your
Excellency will observe, that in his reply to me he has either
misunderstood, or has affected to misunderstand the part of
his former letter to which I referred; and he has in fact left
the charge of making use of a false pretext where it stood.
I have therefore given him no reply upon that or any other
subject on which he has addressed me. Your Excellency
will likewise find an insinuation of the same kind in a letter
from Monsieur Calvo, dated the 19th instant, of which and
of my answer of the 20th I enclose copies. These letters
contain nearly the substance of a conversation I had with
Monsieur Calvo on the evening of the 19th; and I assure
your Excellency, that at the moment Monsieur Calvo was
writing his letter from Truxillo, stating the contents of the
magazine of that place, on which statement he founded his
insinuation that I was withdrawing from Spain upon a false
pretext, Lieut.-Colonel Waters delivered to me a return of
the contents of the magazine, made up to the evening of the
19th; from which it appeared, that it did not contain a
sufficiency to feed the British troops even for one day; and
if the magazine had contained a sufficiency of food, there
was no means of transport to remove it to the positions which
the troops occupied.

Your Excellency will recollect, that in my correspondence
with General Cuesta and with General Eguia, I stated the
difficulty of settling any arrangement for the division of the
magazine to be formed at Truxillo, in proportion to the
strength of the two armies, because probably both armies,
but certainly the Spanish army, would draw provisions from
other quarters; which provisions could not go through the
magazine: to which answers were given, calling upon me to
rely upon the honour and good faith with which the arrange-

ment to be made should be carried into execution. I now beg to refer you to the enclosed letter (of which I have the original in my possession) from the Alcalde of Guadalupe to Mr. Commissary Downie, in which the Alcalde informs Mr. Commissary Downie, that he had received the directions of Monsieur de Calvo, which he had obeyed, to send to Mesa d'Ibor, the head quarters of the Spanish army, the provisions which Mr. Downie had ordered, and had been provided for the *use of the British army, to be sent to the magazine at Truxillo.*

This is the honour and good faith with which the arrangement respecting the magazine at Truxillo was to be carried into execution! and this Monsieur Calvo is the gentleman in whose assurances I was to place confidence (as if I had not already gone far enough in confidence, in the assurances of the agents of the Spanish Government) that all the contents of the magazine at Truxillo should be given to the British troops, to the exclusion of the Spanish army; and that every thing which the army required, of every description, was on the road from Seville.

I find that it is intended to justify the Spanish Government for their neglect of us, by circulating a report that my complaints of want of supplies, of means of transport, and, I might have added, of the common attention, and even of humanity towards the army, and particularly the wounded, were mere pretexts. This plan has been carried into execution so far, as that Monsieur Lozano de Torres, the Spanish Superintendant attached to this army declared publicly yesterday, that he could prove that the British army, instead of wanting food, had received double rations ever since it arrived in Spain; and yet this same gentleman has expressed to me, in the most indignant terms, more than once, the shame he felt, as a Spaniard, on account of the manner in which we were treated, and the privations we were made to endure; which expressions he acknowledged this day. These reports against me may do very well for the people of Seville, but the British army will not soon forget the treatment it has received; and I know there is not a general officer in it, and I believe not an officer or soldier who does not think I should have neglected its interests, and even should have risked its existence, if I had delayed my departure for another day.

I have the honour to enclose a copy of my despatch to the Secretary of State.

I have the honour to be, &c.

ARTHUR WELLESLEY.

P. S. By a letter from Marshal Beresford I find that he also has been distressed for want of provisions. He informs me that the Marquess de la Romana was still at Corunna on the 5th instant.

P. P. S. I beg leave to draw your Excellency's attention to a fact which has occurred here this day. Your Excellency will observe that Monsieur de Calvo boasts, in his letter of the 19th, that he had here at command means of transport to carry provisions to the British army and its detachments, not less than thirty miles from hence, and the quantity not less than one hundred thousand pounds in weight daily. Some sick had been sent here from Jaraicejo, who had not been considered in the arrangement made for the removal of the sick, and six carts were to remove them, which were required last night from Monsieur Lozano de Torres, another deputy from the Junta, and living with Monsieur Calvo. These six carts have not been given, and I have removed these sick in the best manner I could.

Just to shew your Lordship the difference of the manner in which we are treated in Portugal, I mention that General Liete having heard by accident that our wounded were going to Elvas, prepared to receive them, and the preparations for the hospital were actually made unsolicited, before the officer who was charged to make them arrived with my letter to General Liete, to announce my wish to establish the hospital at Elvas.

In the same manner I must mention, that stores for which the orders did not reach Lisbon till the 18th, will be at Elvas on the 26th, and yet Lisbon is further from the army than Seville is, and the means of transport in Portugal not half what they are in Spain.

[1st Enclosure.]

General Eguia to Sir Arthur Wellesley.

SIR,   Deleytosa, August 18th, 1809.

I sent a despatch this morning to your Excellency, with the communication of the official accounts I had recently received from the Commissaries in Truxillo, of all they had done to provide the subsistence required by the army under your command, for this and for the succeeding days.

While it appeared from the said accounts that the officers named by your Excellency were satisfied with our zeal and services, and while I hoped that your Excellency would consequently feel the same satisfaction, I perceive with surprize that your Excellency persists in abandoning my left, without having been pleased to tell me the place towards which you direct your course, nor any which may assist me in forming an idea of this march.

Your Excellency will allow me to ask this question, formally, for the information of my court and my government, while you will take notice that until I receive a formal explanation on this subject, I shall delay the departure of my troops who are to defend the bridge of Almaraz, which is now occupied by the English vanguard; and it is indeed my duty to declare to your Excellency, with the greatest regret, that if you follow up your system of leaving me alone in the position I now hold, I shall remain in it for a very short time, as it does not enter into the plan of my future operations to maintain it; on ·this question I shall send an account to the government, for its superior approbation.

FRANCISCO DE EGUIA.

[2nd Enclosure.]

General Eguia to Sir Arthur Wellesley.

SIR,   Deleytosa, August 19th, 1809.

I transmit to your Excellency a copy of the express I have just received from the Minister of War : that with reference to its contents, and with the agreement which I am ordered to maintain with your Excellency, on the points it comprehends, you may be pleased to express to me your opinion on the subject, both for my own information and for the purpose of enabling me to satisfy the superior authorities.   God preserve you.

FRANCISCO DE EGUIA.

[3rd Enclosure.]

Don Antonio de Cornel to General Eguia.

(Enclosed in the preceding.)

SIR,   Seville, August 16th, 1809.

By the expresses from your Excellency of the 13th of this month, the Supreme Governing Junta of the kingdom has been informed that nothing new has occurred with respect to the enemy; and has learnt the news communicated to your Excellency by Lieut.-Colonel O'Lawler. It is to be supposed, in consequence of this news, that the army of Soult is in search of that of the Marshal Beresford, which was to have marched by Coria; and in this case it seems that no doubt can remain, that the army of Sir Arthur Wellesley, united with our own, should pass the Tagus; more particularly as it is known, by the observation of Colonel Waters, how few were the forces of the enemy at the bridge of Arzobispo. It would seem likewise expedient that Beresford, by marching into the interior towards Perales and Gata, should attract the attention of the army by which he is followed; since by a calculation of the time which Soult must require for his return, there might be an opportunity of fighting Victor with diminished forces : and in consequence of my communications to your Excellency, by the courier of yesterday, you will be able to make these remarks to Sir Arthur Wellesley, in order that the advantages may not be lost which might result to the just cause which both nations defend in common.

Royal Palace of the Castle of Seville,
16th August, 1809.   CORNEL.

[4th Enclosure.]

General Eguia to Sir Arthur Wellesley.

SIR,   Head Quarters, Deleytosa, August 19th, 1809.

I have received the official note of your Excellency with date of last night, in which you give me notice of your decisive resolution to march to Portugal, on account of the want of subsistence for the army under your command. Your Excellency, as I have already offered shall have all that you require for your troops, and either the article which your Excellency desires to be procured will be wanting in all the magazines, or the English army shall have it; for, I repeat, that the Spanish soldier shall be in want of every thing, in order that nothing may be wanting to our allies. In case your Excellency should not be thoroughly acquainted with my wishes, I have the honour to repeat to you, that there shall be an English Commissary constantly in Truxillo, who shall have a key of the magazine and shall take from the whole the part which has been stipulated, according to the numbers of the British army, and although my own may perish.

I conceive that I shall satisfy the wishes of your Excellency with this positive and conclusive answer; while I likewise observe to your Excellency that I have given my orders in Truxillo, in order that it may be duly effected; if however, notwithstanding this answer, your Excellency should persist in marching your troops into Portugal, I shall be convinced that other causes, and not the want of subsistence, have induced your Excellency to decide in taking such a step. The answer which I wait from your Excellency will determine whether I shall send troops or not, to relieve the posts which are covered by the vanguard of the English near the bridge of Almaraz.

I have the honour, &c.

FRANCISCO D' EGUIA.

[5th Enclosure.]

General Eguia to Sir Arthur Wellesley.

Sir,   Head Quarters, Deleytosa, 19th August, 1809.

I have received the official note of your Excellency, and it is to me a cause of astonishment how your Excellency could have imagined that I can doubt the truth of your expressions, when the experience of the scarcity which is suffered by our own army must convince me that it is equally felt by the troops under your command. But I addressed your Excellency under the supposition of the resources and measures that had been taken, and'in no manner did I doubt of the correctness of your assertions. Your Excellency, by supposing very different from that which it was my intention to write, has obliged me to make this explanation.

I shall send an officer to Juanesso to receive the ammunition, which there is in that village, and I will take care that the park shall receive that which is delivered for it here, as your Excellency informs me in the above-mentioned note.

Information has just reached me, that the enemy talks loudly of our approaching attack by the bridge of Arzobispo. I conceive it my duty to make this known to your Excellency, with an enclosure of a copy of that information.

FRANCISCO D' EGUIA.

[6th Enclosure.]

Sir Arthur Wellesley to General Eguia.

Sir,   Jaraicejo, August 19th, 1809.

I have had the honour of receiving your Excellency's letter of this day's date, and I feel much concerned that any thing should have occurred to induce your Excellency to express a doubt of the truth of what I have written to you; as however your Excellency entertains that doubt, any further correspondence between us appears unnecessary : and accordingly this is the last letter which I shall have the honour of addressing you.

Although your Excellency has expressed a doubt of the truth of what I have written to you, I entertain none of the truth of what your Excellency has written to me; and I am well convinced that your Excellency has given orders, and that all the contents of the magazine at Truxillo will be given to the British troops, even though the Spanish troops should want food.

But notwithstanding these orders, and an obedience to them, the British troops are still in want; yesterday they did not receive one-third of a ration, and that was in flour ; this day they receive only half a ration, and that likewise in flour ; and on neither days have the horses of the army received any thing.

These deficiencies arise not from want of orders of your Excellency, or of your faithful execution of your promise to me, but from the want of means in the country, and from the want of arrangement in the government in the adoption of timely measures to supply the wants, which they were informed long ago existed. But to whatever cause the deficiency of means of supplying the troops with provisions may be attributed, it is obvious that it exists; according to the return of the state of the magazine at Truxillo, sent to me by your Excellency yesterday, it did not contain a sufficiency to feed even the British army for one day. This being the case, the wants of the army must continue; I must continue to lose horses and men daily; and in order to ease my army, I must remove to a country in which I know I shall get food, and other assistance which I require. Whatever your Excellency may think of the truth or falsehood of my assertion, I repeat that want, and the apprehension of its further consequences, are the only reasons for my quitting Spain. I have the honour to inform your Excellency, that besides the ammunition left at Deleytosa, I shall be obliged to leave here a large quantity for the want of means of moving it.

I will send an officer to Deleytosa to-morrow, to deliver to the Officer whom you will appoint to receive it, the ammunition which is there; and if you will send an officer here in the course of this day, he shall receive charge of the ammunition which will be left here, if your Excellency wishes to have these articles; if you should not wish to have them, I propose to destroy them, as I have no means of moving them from hence.

I have the honour, &c.

ARTHUR WELLESLEY.

P. S. I have just received your Excellency's second letter of this date, enclosing one of the 16th of August from the Minister of War at Seville. The Minister of War is entirely misinformed of the actual situation of the French armies; a large corps has marched to Salamanca; another is at Placentia; Marshal Mortier, with a part of Victor's corps, is at Talavera, Oropesa, and Arzobispo, and the remainder of Victor's corps, with Sebastiani's, is in La Mancha.

Marshal Beresford is on the frontiers of Portugal, near Salvatierra. Under these circumstances, there might be an opportunity of striking a blow with advantage, although no permanent good be produced till the corps of the Marquess de la Romana, or some other corps, could be brought forward. But the Minister of War forgets that we have no food; that our cavalry, from want, are scarcely able to move from the ground; that our artillery horses are not able to draw the guns, and that I have no means of moving; and I am actually obliged to leave here my ammunition from the want of means of moving it; and above all, that the soldiers are worn down by want and privations of every description.

It is extraordinary that the minister did not advert to these circumstances, which have been frequently laid before him, or that adverting to them, he should propose to me any operation of any description to which he must have known I was unequal; but his having omitted to advert to them, sufficiently accounts for their continued existence.

A. W

[7th Enclosure.]

M de Calvo to Sir Arthur Wellesley.

SIR,   Truxillo, August 19th, 1809.

When I manifested to your Excellency, verbally, the very distinguished esteem which my government entertained towards your Excellency and your deserving army, and the grief it had felt for the privations which that army had endured for some days, arising no less perhaps from the nature of the last movements, which have been executed by the combined arms, than from other causes, which had not come to its knowledge until a few days from the present; I have assured you that they should cease immediately; and that by means of their disappearance, and of the considerable remittances of articles of subsistence, which all the towns of this province began to make collectively, in consequence of the vigorous orders which I had addressed to them, there would be shortly an abundance of all things in the armies, and that their supplies would be regulated for the future in a manner by which the return of scarcity would be avoided.

Your Excellency has not been pleased to trust to their assurances, and has disclosed to me your resolution to return immediately to the kingdom of Portugal; and although I have repeated to you those offers, giving to them non-limitation, since I have chosen to bind myself to provide, within three days, your army with all the rations it may require; while at the same time it should want nothing in the interval which could be applied to its use, although the Spanish army were to be left with nothing; and within the fifteen first days it should have, in magazines situated where your Excellency directs, all the articles which your army could be supposed to consume in one or two months; all the carts and mules of draft and burthen which could be required for the transport of those magazines, being likewise provided.

Your Excellency has not judged these new proposals to be more worthy of reliance than the former; and while you qualified them as proceeding from the best intention, you have declared that you had no reason for believing that they would be realized. You therefore persisted in your intention of effectuating your retreat. At the instant of my return I have arranged in such a manner, that from this time seven thousand rations of bread, fifty thousand pounds of flour, two hundred and fifty *fanegas* of barley, fifty of rye, one hundred of wheat, and sixty *arrobas* of rice, which can be sent on all the mules of burthen and carts which are here; and which, together with those your Excellency already possesses in your army, will be more than competent to transport those articles before the noon of to-morrow to the positions occupied by your troops. I do not speak of flesh, because your Excellency has told me that you had always an abundance of that article, as you have at present; if, however, your Excellency is pleased to have a remittance of it, it shall be done to-morrow in sufficient quantity for the consumption of eight days. My activity should not rest until continual remittances of the same article

shall have been multiplied, in order to prove that my promises were not
in vain, and that your Excellency ought to have confided in them, although the sphere of my operations would be much limited by the circumstances.   There are various towns of this province, in which the
demands of the commissaries of your army, incessant and direct convoys
of bread, flour and flesh, are carried on.   If, indeed, there was in the
intentions of your Excellency any disposition to vary your purpose of
retreat, I am certain that I should obtain for myself the satisfaction of
hearing your Excellency yourself confess, that I had surpassed your hopes.
But in case your resolution of marching to Portugal should be the off-
spring of other political or military motives, and not precisely of the
want of means of subsistence, permit me to remark to you the fatal consequences which the immediate execution of it might cause, without the
delay of some days, during which the Spanish army would be familiarized
with the idea of being abandoned by those troops who so much sustained
its martial spirit, and who had recently inspired it with so much confidence by the valour of their conduct in the fields of Talavera; since its
immediate dispersion may be considered as inevitable; which would be
followed by the loss of all its artillery, and of the boats which formed the
bridge of Almaraz.   These are not imaginary fears; they are founded on
a knowledge of the present moral condition of our troops; and your Excellency cannot view them with indifference, as you know the sad results
to which the common cause of the two allied nations would be exposed.

I entreat your Excellency to have the goodness to answer me by the
same courier, the bearer of this letter, and to accept the sentiments, &c.
&c. &c.

LORENZO CALVO.

[8th Enclosure.]

Sir Arthur Wellesley to M. de Calvo.

SIR,   Jaraicejo, 20th August, 1809.

I have had the honour of receiving your letter of the 19th from Truxillo, to which I write this reply, notwithstanding that I hope to have the
pleasure of seeing you at Truxillo in the course of this morning.

I must first beg leave to inform you, that I have no motive for withdrawing the British army from Spain, whether of a political or military
nature, excepting that which I have stated to you, viz. a desire to relieve
it from the privations of food which it has suffered since the 22nd of last
month; privations which have reduced its strength, have destroyed the
health of the soldiers, and have rendered the army comparatively inefficient.   You gave the assurances yesterday, which you have repeated in
your letter, that these privations shall not continue; that in three days
there will be plenty of provisions, and that in the meantime we shall
have all that the magazine at Truxillo contains.   In answer I have to observe to you, that I have received the same assurances from every Spanish
Commissioner who has been employed with the British army; each in his
turn has disappointed me; and although your rank is higher, and your

powers are greater than those of the other Spanish officers who have been with me, I acknowledge, that in a case so critical as that of a starving army, I feel no confidence in your assurances, and I give no credit to the accounts of existence of resources said to be on the road, in which place not known, or of any others in the magazine of Truxillo.

In respect to the magazine at Truxillo, according to the accounts of its contents yesterday evening, which I received last night, it does not contain enough to feed the British army only one day, and the provisions for the Spanish army must likewise be drawn from it. You tell me that the British troops shall have every thing, and the Spaniards nothing; to which I reply that its execution is utterly and entirely impracticable, and is certainly very inconsistent with what has taken place hitherto. Till lately I know the Spanish troops received their rations regularly, while the British troops were starving. I am not so well aware of the manner in which the Spanish troops have been supplied lately; but I know from the best authority, that of the Commander-in-Chief of the Spanish army, that the Spanish cavalry were receiving at least half a ration of barley while the British cavalry had none; and I imagine that they have been well supplied with other provisions, as I have in my possession a letter from yourself, stating that you had ordered to the Mesa d'Ibor, for the use of the Spanish army, all the provisions required for the British army by Mr. Downie, the British Commissary, and provided by the town of Guadalupe and its neighbourhood.

I cannot, therefore, give credit to the execution of any plan which shall go to give provisions to the British army to the exclusion of the Spanish troops; and I conceive the proposal to have been made to me only as an extreme and desperate measure to induce me to remain in Spain.

But supposing the plan to be capable of execution, I could not give my sanction to it.

The Spanish army must be fed as well as the British army; neither otherwise will be of much use in the positions which they have hitherto occupied. If the Spanish army is to be fed, and it cannot be otherwise, the magazine at Truxillo will be found not to be equal to one-third of the demand of the British army for one day, according to the official return I received last night of its contents yesterday. But, besides provision, the army requires other assistance, for which I have called in vain, and for the want of which I am now obliged to leave behind me my ammunition, and to deliver it to the Spanish Commander-in-Chief.

I am fully aware of the consequences which may follow my departure from Spain; not that I apprehend those to which you have referred, for in point of fact there is now no enemy in our front. But I am not responsible for the consequences, whatever they may be. Those are responsible for them, who, having been made acquainted with the wants of the British army more than a month ago, have taken no effectual means to relieve them; who have allowed a brave army, which was rendering gratuitous services to Spain, which was able and willing to pay for every thing it received, to starve in the centre of their country, and to be reduċed by want almost to a state of inefficiency; who refused or omitted to find carriages to remove the officers and soldiers who had been wounded in their service, and obliged me to give up the equipment of the army for the performance of this necessary duty of humanity.

I have one more observation to make, in reply to your letter, in respect to the requisitions made by the British Commissaries for provisions in the villages. There is but one Commissary now so employed, and he is at Caceres. Indeed all the villages in this neighbourhood are occupied by the Spanish troops, and it would be useless to send a British Commissary to endeavour to procure any thing from them. But I shall be obliged to you to state where this Commissary is, supposing the report made to you to be founded in fact, that while the British army is starving, it may be allowed to a Commissary to endeavour to obtain some relief for the troops for whom he is bound to provide, paying for what he receives.

I have the honour to be, &c.

ARTHUR WELLESLEY.

[9th Enclosure.]

A. Calderone Aguadelo to the British Commissary.

Guadalupe, August 15th, 1809.

His Excellency Don Lorenzo Calvo, Member and Representative of the Supreme Central Junta, has addressed to me a recent order, dated Medellin, the 14th of the present month, to send away the requisitions of all the provisions which you have had made in this town and in the neighbouring places, to the Mesa d'Ibor and the head-quarters, for the use of the Spanish troops; on which account I do not forward to the city of Truxillo the supplies from this town; and I have made known the same order to the other towns according to my instructions. I communicate this to your Excellency for his information.

ANASTASIO CALDERONE AGUADELO.

XXI.

The Marquess Wellesley to Sir Arthur Wellesley.

SIR,   Seville, August 22, 1809.

1. I have the honour to acknowledge the receipt of your despatch of the 19th inst. which I communicated to M. de Garay immediately after it had reached me; and yesterday evening I presented the note of which a copy is enclosed in this despatch.*

2. Although M. de Garay and this government must have been prepared to expect the early notification of your return to Portugal, from every communication which I had made since my arrival at Seville, and especially from your recent

---

* See p. 46.

despatches (which I had regularly put into M. de Garay's hands) the most violent emotions of alarm and consternation seemed to be excited by the near approach of an event so long foreseen.

3. M. de Garay declared to me, with expressions of the deepest sorrow and terror, that if your army should quit Spain at this critical moment, inevitable and immediate ruin must ensue to this government; to whatever provinces remained under its authority; to the cause of Spain itself; and to every interest connected with the alliance so happily established between Great Britain and the Spanish nation.

4. These expressions were mixed with the most cordial sentiments of personal respect and gratitude for your great and splendid services in the cause of Spain, and with the highest admiration of the character and conduct of the British troops under your command.

5. M. de Garay proceeded to express the affliction of this government for the sufferings of your gallant army; he protested that great efforts had been made for your supply; that this Government was ready to adopt any plan for that object which you or the British Ambassador would suggest; that at this moment the most active exertions were actually in progress for the purpose of furnishing you with provisions and the means of transport; that all the resources of these provinces were called forth for that sole end; and that he trusted that the exigencies of this moment were not so irresistible, as not to admit of your remaining within the Spanish frontier until you had ascertained the result of the efforts which this government had made for your supply, since the period of my arrival at Seville.

6. The enclosed notes* contain the substance of the observations which I offered in reply to M. de Garay's earnest solicitations; I found however that no argument, which occurred to me, produced the effect of diminishing the urgency of his entreaties, and I have ascertained that his sensations are in no degree more powerful than those of the government, and of every description of the people of Spain within this city and its vicinity. I am also informed, that the

---

* See pages 43, 45.

rumour of the return of the British army to Portugal, had reached Cadiz some days ago, and had occasioned an equal degree of alarm in that quarter.

7. I am aware that these painful occurrences have not been unexpected in your view of the consequences of your retreat into Portugal, and that the absolute necessity of the case, is the sole cause of a movement so entirely contrary to your inclination.

8. I am also fully sensible not only of the indelicacy, but of the inutility of attempting to offer to you any opinion of mine in a situation where your own judgment must be your best guide, and when no useful suggestions could arise in my mind, which must not already have been anticipated by your own experience, comprehensive knowledge, and ardent zeal for the public welfare.

9. Viewing however so nearly, the painful consequences of your immediate retreat into Portugal, I have deemed it to be my duty to submit to your consideration the possibility of adopting an intermediate plan, which might combine some of the advantages of your return into Portugal, without occasioning alarm in Spain, and without endangering the foundations of the alliance between this country and Great Britain.

10. Under this impression I have delivered the note to M. de Garay, and I request your favourable attention to that note, and to the Enclosures which it contains.*

11. I am inclined to hope that this government will adopt the plan proposed for the improvement of the supply and means of transport of your army, and that in the meanwhile every possible effort will be made to diminish the pressure of your present distress, until the principles of the proposed plan can be brought into full operation. It is to be hoped that in the position proposed for your army, the supplies which you have provided in Portugal would be within your reach.

12. But it would be vain to urge these considerations beyond the extent in which they may be approved by your judgment. It will be sufficient for me to receive an early intimation of your opinion, and to be enabled to state it dis-

---

* See p. 42.

tinctly to this government; which looks to your decision on the present occasion, as the final determination of its fate, and of the existence of the Spanish nation.

13. That decision I am persuaded will be founded on the same principles of wisdom, justice, and public spirit, which have already obtained the respect, esteem, and confidence of the Spanish nation; and it will be my duty to endeavour to satisfy this government (whatever may be the exigency of the crisis) that no change has taken place in the sentiments or motives of action which have so cordially engaged their affection and admiration.

I have the honour to be, &c.

WELLESLEY.

No. XXII.

Sir Arthur Wellesley to the Marquess Wellesley.

MY LORD,   Miajados, August 22nd, 1809.

I have this day had the honour of receiving your Excellency's despatch of the 20th.

My former letters will have apprised your Excellency, that I was aware that Marshal Ney's corps was gone to Talavera; in respect to the intelligence from General Vanegas, it appears to me that the enemy have no intention to make any progress in that quarter beyond the foot of the mountains. If they entertained any intention of proceeding farther, they would have gone in greater strength.

However, whatever may be the enemy's design in that quarter, my former despatches must have convinced your Excellency, that I was unable to co-operate in any movement in this quarter, which should have for its object to draw the enemy from La Mancha, or indeed in any other movement of any description, excepting that which I am now making; having no provisions, no horses, no means of transport being overloaded with sick, the horses of the cavalry being scarcely able to march, or those of the artillery to draw their guns; and the officers and soldiers being worn down by want of food and privations of every description.

The Spanish Ministers cannot have adverted to what I have repeated to them through different channels frequently since the 17th of last month, viz. that if I was not supplied with what I required, not only I should not co-operate in any forward movement, but must withdraw from Spain; or they would not give credit to the existence of the wants of the British army; or they must believe me to be so exceedingly desirous of serving them, that whatever might be the consequences to the army, I should make it march and fight as long as two men could remain together.

Nobody feels more sorely disappointed and hurt than I do, that so little attention has been paid to the demands which I have frequently made; and whatever may be the consequences of the steps which I have been compelled to take, I am in no manner responsible for them.

I have now proceeded three marches in the rear from Jaraicejo since the 20th, and have not met a supply of any description on its way to the army; so that if I had remained at Jaraicejo so long, it would have been the 26th before the army would have received any of the supplies from Seville; and yet Monsieur de Calvo undertook that the army should be fully supplied on every day after the 19th, and was much surprised that I had no confidence in his promises of the arrival of supplies, respecting the progress of which upon the road, or even their having quitted Seville, he had no information.

I have the honour to be, &c.

ARTHUR WELLESLEY.

No. XXIII.

The Marquess Wellesley to Don Martin de Garay.

SIR,   Seville, August 23, 1809.

Your Excellency will not be surprised to learn my extreme solicitude, in consequence of the silence which this government has observed since the receipt of my note marked 21st of August, containing a proposition for the improvement of the system of supplying the army in the field.

I most earnestly request that I may be favoured as soon as possible with the reply of the Supreme Central Junta to that proposition, on the result of which, as your Excellency has repeatedly stated, the security of Spain essentially depends.

Availing myself of this opportunity to renew to your Excellency the assurances of my high consideration and esteem,

I have the honour to be, &c.

WELLESLEY.

No. XXIV.

Sir Arthur Wellesley to the Marquess Wellesley:

MY LORD,   Merida, August 24, 1809.

I had the honour of receiving last night, at Medellin, your Excellency's despatch, dated the 22d instant.

From all that I have heard of the state of the Government at Seville, I am not surprised that they should have been astonished and alarmed when they heard that I had at last determined to adopt the measure which I had so frequently informed them I should adopt.

Although I was desirous to avoid as long as possible withdrawing into Portugal, and certainly remained in the position upon the Tagus as long as it was practicable, and longer probably than was consistent with the anxiety which I have always felt for the welfare and comfort of the troops placed under my command, I am of opinion that having been compelled to withdraw, it becomes a question for serious consideration whether any circumstances should now induce me to remain in Spain, and to hold out hopes of further co-operation with the Spanish troops, to be decided on grounds very different from those which were to lead to a decision whether, being joined in co-operation with the Spanish army, I ought or ought not to separate from them. I beg to lay my ideas upon this point before your Excellency, and to request the aid of your superior judgment, to enable me to decide upon it in the manner which will be most beneficial to the national interests.

When the two armies were joined, this implied engagement existed between them, that as long as the operations were conducted by mutual consent they were to continue in co-operation.

I should not have considered myself justified in separating from the Spanish army unless Portugal should evidently have required the protection of the British army, or unless the

Spanish army should have been under the necessity of adopting a line of operation to follow which would separate me
from Portugal, or unless driven as I was to separate by
necessity, or unless the Spanish army had again behaved so
ill as a military body as it did in its shameful flight from the
bridge of Arzobispo.

I conceived this last case would have made it so notorious
that it was necessary for me to separate; that I had determined that it should induce a separation equally with the
occurrence of any of the other three; and I should have stated
it broadly and fairly as my reason for withdrawing the British
army from all communication with a body endowed with qualities as soldiers in a degree so far inferior to themselves.

Your Excellency will observe that my conduct in continuing with the Spanish army would have been guided by a fair
view of our reciprocal situation, and by a consideration of
what they might consider an engagement to act with them,
as long as it was consistent with the orders I had received,
to consider my army applicable to the defence of Portugal;
with which orders the Spanish Government are fully acquainted.

At the present moment however I have been compelled to
separate from the Spanish army, and the question now is,
whether I shall place myself in co-operation with them again.

The first point which I should wish your Excellency to
consider is the difference of reasoning by which the decision
of this question must be guided, from that which I have above
stated would have guided, and did in fact guide me in the
decision on the other; in that case I considered the armies to
be under an implied engagement to each other, not to separate except on certain defined or easily definable grounds;
but in this case there is positively no engagement of any description; there is none in the treaty between his Majesty and
the Spanish Government; there is none implied or expressed
by me; indeed the argument would lead the other way, for
his Majesty having offered the Spanish Government the services of his army upon certain conditions, the conditions were
refused, and it must have been understood that his Majesty
would not give the aid of his army; and accordingly his
Majesty has never ordered, but has only permitted me to
carry on such operations in Spain as I might think proper

upon my own responsibility, and as were consistent with the safety of Portugal.

The question then comes before me to be decided as a new one, whether I shall join in co-operation with the Spanish army again.

I must here take into consideration, as I did upon the first occasion, the objects of such co-operation, the means which exist of attaining those objects, and the risks which I shall incur of loss to my army, and of losing sight of Portugal, for the defence of which country the British army has been sent to the Peninsula.

The object held out in your Excellency's despatch, and which I consider as only the first and immediate object (for I am convinced your Excellency must look to offensive operations as soon as the means will be prepared for them) is the defence of the Guadiana.

Upon this point I must inform your Excellency, that in my opinion the Guadiana is not to be defended by a weaker army against a stronger. It is fordable in very many places, and it affords no position that I know of; and the result of withdrawing the Spanish army from its present position to that which has been proposed to your Excellency for them, would be to expose them to be defeated before I could assist them.

The Spanish army is at this moment in the best position in this part of the country, which they ought to hold against any force which can be brought against them, if they can hold any thing; as long as they continue in it they cover effectually the passages of the Guadiana, which they would not cover by the adoption of any other position; and their retreat from it in case of accidents must always be secure, there is no chance of their being attacked by superior numbers; I have reason to believe that Soult, as well as Ney, has passed through the mountains into Castille, and there remains only Mortier's corps and two divisions of Victor's in Estremadura, the total of which force cannot amount to 25,000 men.

The subsistence of the Spanish army in their present position, particularly now that we have withdrawn, cannot be very difficult.

Upon the whole then I recommend that they should remain in their present position as long as possible, sending away to Badajoz the bridge of boats which is still opposite to Almaraz.

According to this reasoning, it does not appear to be necessary, and it is not very desirable, that the British army should be involved in the defence of the Guadiana.   But it may be asked, is there no chance of resuming the offensive? In answer, I have to observe, that at present I see none, and hereafter certainly none.

Your Excellency is informed of the history of the causes which led to the late change in our operations; from the offensive, after a victory, to the defensive.   The same causes would certainly exist if we were to recommence our operations.   The French have as many troops as we have; indeed I am not certain that they are not now superior to us in numbers, as they are certainly, at least to the Spanish army, in discipline and every military quality.   Unless we could depend upon the troops employed to keep the passes of the mountains, we could not prevent the French corps in Castille from coming upon our rear, while those in Estremadura and La Mancha would be in our front ; but I certainly can never place any reliance upon the Spanish troops to defend a pass, and I could not venture to detach from the British army, British troops in sufficient numbers to defend the passes of Baños and Perales.   Even if we could, however, by the defence of those passes, prevent the enemy from attacking us in the rear, we could not prevent him from penetrating by the passes of Guadiana or Avila, and adding to the numbers in our front.

To this add, that there are no troops in the north of Spain which could be employed to make a diversion.   Blake has lost his army, the Marquis de la Romana's is still in Gallicia, and he cannot venture to quit the mountains, having neither cavalry nor artillery.

The Duque del Parque has very few troops, and, as he has shewn lately, he does not like to risk them at a distance from Ciudad Rodrigo.   But I come now to another topic, which is one of serious consideration, and has considerable weight in my judgment upon this whole subject, and that is, the frequent, I ought to say constant, and shameful misbehaviour of the Spanish troops before the enemy.   We, in England, never hear of their defeats and flights; but I have heard of

Spanish officers telling of nineteen or twenty actions of the description of that at the bridge of Arzobispo, an account of which I believe has never been published.

In the battle at Talavera, in which the Spanish army, with very trifling exceptions, was not engaged, whole corps threw away their arms, and ran off in my presence, when they were neither attacked nor threatened with an attack, but frightened I believe by their own fire. I refer your Excellency for evidence upon this subject, to General Cuesta's orders, in which, after extolling the gallantry of his army in general he declares his intention to decimate the runaways; an intention which he afterwards carried into execution. When these dastardly soldiers run away, they plunder every thing they meet; and in their flight from Talavera, they plundered the baggage of the British army, which was at the moment, bravely engaged in their cause.

I have found, upon inquiry and from experience, the instances of the misbehaviour of the Spanish troops to be so numerous, and those of their good behaviour so few, that I must conclude that they are troops by no means to be depended upon; and then the question arises again, whether, being at liberty to join in co-operation with those troops or not, I ought again to risk the King's army. There is no doubt whatever that every thing that is to be done, must be done by us; and certainly the British army cannot be deemed sufficiently strong to be the only acting efficient military body to be opposed to a French army, not consisting of less than 70,000 men.

Upon every ground, therefore, of objects, means and risks, it is my opinion that I ought to avoid entering into any further co-operation with the Spanish armies, and that at all events your Excellency should avoid holding out to the Government any hope that I would consent to remain within the Spanish frontier with any intention of co-operating with the Spanish troops in future.

At the same time I see the difficulty in which the Government may be placed. Their army may be seized with one of those panic terrors to which they are so liable, and may run off and leave every thing exposed to instant loss. To which I answer, that I am in no hurry to withdraw from Spain. I want to give my troops food and refreshment; and I shall not withdraw into Portugal, at all events, till I shall have received your Excellency's sentiments upon what I have submitted to your judgment.

If I should withdraw into Portugal, I shall go no further than the frontier (but for this I should not wish to engage) and I shall be so near that the enemy will not like to venture across the Guadiana, unless he comes in very large force indeed, leaving me upon his flank and his rear; I shall therefore, in effect, be as useful to the Spanish Government within the Portuguese frontier as I should be in the position which has been proposed to your Excellency, and indeed more useful, as I expect that the nearer I shall move to Portugal, the more efficient I shall become; at the same time, that by going within the Portuguese frontier, I clear myself entirely from the Spanish army, and should have an opportunity hereafter of deciding whether I will co-operate with them at all, in what manner, and to what extent, and under what conditions, according to the circumstances of the moment.

I have the honour to be, &c.

ARTHUR WELLESLEY.

P. S. Since writing the above Lieut.-Colonel O'Lawler has received a letter from General Eguia, stating that he has received orders from the Government to retire upon Villa Nueva de la Serena, in consequence of the movements made by the troops under my command.

If he should retire so far, it will be necessary that he should fall back still further to Monasterio, having no position on the Guadiana.

I have also to observe to your Excellency, that even if I should remain in Spain, it will be impossible for me to take up the position which it has been proposed to your Excellency that I should take up, as in case of the further retreat of the Spanish army, I should find it difficult to get into Portugal: indeed, at all events, the best way for me to cover the Guadiana and Seville, is by a position on the enemy's flank.

No. XXV.

The Marquess Wellesley to the Right Honourable George Canning.

SIR,   Seville, August 24th, 1809.

1. The last despatch which I had the honour to address to you was dated on the 15th inst. ; since that period of time my attention has been principally engaged by the continual distresses of the army under the command of Sir Arthur Wellesley.

2. The enclosed letters from Sir Arthur Wellesley (under dates from the 13th to the 18th inclusive),* contain the details of that calamity and of its unfortunate consequences, which have ultimately reduced him to the necessity of withdrawing towards the frontiers of Portugal, according to the intimation which he had repeatedly made to the Spanish General, to Mr. Frere, and to me, and which had been regularly communicated to this Government.

3. From Sir Arthur Wellesley's letters you will perceive, that notwithstanding the promises and professions of this Government and of its officers, the sufferings of the British army had not been alleviated from the 12th to the 18th inst., that no satisfactory proposition for the relief of the wants of our troops had been offered to Sir A. Wellesley by the Spanish civil or military officers in the vicinity of his army, and that he entertained no expectation of seasonable relief from any effort which the Supreme Central Junta had engaged to make in consequence of my applications to that authority.

4. Sir Arthur Wellesley's letter of the 18th of August, announcing his positive determination to withdraw into Portugal, and requesting that I would give notice of that determination to this Government, reached me on the 20th in the evening, when I communicated the original to M. de Garay.

5. Although the notification which I made to M. de Garay on the 20th inst. must have been expected, it was received by him with the strongest indications of alarm, and I had every reason to believe that the rumour of the return of the British army into Portugal had excited a general sensation of a similar description. Attempts had also been made with

---

* See previous pages.

some success, to prejudice the public opinion with respect to the real causes of the retreat of our army, which were stated to be not any deficiencies in our means of supply or of movement, but certain political considerations, inconsistent with the security and honour of Spain, and with the good faith of Great Britain. Rumours were circulated of demands made in his Majesty's name for the cession of Cadiz, of the Havannah and the Island of Cuba, and for changes in the form of this Government as preliminary conditions to the further operations of the British troops in Spain, and it was suggested that the rejection of these conditions by this Government had occasioned the retreat of Sir Arthur Wellesley's army.

6. It is unnecessary to inform you that I have asked nothing from Spain, excepting subsistence for the brave army employed in her defence.

7. M. de Garay and this Government possess abundant proofs of the severe and urgent distress of the British army, and they know (according to M. de Garay's repeated admission in his conferences with me), that Sir Arthur Wellesley with the gallant army under his command, was animated by the most ardent zeal for the completion of his glorious successes, and that he never would have fallen back on the resources of Portugal while any prospect remained of obtaining subsistence in Spain.

8. But a strict observation of the proceedings of the Junta and of its officers has convinced me that I had formed too sanguine an expectation of their exertions, and too favourable an opinion of their sincerity.

9. This Government is conscious of the real causes of the distress of our troops; public opinion has loudly, and I fear too justly, imputed this calamity to the weakness or negligence of the executive power in Spain; no insinuations therefore have been discountenanced by the Government which might tend to avert from themselves the indignation generally excited by the unfavourable issue of a campaign commenced with such auspicious hopes.

10. On the 20th and 21st instant the opinions of M. de Garay, of this Government, and of the public within these provinces, certainly tended to establish a general apprehension of immediate danger to this quarter of Spain from the

French forces, in the event of the retreat of the British army to Portugal. The judgment of Sir Arthur Wellesley however did not confirm this apprehension. He thought it improbable that the enemy would venture with his present force to advance into Andalusia, and as far as the designs of the enemy could be conjectured from recent movements, it did not appear to be his immediate object to pursue offensive operations in the southern provinces.

11. But although these opinions of the intentions and power of the enemy may prove just and rational, they have not calmed the popular apprehension; and the prevalent sentiment (not discouraged by the Government) appears to be, that the British army without necessity is about to relinquish the protection of Spain in a crisis of imminent danger.

12. In this distracted state of the public mind, and in the confusion and consternation of the Government, it appeared to me to be my duty to endeavour to suggest some plan which might check the rising spirit of discontent and alarm, and might confirm the principles of the British alliance without exposing our army to further peril.

13. Accordingly on the 21st inst. I addressed to M. de Garay the notes of which I have the honour to enclose copies,* and on the 22d I forwarded to Sir Arthur Wellesley a despatch, of which also a copy† is enclosed.

14. In the notes addressed to M. de Garay I endeavoured to explain the nature and causes of the distress of our troops; to suggest to this Government a plan for better securing the supply and movement of our army in Spain; and (under the condition that this plan should be immediately carried into execution with celerity and vigour; and in the belief that sufficient exertion had already been made for the intermediate relief of the British army); I proposed to submit to Sir Arthur Wellesley the expediency of occupying a position in Spain from which he might communicate with Portugal, and at the same time might try the result of the promised efforts of this Government for the subsistence of his troops.

15. The despatch to Sir Arthur Wellesley submits these several plans to his consideration without attempting to press them upon his judgment beyond the limits of his own opinion.

---

* See pp. 42-3, &c. .qq   † See p. 60.

16. M. de Garay and this Government eagerly adopted that part of the plan which suggested the detention of the British army in Spain, and repeated the most positive assurances of the exertions already made, and of those intended for the seasonable supply of the army. But in the meanwhile my confidence in these assurances was diminished by the communications which I received from Sir Arthur Wellesley, whose letters (of which copies are enclosed) of the 21st and 22nd inst.* announced to me, not only the encreasing distress of his troops, but the proceedings of M. de Calvo (a member of the Junta especially commissioned to superintend the supplies of our army), tending to aggravate the existing distress, and even to cast suspicion on the sincerity of the Spanish Government.

17. I take the liberty of recommending the whole of Sir Arthur Wellesley's correspondence to your particular attention; it contains a full and detailed statement of the extent and causes of his distress, and exhibits a view of the state of this country, and of the temper and conduct of the Spanish civil and military authorities, which cannot fail to be useful in forming any plan of future operations in Spain.

18. During the period of my residence at Seville, I have received several notes from M. de Garay containing, by order of the Supreme Central Junta, the most strenuous exhortations for the immediate advance of the British troops against the enemy; and in our conferences he has advised the expulsion of the French beyond the Pyrenees: I have enclosed translations of these notes according to the order of their date. While the British troops remained destitute of the means of transport and of the most important articles of supply, it was at least superfluous to propose active operations; and the letters of Sir Arthur Wellesley afford sufficient evidence of the degree of assistance which our troops might have expected from the Spanish generals and armies in any forward movement. I have not attempted to expostulate with M. de Garay on these unpleasant topics, although I have represented to him in the most unreserved manner the inability of our army to execute the projects recommended by the Junta. M. de Garay however is compelled by the orders of the Junta to repeat to me in the course of every

* See pp. 49-63.

day the same exhortations expressed nearly in the same words.

I have the honour, &c.

WELLESLEY.

No. XXVI.

Don Martin de Garay to the Marquess Wellesley.

MY LORD,   Seville, August 25, 1809.

I have the honour to transmit to your Excellency the arrangements made by the Minister of War, with reference to the official notes which your Excellency was pleased to address to me on the 21st of this month;* these arrangements have been made known to me by the Secretary of that office, in the following terms:

" In consequence of the royal order, which your Excellency was pleased to communicate to me with the date of yesterday, to the intent that the Section of War and the Military Junta should take into their consideration the notes which had been transmitted by the Marquess Wellesley, relating to the establishment of the magazines for the subsistence of the armies; to the positions which it would be useful to take, and to the wish that the Spanish General should receive from Sir Arthur Wellesley the suitable instructions, as well for defensive as for offensive operations; they have been examined with all the consideration which the alliance and constant harmony between the two nations, together with the actual circumstances, can require.

" The Section and the Military Junta are firmly persuaded, that it is the intention of our worthy allies to resume the offensive, from the moment that the armies shall possess a secure subsistence, since the advantage of a hostile movement is well known, and does not require demonstration.

" With this supposition the paper marked (A) has been examined : it demonstrates the necessity of a regulation of provision; and as the ideas of the Ambassador are much in conformity with those prescribed in the enclosed regulation which had been already formed for the subsistence of armies

---

* See p. 43.

in operation (the sole variation consisting in the mode of serving the magazines) the Junta and the Section are of opinion that a copy of the said regulation should be transmitted to the Marquess Wellesley, in order that his Excellency having seen it, may state the objections that occur to him; and for this purpose I enclose the said copy to your Excellency.

" The Section and the Military Junta are equally of opinion, that the positions marked out in the paper (B) viz. to place the armies on the left bank of the Guadiana, are well adapted for the purpose of maintaining the defensive, the troops occupying the ground from Villaneuva de la Serena to Badajoz; they however conceive that such positions should be temporary, and limited to the moment when the armies shall have been supplied; since when this point has been accomplished, it is absolutely necessary to move on the Tagus, for the purpose of carrying on active operations against the enemy. As it is expedient that, in that case the armies should act in combination, and for the same reasons that each army should possess an imposing force, the Section and Military Junta are of opinion, that the Spanish army of Estremadura should be divided in the following manner. This arrangement being founded on the claim which Sir Arthur Wellesley has merited to the entire confidence of our Government, by his eminent qualities of wisdom, activity, and valour, and by his superior attachment to the just cause; all these qualities he has displayed in the highest degree in the battle of Talavera.

1. " The command of the combined army shall be conferred on Sir Arthur Wellesley; it shall be composed of the whole British force, and of 12,000 infantry, 2,000 cavalry, and twelve pieces of cannon from the Spanish army; this corps shall be commanded by a Lieut.-General, three *Mariscales de Campo*, and a corresponding staff. The Spanish General shall consult with Sir Arthur Wellesley on the political department, and interior regulations of his regiments, and shall be under his orders in military operations.

2. " Experience has shewn the necessity of strengthening the positions of the Sierras, in order to anticipate any unfortunate occurrence. Six thousand men of the remaining army in Estremadura shall come to Monasterio and Santa Ollala; the whole of the said army shall be incorporated with that of

General Vanegas ; when he moves forward, the many positions of the Sierra Morena would thus be always protected,
and the army would have a force sufficient for offensive
operations, and for acting in combination with the troops of
Sir Arthur Wellesley.

3. " The troops from Gallicia, those which can be collected
from the Asturias, together with those of Marshal Beresford,
shall also co-operate in combination; assuming the offensive
or defensive according to circumstances, against the troops of
the enemy, which have retired from Castille."

The Supreme and Central governing Junta of the kingdom,
being informed of these opinions of the Section of War, and the
Military Junta, has given its approbation to them; and by a
royal order I make this known to your Excellency, with an enclosure of the copy of the regulations of magazines. Your Excellency will be pleased to examine them, and to give me notice
of any objection which you may find to carrying them into
effect. His Majesty, in the high confidence which he reposes in
your Excellency, entertains no doubt that you will omit nothing
to contribute to that conformity with this plan, which so much
confirms the unalterable harmony between his Majesty and
his allies.

I have the honour to be, &c.

MARTIN DE GARAY.

[Enclosure.]

Translation of a Plan for insuring supplies of Provisions, &c. to the Armies.

Rules which ought to be observed by the Minister of Finance, and the
Commissary or Inspector of Provisions.

1. The stores of provisions should be placed under the care of a Minister of activity, zeal and knowledge in the business, and this Minister of
Finance or Inspector ought to have every information respecting the state
of the magazines under his care, and to see that they are properly provided with every thing necessary for the good and punctual assistance of
the troops; and that the Storekeepers and all those employed execute
faithfully his orders, entering into immediate communication with the
Intendant of the army, to whom he should give accurate intelligence of
any thing new or doubtful which may occur, and to which his attention
may be necessary.

2. He should be well acquainted with the quantity of provisions in such
magazine, the points which are furnished by it, the troops stationed at
those points, and what quantity of provisions may be necessary for their
perfect supply; for which purpose he should take care, that the Store-

keeper of each respective magazine under his superintendence sends him a daily account, expressing what effects and funds may have been left of the day before; what has been received, distributed, and consumed on that day, and what may remain for the following (in the manner marked in No. 5,) all which should be communicated likewise to the Intendant of the army; by which means the state of each magazine will be daily known, in order to the making such arrangements as may be expedient.

3. Every week (more or less as may be convenient) a report should be drawn up from the above statement, of the provisions distributed to the troops at each point, (as marked in No. 2,) and from which report, which also should be sent to the intendant of the army, an estimate will be formed of the provisions necessary for each of the above-mentioned magazines, in order to their regular and exact supply.

4. He should examine, as often as he may judge proper, whether there really exist the effects and money in each magazine which there ought to be, and the state of them.

5. He should take care that the distributing Storekeepers place frequently in the entry-book, the produce of the sales, so that there never shall remain any considerable sum in their hands.

6. Whenever the corps receive provisions without money, he will take care that it is made good at the end of every month, encouraging the corps to the same.

7. As being immediately at the head of this branch, he should have a list of every individual employed, of which there should be one in each magazine, expressive of their situation and pay.

8. He should inspect the accounts of the pay and expences of the magazines, whether monthly or weekly.

9. He will take care that in no case there shall be a want of effects in the magazines, and that they are of a good quality, and such as the troops cannot complain of.

10. Care should also be taken to select convenient buildings for the magazines, dry, well aired, and with good floors, that the articles may not spoil or rot.

11. It will be always proper *in campaign* to value the houses taken for magazines, because often upon an attack of the enemy, and a sudden retreat becoming necessary, it is expedient to burn the buildings and effects, which gives rise to law-suits to make them good. The price of the rent should also be fixed, and for the same reason it is right to make a declaration of the state they are in, because when the owners require them to be placed in the same, without such a declaration, neither the state of the house is known nor what is necessary to be done.

Rules to be observed by the Keepers of the Magazines of Provisions.

1. Each Storekeeper should keep two master books, properly numbered and dated. In the first, he will set down (distinguishing provisions from other articles) whatever he may receive in his magazine, every line being in a separate sheet.

2. He will carefully mark who sends the article, and who delivers it, and if it agrees with the account sent in ; and if it should prove to contain more than is expressed therein, he will take charge of the overplus, marking it very accurately in the receipt at the bottom, and vice versâ when there shall be less, giving instant notice of it to his immediate chief, in order to his taking the necessary steps in consequence.

3. He will note in this book if the effects received came in carts or on horses, whether bargained for, or pressed, in órder that the royal finance may not suffer, and if he sends any thing back by the same conveyance he will mark it in the bill.

4. The following is the way to make these entries :

" Of such an article sent from such a place— on such a day—by such a person, native of . . . . . . in so many sacks, cloths, barrels, hampers, &c. pressed or bargained for." When these things are sent back it is to be marked.

5. This book must have as many lines as there are articles received, and at the least must have the following : bacon, oil, salt-fish, rice, pease, beans, French-beans, salt, wine, brandy, and vinegar : these being articles of first necessity in a province where the army has nothing else to live upon.

§ 2. 1. In the second book he will set down the produce of the daily sales, making the same divisions under different heads ; placing at the beginning of the margin the quantity of the article, and carrying over the amount of what it may have fetched.

2. Besides the heads already mentioned for the first, should be added to the date the following :

Articles delivered by superior orders.—Here should be marked such deliveries as may be made by order of the Intendant or other Minister of Finance, including in the delivery the receipt of the person to whom it is made ; which should be given in to the Minister at the end of every month, in order that he may transmit it to the proper person to solicit the bill of payment, which he will keep, and before giving the receipt he will make the entry in his book.

Extraordinary Disbursements and Expences.—Here should be put down with their dates whatever expences may occur, and which are disbursed, by order of the above Minister, for the repair of the magazine, hire of the same ; accidental jobs, embargoes of wine and brandy to refresh the troops, which often take place in advancing, attacking, retreating, on account of bad nights, stormy weather, or from any other motion, when the General shall please to order it, and lastly, the monthly pay which may be earned by persons employed. In all these documents the *vú bon* of the above Minister must be obtained before he collects them and puts them by.

Utensils which are sent.—Under this head should be marked the sacks, the cloths, bundles, bags, barrels, hampers, or any other article not returned, but detained to keep the articles in ; as well as those which not being wanted, were sent empty, with the horses or carts agreed for which return without a load or capital. Whenever this is done, a bill should be drawn out, saying that they are sent to the person pointed out by their head; which bill with this person's receipt should be returned to him; and if compliance is refused in this particular, notice should be given of it to the above Head or Chief, in order that the Intendant, being made acquainted with it, may enforce its execution. Before he sends it, a bargain should be made expressive of the name and habitation of the person charged to convey it, and when returned to him he should put it with the other monthly documents, as it ought to accompany the bill.

Sending Provisions to other Magazines.—Under this should be set down such articles as are sent by an order of the Intendant, or of the Commander of the troops, to any other magazine or point where the case required it, distinguishing the different sorts, making out a bill with the name of the person who is to convey them, and expressing what kind they are of, marking it arithmetically in the margin, with the number of sacks, barrels, &c. and collecting together these bills, together with the receipts, he should file and keep them, as they are to serve for his justification when the accounts are settled.

3. Besides these two master books, a monthly ledger should be kept, an annual account book, and an account current, all with the rubrick of their immediate chief.

4. The first should consist of five or six sheets of common paper, where will be marked down the various deliveries which may be made him, and those which he may make daily himself, and should be entitled, *" Ledger of such a month and date;"* the daily amount of these will be transferred to the respective master books, and should be kept till the accounts are passed, in case any kind of doubt should arise. If by mistake any false entry should be made in this ledger, it may be rectified by a marginal note; but no scratching out should in any case be admitted.

5. The second should be a little annual account book confined to the money chest, and might be labelled *" The produce of this magazine."* In it should be entered the daily produce of the sale, and monthly the quantity he may have delivered on a superior order; the extraordinary expenses which may occur, and the pay of the persons employed; which quantity he should balance by an account of receipt and expenditure, so that the state of the funds may always be known.

6. The third should be a book of about twenty-five leaves, where should be entered daily, and with the same distinction, the provisions which may be distributed to officers and dependants of the army at the fixed price. It should be kept with the same accuracy as the master books, as it should be sent in with them for the better justification of the accounts; and its title should be *Book of Provisions, furnished to the officers and dependants, beginning with*

7. If provisions are distributed without money to the army, a large book should be kept, where should be distinctly marked the kind of article, the regiments, squadrons, battalions, parties, &c. what are drawn daily, noting the quantity in the same way as in the master book, and taking particular care that no receipt is lost.

These will not be admitted if not presented according to the order of the superior who directed them to be given without funds; and when any corps shall account for the amount of provisions furnished without money, the contract or settlement should be made with this book open, and the daily receipts by which they were made; thus balancing the amount so that no one can suffer, he will deliver all the receipts, and collect one general one which shall express *en gros* the quantity of provisions and money the whole amounts to, and that they are satisfied; and shall transfer it to the master book in the same way as if it had only been verified in that act; putting them with the rest which he shall distribute the same day with money, remarking in the above book at the end of each line that the corps is satisfied; or he will include the produce in the daily statement, and in the little book, but not the provisions, because they should be given with the daily supply without money.

8. If there should be any magazine dependent on him, he will oblige him to give in the account weekly, which should be accompanied by the receipts which he may have distributed to the troops; and the money which the sale may have produced is to be marked in his book, as if it was distributed by him, but remarking that the articles were sold by the sub-storekeeper, which will be marked down in the book of daily produce. The following is the way to keep the account with the subaltern. They inform him of what has been sent in the eight former days, accompanied by the book and bills as vouchers; such parts are admitted as appear by the receipts to have been distributed on those same days, the amount is drawn, and the remainder is accounted for with him. If the sub-magazine is established in any encampment, or any point which may endanger it being attacked by the enemy, he will be compelled to transmit an account of the produce every two days, and a detail of the consumption of provisions by the troops, as he ought to have a perfect knowledge of the effective force; and the Minister of Finance, or in default of him, the Major-General of the Encampment will pass it for him.

9. In the sub-magazine, if there is no superintendant, he will take particular care that the weights and measures are kept clean, as well to avoid all disgust to the troops as to insure their justice and accuracy.

10. No provisions shall be distributed without the receipts being given in the form marked No. 3, as if there are any alterations or scratchings out the accounts will not pass.

11. The account of any extra-gratuitous refreshment of brandy, bread, wine, or cheese, should be viséd by the Commissary of War who ordered it, or by the orders of the General.

12. Great attention should be paid to whether any corps draws for more provisions than it uses or has a right to, which should be compared with the individual details; and if it should be discovered that it exceeds what it ought, he should inform his Chief of it, in order to apply the necessary remedy; and he should bear well in mind that the peasantry cannot draw any thing, the King only allowing this favour to his army and its dependants.

13. The object being that the troops shall not want for the principal succours, and that they shall enjoy them with all possible benefit, he shall take care that in the distribution of provisions the greatest accuracy is ob-

served in the weights; and as it is possible that in some of these there may be defects and decay, it shall be made good to the storekeepers in their respective accounts 2 p. $\%_0$ of common bacon, which they may distribute, and upon salted bacon 3 per cent., 1 per cent. for rice, and 3 per cent. for salt fish.

In the rest of the articles there should be none, if all act with care and good faith.

14. In all the magazines inventories shall be kept of the scales, weights, measures, chairs, tables, ink-stands, bags, baskets, and other articles for their use, of which copies shall be sent to the above-mentioned Chief, signed by the respective storekeeper.

15. Lastly, neither the storekeeper, nor any other person employed, can sell on his account any article for the troops, and still less buy from them at a lower price, in order to sell it at an advanced one, nor under any other pretence whatever.

16. In any case not provided for in this instruction, they shall consult with their immediate Chief, the Minister of Finance, and shall abide by their decisions.

3. *Daily operations of the Storekeeper.*

He is to examine carefully the different articles, and if there should be any defect or deficiency, report to his Chief, in order that he may take the necessary measures in consequence; the same he will do with the produce of the sale.

4. *Duties of the Superintendant.*

1. To watch over the proceedings of the storekeeper.
2. To keep his books in the greatest order and regularity.
3. To be very particular with respect to the weights, &c.
4. To keep a constant and watchful eye over all royal effects.
5. To keep a key, conjointly with the storekeeper, of the money chest, marking down in the book whenever he may have occasion to take out any money, and for what purpose.
6. If he absents himself on duty or otherwise, to give over the books to the storekeeper, who is responsible for any deficiency that may appear on his return.
7. To superintend the conduct of the inferior officers, and see that they do their duty.

Inferior Officers.

To be entirely subservient to the storekeeper and superintendant   In the absence of the former the adjutant will supply his place.

No. XXVII.

The Marquess Wellesley to Don Martin de Garay.

SIR,   Seville, August 28th, 1809.

I have the honour to acknowledge the receipt of your Excellency's note of the 25th instant,* and I have examined with great attention the communications from the Department of War which your Excellency has been pleased to make to me by order of the Supreme Central Junta.

The first and most important point stated in my notes of the 21st instant,† related to the establishment of a more efficient system for furnishing the means of supply and movement to the British army in the field. For this indispensable object, I submitted to your Excellency a detailed plan, which I requested the Government to carry into effect with all practicable celerity. In reply to this proposal on my part, your Excellency has not stated to me any measures which have yet been adopted for the effectual establishment of the plan which I took the liberty of recommending, but your Excellency, by the order of the Supreme Central Junta, has communicated to me the copy of " a royal instruction for the management of magazines of provisions for armies in the field," and my opinion is desired by the Government, with respect to any alteration which it may be proper to suggest for the amendment of that instruction. The instruction contains nothing more than a series of rules and orders for the internal management of magazines relating merely to the details of that branch of service.

The general superintendence of the economy of the magazines is very properly confided, by the first article of the instructions, to an officer of the Department of Finance.

I have the honour to inform your Excellency that I perceive no objection to the rules and orders contained in this instruction ; but I must observe that this regulation alone would not be sufficient to correct the existing defects in the system of supplying the armies in the field. If this regulation is intended as a substitute for the plan which I have presumed to offer to your Excellency, I must declare with the freedom which your Excellency has permitted me to use, that I cannot expect any substantial correction of those evils which

---

* See p. 75.   † See p. 43.

have occasioned such calamities during the present campaign. Your Excellency's note, to which I have now the honour of replying, blends the suggestions which I proposed for an improved mode of subsisting the army, with a detailed consideration of its future operations.

I request your Excellency's permission to separate these points, for the purpose of considering each distinct question with more perspicuity and accuracy.

I have therefore confined this note to the separate object of requesting to know from your Excellency, whether the plan which I submitted to you on the 21st instant for the supply of the army in the field, is approved by the Government, and whether any steps have been taken for the purpose of carrying it into execution.

I avail myself of this occasion to renew, &c.

WELLESLEY.

No. XXVIII.

Sir Arthur Wellesley to the Marquess Wellesley.

MY LORD,   Merida, August. 28th, 1809.

I am anxious to receive your Excellency's sentiments on the points described in my despatch of the 24th instant (No. 14,)* as it will be necessary that I should make early arrangements to draw out of Portugal the supplies of ammunition, stores, and necessaries for the troops, which I have reason to believe are already collected at Elvas.

Having been able to separate the army, the troops have received their regular rations since the 25th instant, with the exception of the horses of the cavalry. I have to inform your Excellency, however, that none of the supplies, either of provisions or means of transport, which Monsieur de Calvo informed me, and the Spanish Minister informed your Excellency, were so near the army, have yet reached Merida, which is at least four marches from Jaraicejo, and I entertain doubts whether any of them were even ordered till your Excellency presented your first note to the Minister.

The officers and troops are still very unhealthy, and I fear that I shall find it difficult to remove them from hence to Elvas, where the British hospital is established for want of

* See p. 65.

carriages, and I can get none here. The loss of horses likewise continues to be very great, on account of the necessity of giving them wheat instead of barley.

I have the honour to be, &c.

ARTHUR WELLESLEY.

No. XXIX.

The Marquess Wellesley to Don Martin de Garay.

MY LORD,   Seville, August 30th, 1809.

My reply to that part of your Excellency's note of the 25th instant, which relates to the position and operations of the army in Estremadura, has been delayed until I could receive accurate intelligence of the condition of Sir Arthur Wellesley's army, and until I could possess the advantage of a full knowledge of his sentiments.

I have received despatches from Sir Arthur Wellesley to the date of the 28th instant, when he remained at Merida in consequence of my suggestion.

When I forwarded to Sir Arthur Wellesley the suggestions contained in my note to your Excellency of the 21st instant, I relied on this Government, that the plan for improving the means of supply and movements of the army, would have been carried into immediate effect. I also hoped that the exertions which your Excellency assured me this Government had already made, might have afforded some aid to the British troops; without these expectations and hopes, I should not have ventured to suggest to Sir Arthur Wellesley any delay in the execution of his intention to fall back upon the supplies provided in Portugal.

In the despatch I received from Sir Arthur Wellesley this day, he informs me, that none of the supplies, either of provisions or means of transport, promised by this Government to the British army, had reached Merida; and that it was absolutely necessary, for the security of his army, that he should not postpone any longer the completion of his arrangement for drawing his supplies from Portugal.

While I receive this distressing intelligence from Sir Arthur Wellesley, I suffer the additional regret of observing, that this Government has not yet given effect to any system for the better management of the subsistence or movements of the army.

Under these circumstances, I find myself compelled not only to concur with Sir Arthur Wellesley in those considerations which have induced him to form the intention of retiring to the frontier of Portugal, but I have strongly advised that officer not to delay the execution of a measure now rendered indispensable for the security of the remainder of that gallant army, which has already endured such sufferings in the cause of the Spanish nation.

I therefore have the honour to request your Excellency to inform the Supreme Junta, that in consequence of the total failure of the means of supply and transport necessary to enable the British army to act in Spain, that army with my entire consent will immediately move towards the frontier of Portugal.

It will remain for the wisdom of the Supreme Central Junta to consider what system shall be adopted to prevent in future the embarrassments which have impeded the operations of the British army during this campaign.

Your Excellency will perceive, that under the circumstances stated in this note, the plan of operations, and the arrangements proposed in your Excellency's note of the 25th instant, are become impracticable in the present moment.

It is difficult to ascertain the immediate causes of the distress which has been suffered by our army since the hour of its arrival in Spain; it is however perfectly evident, that unless some change be effected in the mode of conducting the military department, the greatest danger is to be apprehended to the interests and honour of Spain.

I avail myself of this occasion to repeat to your Excellency the assurances of my high consideration and esteem, and

I have the honour to be, &c.

WELLESLEY.

No. XXX.

The Marquess Wellesley to Sir Arthur Wellesley

SIR,   Seville, August 30th, 1809.

1. I now have the honour of replying to your despatch (No. 14,) of the 24th instant; I have received your despatch (No. 15,) dated 28th of August.*

2. In submitting to your consideration the plan proposed for occupying a position on the line of the river Guadiana, I did not intend to suggest that position as a permanent station of defence against the enemy. I entertained a hope that, under all the circumstances of the actual situation of the enemy's force, the position suggested might be safe, for a sufficient time, to enable you to try the result of the plan of supply for your army, which I had offered to this Government, and that the supplies which were provided in Portugal would at the same time be within your reach.

3. The resumption of offensive operations certainly appeared to me to be highly desirable, whenever it might become practicable, within the line drawn by your instructions from Lord Castlereagh of the 25th of May, but I was sufficiently apprized, by the intelligence which I had already received from you, that some time must elapse before your troops could recover the effects of the severe distress which they had suffered.

4. My opinion entirely coincides with that which you have stated, that no engagement exists either in the treaty between his Majesty and the Spanish Government or in the spirit of the alliance, or in any assurance authorized by you, to entitle the Spanish Government to demand the aid of a British army in Spain.

5. Your entrance into Spain was a favour conferred upon the Spanish Government, entirely beyond the conditions of the treaty, and the general obligations of the alliance, and you were justified in confining the extent of your operations within such limits as you might deem most advisable, consistently with the tenour of your instructions.

6. From the junction of your army with the Spanish troops, a species of implied engagement certainly arose, under which

---

* See pages 65-84.

it would not have been proper to have separated your army from that of Spain, without an absolute necessity, founded either on the obligation of your instructions (which have been previously explained to the Spanish Government) or in such an exigency of the case as must evidently have rendered further concert and co-operation with the Spanish army impracticable. Under the first consideration, the defence of Portugal must have formed the invariable object of your attention, and must have directed and limited the line of your operations. Under the second consideration, the failure of the Spanish Government, either in providing you with the necessary supplies and means of movement, or in affording to you the effectual co-operation of such a Spanish force as might enable you to oppose the enemy with a chance of success, must have dissolved any implicit engagement for the continuance of your army in Spain.

7. In my judgment, all these considerations now concur to release you from any such engagement. The mismanagement of the Spanish Government, added to the misconduct of the Spanish generals and troops, exposes your army, &c. to certain destruction, if you should attempt to remain in Spain. This case, indeed, does not appear to have been contemplated in your instructions, but it evidently involves every consideration which can be supposed to affect the safety of Portugal; for it must be evident, that the defence of Portugal would be entirely abandoned, by any act which should expose your army to risk, without any reasonable prospect of advantage to the common cause.

8. The inexpediency of contracting any new engagement to co-operate with the Spanish forces, is proved by the same considerations which have left you free to exercise your judgment upon that question.

9. When I forwarded to your Excellency the suggestion contained in my note of the 21st instant, I relied on this Government that the plan for improving the means of supply and movement of the army, would have been carried into immediate effect; I also hoped that the exertions (which I was assured had already been made by this Government) would have afforded you some degree of intermediate relief; without these hopes and expectations, I should not have attempted to induce you to hazard any further delay in Spain, but I have been entirely disappointed by the conduct of this

Government. By your despatch (No. 13,) dated the 22nd of August, it appears that you have received no intermediate aid; no plan for the improvement of your supplies has been yet adopted; the foundation therefore of my prop sitions of the 22nd of August has failed.

10. Until I received your despatch of the 24th instant, I had entertained a less unfavourable opinion of the Spanish army than you have stated, but I was convinced that it was vain to expect co-operation from any body of Spanish troops which should not be placed effectually under your command : if your army could have recovered its efficiency, if a proper system for your future supply could have been established, and if an adequate Spanish force could have been placed under your orders, I entertained a hope that offensive operations might have been resumed within a reasonable time with a prospect of success, and that the success of such a combined force under your command, and the manifest advantages of an improved plan of subsistence and transports, might have formed an example from which useful and practicable principles might have been derived for the amelioration of every branch of the Spanish Government, and especially of the military department, reviewing however the events which have passed under my observation, the facts which you have stated, the condition of your army, of the Spanish armies and government, and the relative strength and position of the enemy's force, I am reluctantly compelled to declare, that it would not be advisable to attempt to resume offensive operations in Spain in the present moment, or within any period of time which can now be calculated.

11. Your despatch (No. 14,) has satisfied me that the defence of Andalusia and of these provinces may be aided as effectually by the position of your army in the frontier of Portugal, as by any other station which such a force could now occupy.

12. I have not therefore encouraged this Government to expect either that you should remain within the Spanish frontier, or that you should return within any stated time for the purpose of co-operating with the Spanish army in any plan of a defensive nature; my note of this date to M. de Garay contains the only communication which I have made to the Government on this question.

13. In this state of affairs it is a matter of some delicacy to attempt to recommend to the Spanish Government the most eligible position for their army; this point must be left to their own discretion, as far as I have been enabled to collect the opinions of this Government, they do not accord with yours, and it is not to be expected that the Spaniards should be inclined to relax any of these prejudices in the moment of the retirement of our army to the frontier of Portugal.

14. Although it is evident that the retirement of the British army to Portugal is a measure of absolute necessity, created by the mismanagement of the Spanish Government, by the misconduct of the Spanish generals and troops, and by circumstances in the state of the country which cannot in any degree be attributed to us, it is to be expected that the most unfavourable impression will be produced by this movement upon the minds of the Government and people of Spain.

15. Impressions of this description are not governed by strict principles of reason or justice, but it is necessary to consider the influence and consequences of such prejudices in forming an estimate of the probable result of any course of public action.

16. It would therefore have been highly desirable to have been enabled to alleviate the force of these unfavourable circumstances, by any promise or hope of the future co-operations of a considerable British force in Spain, under the condition that proper remedies should be applied by the Spanish Government to those evils which have compelled your Excellency to forfeit the advantage of the glorious successes obtained by his Majesty's forces under your command; but it would be unwarrantable to encourage any definitive expectation of such assistance; and I am apprehensive that the general terms in which any suggestion of this description must be expressed, will not be sufficient to induce the Spanish Government to commence with spirit and ardour those systematic efforts which would be required for the purpose of drawing forth the military resources of the country, and of applying them with vigour and effect against the hostile power of France.

17. It would certainly diminish the alarm and ill temper of the present moment in Spain, if it were even possible to assure this Government that your army would remain on the

frontier of Portugal, and would be ready to act against the enemy in any case of necessity; but I am aware of the danger of entering into such an engagement, and I shall therefore abstain from any expression which may warrant that conclusion in the minds of the Spanish ministers.

18. The consternation which prevailed in the first moment of your movement towards Portugal, has abated in some degree by your continuance at Merida, and by the apparent dispersion and inaction of the enemy's force.

19. It is to be hoped that the dreadful apprehensions entertained by this Government, at the time when I wrote my despatch of the 22nd of August, may not be realized so soon as to preclude us from considering the means of affording aid to the Spanish cause, under such conditions and arrangements as may render our assistance useful to Spain, without involving injury or danger to the interests of Great Britain.

I have the honour to be, Sir,
your Excellency's, &c.
WELLESLEY.

No. XXXI.

Don Martin de Garay to the Marquess Wellesley.

MY LORD,   Seville, 30th August, 1809.

I have given an account to the Supreme Central and governing Junta of the kingdom, of the official note of your Excellency, under date the 28th of this month;* in which you are pleased to reply to that which by an order of His Majesty I had the honour to address to you, with the date of the 25th of the same month; in which I transmitted to you the communications I had received from the ministers of war, with reference to the plan proposed by your Excellency for the establishment of magazines of subsistence for the armies in the field: and I enclosed the royal instructions for the regulation of the said magazines.

Your Excellency has laid before me the considerations which suggested themselves to you respecting these instructions, and has expressed your desire to know if the plan proposed by your Excellency has been approved by the

* See p. 83.

Government, and if any steps have been taken for the purpose of carrying it into effect.

His Majesty having taken the whole question into consideration, has decided on giving his approbation to the plan, which has been referred to, in all its parts; and in consequence a copy of the same is to be despatched immediately to the Secretary of the Office of Finance, with the corresponding royal orders, to the intent that the most active and effectual measures be instantly adopted for carrying it into execution; and that as many persons as are necessary for the purchase of grain, both in Estremadura and Andalusia, may be named: as also for the several lines of magazines proposed by your Excellency, and approved by His Majesty.

I lay before your Excellency this information for your guidance, and for the effects which you may conceive best adapted for the royal service of your Sovereign, and for the defence of the just cause in which His Britannic Majesty and your Excellency have displayed so much interest.

I am ordered by His Majesty to lay before the consideration of your Excellency (in the supposition that the question of the establishment of the magazines of subsistence for the armies is already agreed upon) the urgent necessity of an answer from your Excellency, respecting the active part in the military operations required by the actual and critical circumstances, which he may depend upon the English troops for taking. As the Secretary of the War Office informs me, with the date of yesterday, that according to all the accounts which have been forwarded to him by the scouts of the army of Estremadura and La Mancha, the enemy was in retrograde motion; that this movement might have originated in the accounts which have been received from the north, which compel them either to advance into the interior of France, or to take up a position nearer to the Pyrenees; but that it might likewise have for object, the occupation of Old Castille; in which case, the troops of Gallicia, the Asturias, and Ciudad Rodrigo, would be very much exposed; and that for these reasons the Secretary of War, with the approbation of His Majesty, is of opinion, that the armies should move with the greatest activity; whether to observe the movements of the enemy more closely, or to attack him when circumstances may render it expedient.

I make this communication to your Excellency by a royal order; and His Majesty, knowing the zeal of your Excellency, and your attachment to Spain, does not doubt of your promptitude in making the arrangements which are best adapted, in your opinion, for sustaining the interests of this nation, and for defending the just cause of its liberty and independence, in which our respective Sovereigns are so deeply engaged. Your Excellency will communicate to me the determinations which may best accord with your sentiments.

I have the honour to be, &c.

MARTIN DE GARAY.

No. XXXII.

Don Martin de Garay to the Marquess Wellesley.

MY LORD,   Seville, 31st August, 1809.

The Secretary of the War Office has sent me the following information, under date of yesterday:

"I enclose to your Excellency by a royal order, a copy of the official note which has been transmitted by the Marquis of Malespina to Don Francisco d'Eguia, that you may make it known to the Ambassador of England, and that you may be acquainted with the decision of Sir Arthur Wellesley to march into Portugal; as likewise his doubts that the proposal for placing the armies behind the Guadiana, had been made by the Ambassador himself; and as the actual circumstances require that our armies should move, it is necessary to know definitely whether the English co-operate or not."

By order of the Supreme Central and Governing Junta of the Kingdom, I make this communication to your Excellency, and enclose the above mentioned copy, in order that your Excellency, being fully acquainted with its contents, may be pleased to reply to me as best accords with your wishes, and that I may be enabled to make known that reply to the Secretary of the War Office, for his guidance, and the requisite effects.

I have the honour to be, &c.

MARTIN DE GARAY.

No. XXXIII.

Sir Arthur Wellesley to the Marquess Wellesley.

MY LORD,   Merida, August 31st, 1809.

The Spanish Government have lately sent forward a large number of shirts and sheets, for which I had applied through Mr. Frere, for the use of the hospitals; I shall be very much obliged to your Excellency if you will give directions that I may be furnished with an account of the expense of these articles, stating to whom I shall order payment to be made for them.

The persons who brought them have run away, with their mules, and I am apprehensive that I shall be obliged to leave here the shirts and the sheets. But there is no reason why the Spanish Government should not be paid for them.

After I had written to your Excellency on the 28th instant, nine carts arrived here from Seville loaded with biscuit for the use of the British army; and the carts are marked as intended for our service. It is very desirable' that I should be informed by the Government on what terms these carts are to be received into the service, whether to be purchased or hired, and at what rates. I propose now to employ them in the removal of the men, who have lately been taken ill, to the hospital at Elvas; but if the Spanish Government should be of opinion that when the British army will be in Portugal, it ought not to enjoy the advantage of the means of transport which have been procured for it in Spain, these carts shall be sent back; notwithstanding that if the Government and the people of Portugal had acted upon the same principle when the British army entered Spain, the army could not have made one march within the Spanish territory.

I am very anxious to receive your Excellency's sentiments upon the points which I submitted to you in my letter of the 24th, (No. 14,) that part of the British army (the cavalry particularly) which had moved by the road of Caceres, having been pressed for provisions, and not having received, by some accident, the notification of my intention to halt here for some days, had marched on, and has actually arrived within the Portuguese frontier. In the mean time the

Spanish army has, I understand, marched to take up its position behind the Guadiana, and it will probably arrive at La Serena this day. This being the case, it is necessary that I should get the British army in a more collected state, either in Portugal or within the Spanish frontier; and as the opinions entertained in my despatch (No. 14,) of the 24th instant, are strengthened by reflections since I addressed you, I propose to commence to move to Badajoz on the day after to-morrow, unless I should in the immediate time receive from your Excellency a communication of your sentiments which shall occasion an alteration of my opinion.

The bridge which had been on the Tagus near Almaraz arrived here last night, on its way to Badajoz. I cannot avoid to take this opportunity of drawing your Excellency's attention to the ease with which all the services of this description required for the Spanish army, have been performed; at the same time that nothing of the kind could be done, on the most urgent requisitions of service as well as of humanity, for the British army.

When the guns taken from the enemy at the battle of Talavera were given up, there was no difficulty about drawing them off; when the British army laid down its ammunition for want of means of conveying it, there was no difficulty about transporting it, and there has been none in providing the means to remove the bridge from the neighbourhood of the Tagus at Almaraz to Badajoz. Yet the application of these means at any period of the service of the British army, would have relieved many of the difficulties under which we laboured, and would certainly have prevented its separation from the Spanish army at the moment at which it was made. But I beg your Excellency to observe, that among all the offers which are pressed upon me to divide the contents of the magazine of provisions at Truxillo, to take what I pleased from it, nay, to take the whole even at the risk of starving the Spanish army; offers, of which I knew, and explained, and have since been able to prove the fallacy of, not one was even made to assist the British army with a cart, or mule, or any means of transport, which abounded in the Spanish army.

I have the honour to be, &c.

ARTHUR WELLESLEY.

No. XXXIV.

Sir Arthur Wellesley to the Marquess Wellesley.

MY LORD,   Merida, September 1st, 1809.

I have the honour to acknowledge the receipt of your Excellency's private letter of the 29th of August, containing a copy of Monsieur de Garay's note of the 25th August and of your Excellency's answer of the 28th, and of your despatch, of the 30th and of your despatch (marked separate) of the same date.

I am happy to find that your Excellency concurs with me in the opinions which I laid before you on the 24th, and I propose to-morrow to commence my movement from this place.

I intend that the greatest part of the army shall remain within the Spanish frontier, if I should be able to maintain it in that position, and I will apprise your Excellency of the exact positions which I shall occupy, and hereafter of any change which I may think it necessary to make.

My reason for wishing not to engage to remain on the Portuguese frontier, is, that the principal magazines of the British army are at Abrantes, Santarem and Lisbon; and notwithstanding the good will of the Portuguese Government, and the inclination of the people to give us every assistance in their power, Alentego being a poor country, I might find it impossible to maintain the whole army at such a distance from the magazines as the positions which they will occupy upon the frontier. I besides think that it is desirable that the Spanish Government should be induced to look into and acquire an accurate knowledge of their real situation compared with that of the enemy, and that they should be induced to make such an exertion as will at least provide for their defence by their own means.

On this account, and as I think I ought not to involve his Majesty's army in any system of co-operation with the Spanish troops, for the reasons stated in my despatch of the 24th, I beg to decline to accept the honour which the Government have offered to confer upon me, of the command of the corps of 12,000 men, to be left in this part of the country.

I could not have accepted this command under any circumstances without his Majesty's permission, excepting for the time that I should have considered myself authorized by the instructions of his Majesty's Ministers; or should have been enabled by circumstances to continue in co-operation with the Spanish army; but, having been obliged to separate from them, and considering it advisable that the British army should not at present enter upon any system of co-operation with them again, I cannot take upon myself the command of any Spanish corps whatever. In respect to offensive operations in future, it is desirable, that the means actually existing in Spain, of the French and of the allies should be reviewed, and the advantages which each party possesses in the use of these means should be weighed.

I estimate the French force in Spain, disposable for service in the field, to amount to 125,000 men, well provided with cavalry and artillery; in which number I do not include the garrisons of Pampeluna, Barcelona, &c. I include however the corps commanded by St. Cyr and Suchet, which I calculate to amount to 32,000 men, which are employed in Arragon and Catalonia; and the remainder being 90,000 men, are in Castile and Estremadura. Of this number 70,000 men are actually in the field in the corps of Victor, Soult, Ney, Sebastiani and Mortier; and the remainder are employed in garrisons, as at Madrid, Escurial, Avila, Valladolid, &c. in keeping up the communication with those places; every man of whom might be brought into the field if occasion required.

In these numbers I do not include sick and wounded, but found my calculations upon what I know were the numbers of the French army before the battle of Talavera, deducting a loss of 10,000 men in that battle.

Your Excellency will observe, that there are seven French corps in Spain; I believe there were originally eight, for Suchet's is the 8th corps, and each corps composing in itself a compleat army, ought to consist of from 30 to 40,000 men. Against this force the Spanish Government have about 50,000 men in the two corps of Eguia and Vanegas. Blake may have collected again about 6,000 men, and the Marquess de la Romana has 15,000 men, of which number 1,500 have no arms. The Duque del Parque has 9,000 men in the garrison of Ciudad Rodrigo, but he is unwilling to detach them.

Besides these numbers the British army may be reckoned from 20, to 25,000 men.

I am aware that there are troops in Spain besides those which I have enumerated but they are not in any manner, and cannot be considered disposable for the field. The plan of operations must be founded upon the relative numbers above stated.

But besides considering the numbers it is necessary to advert to the composition, and to the state of efficiency of these different armies.

The French corps are as I have already stated, each a complete army, having probably a greater proportion of cavalry, and certainly of artillery, than they ought to have for the existing numbers of their infantry; and they are well disciplined excellent troops.

The Spanish corps of Vanegas and Eguia have probably between them not less than 10,000 cavalry, which is more than their proportion; and they are well provided with artillery. But the corps of Romana has neither cavalry nor artillery, and for want of these arms is unable to quit the mountains of Gallicia. The Duque del Parque is unable if he were willing to assist him with what he wants.

Blake's corps I believe consists only of infantry. Both infantry and cavalry are comparatively undisciplined; the cavalry are tolerably well clothed, well armed, accoutred and mounted: but the infantry are not clothed nor accoutred as they ought to be, notwithstanding the large supplies of clothing and accoutrements sent out from England.

With these relative numbers, and adverting to the state of discipline and efficiency of the different armies, it would appear impossible to undertake any offensive operations with any hope of success; more particularly adverting to the local difficulties with which the allies would have to contend, and of the advantages of the enemy.

The enemy has it in his power to collect his whole force in Castile and Estremadura at any point north of the Tagus; and can dispose of the parts of it in the front or rear of the armies of the allies as he may think proper.

The allies must move upon the enemy in two distinct corps at least, there can be no military communication between the corps assembled in this part of Estremadura and that which would advance from La Carolina through La Mancha, on account of the chain of mountains on the whole of the left bank of the Tagus, from the Puerto de Miravete to the bridge of Toledo. The only communication which those corps can have, is by the right bank of the river from Almaraz, and by the bridge of Toledo; and it is obvious that a battle must be fought with the enemy's whole force, and won by one of the two corps, before that communication can be established.

This consideration was the reason that in the late operations the march of Vanegas was directed upon Viana and Fuente Dueñas and Arganda. It was impossible to join with Vanegas, before a battle should be fought with the enemy's whole force by one of the armies; and it was thought best to order Vanegas to adopt such a line of march as should be most distant from the combined armies; in relation to which and the combined armies the enemy could not have taken up a centrical position, from which he could have had the choice of attacking either. The enemy would thus have been forced either to detach to oppose Vanegas; or if he had kept his whole force collected to fight the combined corps advancing from this side, he would have lost Madrid; and his retreat would have been cut off.

Vanegas however did not obey the orders he received, I believe in consequence of directions from the Junta; instead of being at Arganda close to Madrid on the 23d, he did not approach the Tagus till the 28th, when he was kept in check at Toledo by 2,000 men, while the whole army were engaged with us at Talavera.

These circumstances will shew your Excellency the difficulty which attends the position of the allies; and indeed ought to have some influence with the Spanish Government in their distribution of their troops at present.

The French having 70,000 men disposable in Castile and Estremadura, may employ them either in opposing the advance of the allies from this side, who could not bring more than from 50 to 55,000 to oppose them; or they would detach 20,000 to oppose Vanegas, and meet the allies with 50,000. The whole would thus be kept in check, even if it could be hoped that one or both corps would not be defeated.

The Marquess de la Romana, the Duque del Parque, Blake, &c. could afford no relief from these embarrassing circumstances, having no cavalry to enable them to enter the plains of Castile, nor artillery.

But even if these first difficulties could be overcome, and the French armies should retire to the northward, the numbers of the allies would be found still more unequal to those of the enemy. The corps of St. Cyr and Suchet would then take their place in the operations; and the Spanish armies would have no corresponding encrease. The difficulties however are not of a nature to be overcome by the means at present in the power of the Spanish Government; they must increase their troops, and discipline, cloath and equip their forces, before they can reasonably attempt any offensive operations against the French; and in the meantime it becomes a question how the troops ought to be disposed of. From what I have already stated, your Excellency must observe the importance of their having a strong Spanish corps in this part of Estremadura. The British army must necessarily be the foundation of any offensive operation the Spanish Government can undertake; and it is obvious that the place of this army must be on the left of the whole, issuing from the frontiers of Portugal.

If the Spanish corps which is to act with the British army should be weak, their operations must be checked at an early period; and in that case I should apprehend that the operations of the larger Spanish corps directed from La Carolina would not be very successful.

But the prospect of these offensive operations may be considered too distant to render it reasonable to advert to them in a disposition of the Spanish army which is now about to be formed, and I would therefore suggest other grounds for recommending that the army in Estremadura should not if possible be weakened.

Your Excellency has observed that Soult entertains a design of attacking Ciudad Rodrigo; which design I understand was discussed and recommended by a Council of War held some time ago at Salamanca.

The success of this enterprize would do more mischief than the French are capable of doing in any other manner. It would completely cut off the only communication the

Spanish Government have with the northern provinces; would give the French the perpetual possession of Castile, and would probably occasion the loss of the Portuguese fort of Almeida.

I should be desirous to make every exertion to ease Ciudad Rodrigo; but if Estremadura should be left with only 12,000 men, it must be obvious to your Excellency that Seville, as well as Portugal, will be exposed while I shall be removed from this part of the country.

I am much afraid, from what I have seen of the proceedings of the Central Junta, that in the distribution of their forces, they do not consider military defence and military operations, so much as they do political intrigue, and the attainment of trifling political objects.

They wish to strengthen the army of Vanegas, not because it is necessary or desirable on military grounds, but because they think the army, as an instrument of mischief, safer in his hands than in those of another; and they leave 12,000 men in Estremadura, not because more are not or may not be deemed necessary, in any military view of the question, but because they are averse to placing a larger body under the command of the Duke d'Albuquerque who, I know, that the Junta of Estremadura have insisted should be employed to command the army in this province.

I cannot avoid to observe these little views and objects, and to mention them to your Excellency, at the same time that I lament that the attention of those who have to manage such great and important affairs as those are which are entrusted to the management of the Central Junta, should be diverted from great objects to others of trifling importance.

I cannot conclude this letter without adverting to the mode in which Don Martin de Garay, in his note to your Excelleney of the 25th instant, disposes of the Portuguese troops, without having had one word of communication with the Portuguese Government, or any body connected with it, respecting them.

In fact those troops have been equally ill, indeed I might say worse treated, than the British troops, by the officers of the Spanish Government, and were at last obliged to quit Spain for want of food; and I will no more allow them, than I will the British troops, to enter Spain again, unless I should have some solid ground for believing that they will be supplied as they ought.

It is a curious circumstance respecting Marshal Beresford's corps, that the Cabildo of Ciudad Rodrigo actually refused to allow them to have 30,000 of 100,000 pounds of biscuit (which I had had prepared there, in case the operations of the army should be directed to that quarter, and for which the British Commissary had paid) and seized the biscuit on the grounds that debts due to the town of Ciudad Rodrigo, by the British army lately under the command of Sir John Moore, had not been paid; although one of the objects of the mission of the same Commissary to Ciudad Rodrigo was to settle the accounts and discharge those debts.

Yet this same Cabildo will call for assistance as soon as they will perceive the intention of the enemy to attack them, having seized, and holding probably in their possession at the moment, the means which, if lodged as directed, in the stores at Almeida, would enable me effectually to provide for their relief.

I have the honour to be, &c.

ARTHUR WELLESLEY.

No. XXXV.

The Marquess Wellesley to Don Martin de Garay.

SIR,   Seville, Sept. 1st, 1809.

I had the honour to receive last night your Excellency's note under date the 31st August, containing, by order of the Supreme Central Junta, a question from the Secretary of the Department of War, respecting the operations of the British army under the command of Sir Arthur Wellesley.

In my note under date the 30th August, I had the honour to state to your Excellency, that in consequence of the total failure of the means of supply and transport necessary to enable the British army to act in Spain, that army, with my entire consent, would immediately move towards the frontiers of Portugal.

I take the liberty of referring your Excellency to the same

note of the 30th August for a further explanation of the necessity which has absolutely compelled Sir Arthur Wellesley
to adopt this measure for the security of his troops.

I have the honour to be, &c.

WELLESLEY.

No. XXXVI.

The Marquess Wellesley to Mr. Secretary Canning.

SIR,   Seville, September 2, 1809.

1. While the intelligence received from Sir Arthur Wellesley to the date of the 24th instant continued to furnish
irresistible proofs of the failure of every promise or effort
made by this Government for the immediate relief of our
troops, no satisfaction was afforded to me respecting any permanent plan for their future supply.

2. On the 21st of August I had submitted to the Government by the express desire of M. de Garay a detailed plan
for the improvement of the subsistence and means of movement of the army. Notwithstanding the assurances of M. de
Garay on receiving my note of the 21st, no answer had been
returned to me from the Junta on the 23d of August; on
that day I requested the reply of the Junta to a proposition
so intimately blended with the safety of Spain and of his
Majesty's troops serving in her cause.* No answer was returned by the Junta until the 25th of August, when I received
a note from M. de Garay with the copy of a voluminous
regulation or instruction,† relating merely to the internal
economy of magazines of provisions, and not extending to
any of the most important defects which required correction
in the mode of supplying the army, nor including the main
objects of my proposition. After an examination of this regulation, and of the unsatisfactory note which accompanied
it, I returned my answer on the 28th of August,‡ expressing
my anxiety to know whether this Government was disposed
to adopt the plan which I had suggested, and whether any
steps had been taken for carrying it into effect.

---

* See p. 64.   † See p. 75.   ‡ See p. 83.

3. On the 26th of August I received Sir Arthur Wellesley's letter dated the 24th, and on the 30th I received that of the 28th. In consequence of those communications, on the 30th I sent a note to M. de Garay,* and on the same day I forwarded to Sir Arthur Wellesley a despatch in reply to his letters of the 24th and 28th.

4. After I had sent my note of the 30th of August to M. de Garay, I received from him a note† under date the same day, which must have been closed before he had received my note of the 30th.

5. From Sir Arthur Wellesley's letters of the 24th and 28th it was evident that his immediate retirement to the frontier of Portugal was indispensable to the recovery and safety of his troops; and the dilatory and inefficient management of the Government at this place had destroyed the foundation of the plan which I had suggested for the purpose of enabling the British army to continue in Spain at any distance from the frontier of Portugal. I therefore signified to Sir Arthur Wellesley in my letter of the 30th of August, my entire concurrence in his determination to continue his march until he should arrive within reach of his Portuguese supplies; and I also approved his intention of avoiding any promise of further co-operation with the Spanish army. In my note of the same date to M. de Garay, I distinctly communicated Sir Arthur Wellesley's intentions and my sentiments upon the whole question.

6. M. de Garay's note of the 30th of August contains indeed the tardy assent of the Junta to the proposal which I had made on the 21st for the establishment of a new system of magazines and means of transport; but this assent, as usual, appeared to be merely formal and verbal. The practical arrangements requisite for rendering any improvement effectual are omitted, and past experience could not justify any hope of substantial benefit from the mere ordinances of the Junta. The ostensible adoption of my plan was also embarrassed by an inadmissible and impracticable condition; for the Government, in approving what I had suggested, expressed its confidence that the British army, together with the Spanish co-operating forces, would immediately make a

---

* See p. 85.   † See p. 91.

forward movement against the enemy.   This proposition accords with the general tenor of those professions of zeal for
active war which have particularly characterized the declarations of the Junta since the army has been deprived of the
means of movement and supply.   Far from affording any just
foundation of confidence in the intentions of this Government,
such assiduous declarations of activity and enterprize, unac-
companied by any provident or regular attention to the means
or objects of the war, serve only to create additional suspicions of ignorance, weakness, or insincerity.   No person acquainted with the real condition of the British and Spanish
forces, and with the relative state and position of the enemy's
armies on the 30th of August, could reasonably advise a forward movement against the enemy with any other view than
the certain destruction of the allied armies.

7. Under the impression of these opinions, I could not
have been justified in recalling either my letter of the 30th
of August, addressed to Sir Arthur Wellesley, or my note of
the same date to M. de Garay.

8. On the 31st of August I received a note from M. de
Garay* containing, from the Secretary for the Department of
War, the report of a very unpleasant conference which had
taken place between Sir Arthur Wellesley and an officer de-
puted by the Spanish General at Merida.   The Secretary
for the Department of War further states that the Spanish
army is to move immediately, and desires that the British
Ambassador may declare definitively whether the British
army will co-operate or not.

9. To this question I replied on the 1st of September,
merely by referring to my note of the 30th of August,† in
which I had stated that the total want of supplies compelled
the British army to retire to the frontier of Portugal.

10. On the 1st and 2nd of September I received Sir Arthur
Wellesley's letters of the 31st of August and 1st of September
from Merida, at which place he had halted from the 24th of
August in consequence of my despatches.   You will observe
that on the 28th of August, after Sir Arthur Wellesley had
despatched his letter of that date, nine carts laden with biscuit
had reached the British army from Seville.   This appears to

* See p. 93.   † See p. 85.

be the first supply received from the Junta in consequence of my applications. I must request your particular attention to the remarks of Sir Arthur Wellesley upon the abundant means of transport existing in the Spanish army, and the unaccommodating temper with which all aid of that description had been denied to him.

11. Sir Arthur Wellesley in his letter of the 1st, announces his final determination to move the next day for the frontier of Portugal, but adds that it is his intention to station the greater part of his army within the Spanish frontier, if he should be able to maintain it in that position, of which he entertains some doubt on account of the distance of his principal magazines within the Portuguese territory.

12. Thus has terminated the important question which has occasioned so much discussion with this Government since the period of my arrival in Spain. The documents to which I have had the honour of referring you in this despatch will furnish you with the most material details necessary for your information; but it may not be useless to submit to your consideration a general view of these extraordinary transactions in a more connected form.

13. After the retreat of Sir John Moore's army, the discussions which had taken place between his Majesty's Minister in Spain and the Spanish Government, relative to the co-operation of a British army within the Spanish territory, seemed to have closed all question of right on the part of Spain to that particular species of assistance from the British Government.

14. The conditions which had been required by the British Government were neither unreasonable nor unjust, nor were they deemed objectionable by the Spanish Government on any grounds of that description. The Spanish Government declined the conditions offered by us for reasons perfectly compatible with the continuance of the alliance, and with the maintenance of an uninterrupted temper of harmony and friendship. It was therefore admitted by both parties that the employment of a British army in Spain was not absolutely necessary to the stability of the alliance, and could not be justly demanded by Spain without a previous arrangement of the conditions under which such aid might be hereafter granted by his Majesty.

15. The instructions to Sir Arthur Wellesley (permitting him to pass the Portuguese frontier, and to co-operate occasionally under certain limitations with the Spanish armies), contain no admission of the right of Spain to any such co-operation. The powers given to Sir Arthur Wellesley are to be exercised according to his discretion with reference to the primary object of protecting Portugal; and the Spanish Government and its officers appear to have been seasonably and distinctly apprized that no operation could be attempted by the British army in Spain which might expose Portugal to hazard, and that any exertion of the British army in Spain would be entirely gratuitous, and must be deemed a favour beyond the obligations of public faith.

16. The Spanish Government and its officers in earnestly pressing Sir Arthur Wellesley to move into Spain, urged no claim of right; in acceding to their request, he neither admitted any such right, nor contracted any engagement to continue in Spain for any period of time, or for any plan of operation exceeding the limits of his instructions of the 25th of May.

17. Sir Arthur Wellesley's intentions of co-operating with General Cuesta against Victor, were known by General Cuesta and by the Junta early in May; and the extension of Sir Arthur Wellesley's discretion, enabling him to enlarge the scale of his operations beyond the provinces on the frontier of Portugal, was notified to General Cuesta and to this Government early in June, 1809. At an early period of June, 1809, this Government declared that orders had been given to collect supplies and means of movement for the British army on its approach to the Spanish territory.

18. On the 8th of July Sir Arthur Wellesley arrived at Placentia in Spain. He had received letters from M. de Garay urging a forward movement, and soon after he had an interview with General Cuesta.

19. On the 16th of July Sir Arthur Wellesley transmitted to Mr. Frere a copy of a complaint addressed to General O'Donohue, an officer of General Cuesta's staff, stating the distress of the British army for means of transport and provisions.

20. From the 16th of July to the 28th of August, the distress of the army appears to have continually increased, notwithstanding the representations of Mr. Frere, those which I

addressed to the Junta, and the repeated promises and professions of the Spanish Government and of its officers.

21. On the 28th of August a supply of biscuit not exceeding the consumption of one day, arrived at Merida, but no augmentation of the means of transport appears to have been supplied at any time, notwithstanding the abundance of the Spanish army and of the country, in those necessary articles. In many instances the Spanish civil and military officers interrupted the supplies of the British army by fraud and by force. During the whole of this period of time, from the entrance of the British army into Spain until the hour of its retirement, the Spanish Generals and armies, with very limited exceptions, not only afforded no effectual aid or co-operation to the British troops, but embarrassed Sir Arthur Wellesley's able and judicious plans, and frustrated the objects of his most important military dispositions; even abandoning the brave British soldiers, wounded in the battle of Talavera, to the mercy of the enemy.

22. The troops of Portugal which entered Spain under General Beresford suffered similar distress and experienced similar ill-treatment; although the efforts of Portugal in the cause of Spain have been as gratuitous as those of Great Britain, and although Spain possesses no claim of any description to the aid of a Portuguese army.

23. If it could be contended, that from the mere act of advancing into Spain, and of co-operating with the Spanish army, any engagement arose to continue that service, until the Spanish Government should be completely satisfied, it is evident that such an engagement could not subsist beyond the moment when the safety of Portugal should be endangered, or when the Spanish Government should be unable or unwilling to secure to the British army the necessary supplies for its movement and subsistence, or the necessary assistance of a co-operating force. In both instances Spain has totally failed, and Sir Arthur Wellesley has returned to the frontiers of Portugal because his continuance in Spain would have exposed the British army, and consequently the kingdom of Portugal, to the most imminent hazard of total destruction, without any prospect of advantage to the cause of Spain, if that exclusive consideration could have justified the sacrifice both of Portugal and of our gallant troops.

24. The British army entered Spain in compliance with

the invitations of the Spanish ministers and officers, and under no obligation of public faith. During its continuance in Spain it not only achieved the most glorious acts of heroism, but saved the Spanish Government from ruin. The Spanish Government and Generals have frustrated every effort of British valour and skill in the field, and have at last compelled that brave army to retreat to Portugal, which they earnestly solicited to advance into Spain.

25. According to the usual course of human affairs, the Spanish Government have reproached us with the consequences of a calamity which they had occasioned, and have endeavoured to ascribe the retirement of the British army to any cause rather than to their own misconduct.

26. These insinuations, however unjust, had produced a general impression which had required attention ; I therefore attempted to afford to the Government an opportunity of retrieving its errors or negligences, and to secure the recovery of our suffering army without injury to the fears or prejudices of this country. But the incredible weakness of the Junta has disappointed every attempt to detain our army in Spain, and I have been compelled to submit to the same necessity which has produced such a result of such splendid military achievements.

27. It cannot reasonably be disputed that the British Government is now at full liberty to exercise its discretion respecting the expediency of permitting a British army to enter Spain for the purpose of co-operating with the Spanish troops.

28. If any obligation to advance into Spain had existed previously to the events of this campaign, those events would have been sufficient to liberate the question from all embarrassment.

29. Under these circumstances, Sir Arthur Wellesley has judiciously determined to abstain from all engagement to occupy even a defensive position in Spain, and I have distinctly explained to this Government my perfect concurrence in the same sentiments.

30. Much ill-temper and some alarm have been occasioned by these communications. The terror however which existed on the first rumour of the retreat of our troops, has been somewhat abated by the prudent and deliberate manner in

which it has been conducted, and by the inaction and apparent dispersion of the enemy's forces in Spain. To these causes of temporary tranquillity may be added the reports of the renewal of hostilities between Austria and France. On this supposed event the Junta build many lofty expectations, which it would be more wise to found on the seasonable correction of their own faults, on the due administration of the great resources of this powerful country, and on the proper direction of the excellent disposition of the Spanish people.

31. Although the retreat of the British army has created many unpleasant sensations in my mind, and has checked the cordiality of intercourse with the Spanish ministers, and in some degree altered the temper of the alliance, I am not without hope that advantage may finally be derived from a misfortune, of which the first aspect was unpromising and melancholy.

32. Whatever delusion may prevail for a moment, the true causes of the retreat of our army cannot long be concealed from the Spanish nation.

33. In this calamity the people of Spain cannot fail to acknowledge the natural consequences of their own weakness, nor to discover the urgent necessity of enforcing a more steady, pure, and vigorous system both of council and action. A relaxed state of domestic government, and an indolent reliance on the activity of foreign assistance, have endangered all the high and virtuous objects for which Spain has armed and bled. It must now be evident, that no alliance can protect her from the inevitable result of internal disorder and national infirmity; she must amend and strengthen her Government; she must improve the administration of her resources, and the structure and discipline of her armies, before she can become capable of deriving benefit from foreign aid : the matchless enterprize and skill of her most powerful, generous, and active ally, have been rendered fruitless in victory by the inefficiency of her own Government and army; and Spain has proved untrue to our alliance because she is not true to herself. It may be hoped that the attention of the Spanish nation will now be turned to the great work of rendering Spain fit to receive the co-operation of an auxiliary force, and to act with those allies who cannot accomplish her deliverance without her own strenuous exertion.   Until some

great change shall be effected in the conduct of the military resources of Spain and in the state of her armies, no British army can safely attempt to co-operate with the Spanish troops in the territory of Spain.

34. The British Government is certainly free from all engagement to incur such a risk; but if arrangements could be devised which might enable us to aid Spain with the services of a British army without positive injury to our troops, it is probable that Spain would now embrace with eagerness the best remaining hope of her deliverance, and in the improvement of her own condition offer the surest pledge of fidelity to her allies.

I have the honour to be, &c.

WELLESLEY.

No. XXXVII.

Sir Arthur Wellesley to the Marquess Wellesley.

MY LORD,   Badajoz, September, 3, 1809.

I have received from Lord Castlereagh copies of Mr. Secretary Canning's despatches to your Excellency, dated the 12th of August, and I have been directed by his Lordship to lay before your Excellency my opinion on the points referred to in those despatches.

The letters which I have had the honour of addressing your Excellency on the 24th of August, and the 1st of September, will have apprised you of my opinion on the first point referred to by Mr. Secretary Canning, the prospect of success in offensive operations against the enemy, which opinions I should equally entertain, even though the British army could be encreased to 40,000 instead of 30,000 men, as long as the Spanish armies will continue of the limited numbers, in the undisciplined and inefficient state, and ill-composed as they are at present.

Your Excellency has before you, in my despatch of the 1st of September, (No. 17,) the detailed information upon which I found my opinion, upon which you may form your own, if the information should be found correct; if it should be found materially erroneous, it may be corrected.

In the existing state of the forces of the enemy, and of the allies in the Peninsula, it would be difficult for the British army, if not impossible, to connect the defence of Portugal with that of Spain, and quite impossible, unless great improvements should be made in the mode of supplying armies in Spain. Hereafter, when it is possible that the existing relative numbers of the armies will be altered to tne advantage of the enemy, it will be quite impossible for the British army to connect with the defence of Portugal that of the south of Spain. The Government have determined to defend Portugal, but if it should be hereafter determined to defend the south of Spain instead of Portugal, I conceive it will be absolutely necessary that the Commanding Officer of the British troops should have the command of the Spanish army; that we should have a garrison in Cadiz; and that the most efficient measures should be adopted to secure supplies and means of transport for the allied armies.

I have the honour to be, &c.
ARTHUR WELLESLEY.

No. XXXVIII.

The Marquess Wellesley to Sir Arthur Wellesley.

SIR,   Seville, September 4, 1802.

1. I have the honour to forward to you by Mr. Wellesley, the copy of a despatch which I have just received from Mr. Secretary Canning, under date the 12th of August.*

2. This despatch contains so full and clear a view of the points to which it relates, and so completely embraces the important questions which have lately been discussed with this Government, that it is unnecessary for me to add any observations upon those subjects.

3. The copy of Mr. Canning's despatch has been made with a view of obtaining the general purport of your Excellency's sentiments with the least practicable delay, and I should esteem it a particular favour if you would return that copy, with such remarks as you may think fit to insert in the margin, by an express courier.

I have the honour to be, &c.
WELLESLEY.

---

* See Appendix.

No. XXXIX.

Sir Arthur Wellesley to the Marquess Wellesley.

MY LORD,   Badajoz, September 5th, 1809.

I had the honour of receiving your Excellency's letter of the 4th instant. I considered my despatches of the 29th of August, and 1st and 3rd instant, as containing my opinion upon all the points referred to in Mr. Secretary Canning's despatch to your Excellency of the 12th of August; and accordingly I sent copies of these despatches to England yesterday, with a letter to Lord Castlereagh, of which I enclose a copy.

I have, however, now written in the margin of the copy which your Excellency has sent me of the despatch of the 12th of August from Mr. Canning, answers upon the points on which I understand from Mr. Wellesley that your Excellency wishes for my opinion.

I have the honour to be, &c.

ARTHUR WELLESLEY.

No. XL.

The Marquess Wellesley to Don Martin de Garay.

SIR,   Seville, September, 8th, 1809.

In my note of the 30th of August I had the honour to inform your Excellency that the British army, under the command of Sir Arthur Wellesley, with my entire consent, would immediately move towards the frontier of Portugal, for the purpose of receiving the necessary supplies, which the government of Spain had not furnished to those generous defenders of the Spanish cause.

The British army accordingly is now stationed near the Portuguese frontier, a part of the army is in Portugal, and the remainder on the Spanish territory, occupying a position which would menace the flank and rear of the enemy, if he should advance towards Andalusia.

I cannot however give the Spanish Government any assurance that the British army will continue in that position.

It may become necessary to approach the British magazines established at distant points within the Portuguese frontier as the immediate defence of Portugal may require the presence of our troops in that kingdom.

In either case, I request your Excellency to understand that the British army will be compelled to withdraw entirely from Spain.

In this situation of affairs, the interests and honour of Great Britain and of Spain, demand a full and distinct explanation of the present condition and the future intentions of both parties.

The despatches which I have received from Sir Arthur Wellesley, and the instructions with which I have been recently honoured by the commands of my Sovereign, enable me to submit to the Supreme Central Junta a declaration of which the grounds, motives, and objects are plain and intelligible.

In the course of the contest with France, Great Britain and her allies have aided Spain—First, by supplies of various descriptions sent into the Spanish ports. Secondly, by powerful military diversions, which have employed the main body of the enemy's force in distant parts of Europe. Thirdly, by the direct co-operation of British armies in the Spanish territory.

From the termination of former discussions, after the retirement of the troops under the command of the late Sir John Moore, the British and Spanish Governments appeared to have agreed to postpone for future consideration that species of assistance which consists in the services of British troops within the Spanish territory.

From that period of time the attention of the British Government had been more particularly and exclusively directed to the security of Portugal, and the confidence which the Portuguese Government had reposed in us, justified the British Government in considering the defence of Portugal as the primary object of our military operations in the Peninsula.

The security of Portugal however did not necessarily confine the British army within the frontier of that kingdom, whenever an occasion might arise of such co-operation with the Spanish armies, as might not leave Portugal exposed to the enemy.

Such was the state of affairs, previously to the entrance of Sir Arthur Wellesley's army into Spain. Neither the terms of existing treaties, nor the spirit of alliance, nor the result of previous discussions, entitled the Spanish Government at that time to demand the services of a British army in Spain.

But the instructions which Sir Arthur Wellesley had received from his Sovereign, permitted him to concede to the Spanish Government testimonies of amity, beyond the positive terms of treaty, on the express obligations of alliance; and he was therefore at liberty to receive the propositions of the Spanish General, and of the Spanish Government, for any plan of occasional concert within the Spanish territory which might tend to promote the interests of Spain, without hazard to the safety of Portugal.

If the British Government had deemed it necessary to insist on the establishment of the regular conditions of a treaty, previously to the entrance of any British army into Spain, even for the most confined operations, it would have been reasonable and just to have required from the Spanish Government,—First, satisfactory security for the supply of provisions and means of movement to the auxiliary force. Secondly, effectual arrangements, not only for the active co-operation of the Spanish force immediately attached to the auxiliary British troops, but for an united and connected system of aid and assistance from the operations of any division and branch of the Spanish army in all the provinces.

If these conditions were not positively required from the Spanish Government, in the form of a treaty, before Sir Arthur Wellesley's army was permitted to pass the frontiers of Portugal, your Excellency cannot doubt that it was presumed to be impossible that the Spanish Government could even consent to receive a British army within the territories of Spain, without having secured the necessary means for its subsistence, and for its action against the enemy.

Your Excellency will observe, that if the Spanish Government omitted these indispensable precautions, or was unable effectually to provide them, it was inconsistent with the safety of Portugal to solicit the entrance of a British army into Spain, even on the most limited and narrow scale of operations. For it is evident that the British army, under such circumstances, could not advance into Spain without imminent hazard to its own existence, and consequently to the safety of Portugal. The same considerations, therefore, which justified the advance of the British army into Spain, must have required its return to Portugal, if the Spanish Government should not furnish it with the requisite supplies, or with the effectual co-operation of the Spanish army.

The British army under Sir Arthur Wellesley entered Spain at the earnest solicitation of this government and of its officers, early notice was given to the Spanish Government of the approach of our troops, and the line of their movement and the limits of their operation were fully concerted and accurately defined in conferences and correspondence with the Spanish officers.

After these solicitations and apparent precautions, it is a melancholy task to examine the situation of the British army, throughout the whole course of its arduous and transcendant achievements, in asserting the independence of the Spanish monarchy, and the liberties and glory of the Spanish nation.

From the hour of Sir Arthur Wellesley's advance into Spain, his troops have wanted the ordinary means of transport, the common necessaries of subsistence, and every article requisite to enable our army not only to move, but even to exist.

The distress of the British troops commenced as early as the 16th of July. It was regularly notified to the Spanish General and to the Spanish Government; the calamity however was not alleviated, it continued to encrease; and since the glorious day of Talavera, Sir Arthur Wellesley has seen the remainder of the brave army which achieved that victory, suffering the extremity of hunger and disease, while the hourly diminution of the means of movement and conveyance precluded all hopes of remedy and all prospect of recovery within the territory of Spain.

The officers ordered by the Spanish Government to aid the British army in obtaining supplies, have not only neglected their duty, but in various instances have deprived the British soldiers of the supplies which had been provided by the British Commissaries.

Great Britain, with the zeal and generosity of sincere friendship, has accumulated supplies of every description in the ports of Spain, and has shed her noblest blood on the Spanish soil.

But the agents of the Spanish Government have seized by violence the subsistence destined for the British army, and have denied the means of conveyance to our sick and wounded soldiers while those means abounded in the camps and towns of Spain.

The troops of Portugal received the same injurious treatment, as soon as these faithful allies entered the territory of Spain, nor could the allied armies of Great Britain and Portugal have suffered greater distress in the country of their most inveterate enemy.

In addition to the want of supplies, I am deeply concerned to be compelled to lament a similar defect of co-operation on the part of the Spanish generals.

No spirit of union, concord or energy has appeared in those who were ostensibly joined with the allies in a common cause, and in an united system of action.

Important plans, previously concerted with the British general, have been suddenly abandoned in the most critical moments of the campaign.

Without previous notice, and without necessity, positions have been relinquished, which were essential not only to the success of offensive operations, but to the common security of defence, and even to the protection of our sick and wounded.

Further instances of the want of co-operation might be adduced, but I wish merely to point your Excellency's attention to misfortunes of which the detailed enumeration might be painful.

These unhappy circumstances however, as well as the facts which I have stated, require the serious notice of the Spanish Government. The interests of the alliance, justice to Great Britain, the honour and safety of Spain, demand an unreserved manifestation of the truth which cannot be suppressed without positive danger to the great cause in which the allies are engaged. With this view, and with sentiments of most cordial attachment to the reciprocal amity of both nations, I declare on the part of the British Government, that the army under the command of Sir Arthur Wellesley, has neither been supplied by the civil authorities, nor aided by the military power of Spain, in any degree sufficient to enable him to contend with the French force opposed to him in the field, and that these causes alone have compelled Sir Arthur Wellesley to retire within the reach of more adequate assistance, and to resume the defence of Portugal as the sole object of his immediate operations.

The British army entered Spain gratuitously, achieved the most glorious actions during its continuance in the Spanish territory, and has retired under irresistible necessity occasioned by no act of the British Government or of its officers.

The government of Spain will now consider the nature of those sufferings which our army has endured, the causes which have deprived our army of subsistence and of co-operation, and the remedies which may be applied to evils of such extensive and imminent danger. Until these evils shall be effectually remedied to the entire satisfaction of the British Government, and until other necessary arrangements shall be made for the security of the British troops, no British army can attempt to co-operate with the Spanish armies within the territories of Spain.

His Majesty however will continue to entertain the most cordial attachment to the cause of Spain, and to the principles of the alliance, and his Majesty will omit no effort consistent with the means and interests of his own kingdom, to aid the exertions of the Spanish nation by every other mode of assistance.

The commands which I have had the honour to receive from his Majesty, authorize me further to express a most anxious solicitude that the Government of Spain should employ every exertion calculated to cultivate and improve the proper resources of this vast and powerful empire, in every branch of its extensive dominions, to draw forth the intrinsic strength of the country, by a due direction of the loyal energies of the people, and to resort to a provident and wise application of the native wealth and powers of Spain, as the only means of her ultimate deliverance, and the only solid foundation of her future security.

In this unreserved advice, the government of Spain will perceive the most unquestionable proof of his Majesty's sincere anxiety for the independence and stability of the Spanish monarchy, and for the prosperity and honour of Spain; since it is evident, that the independence of a nation must rest on the basis of her own internal force and public spirit, and that no country can attain or preserve happiness or glory by implicit reliance on foreign aid.

For these great objects I should view with the most lively satisfaction, any regular, deliberate, and systematic attention to the increase and management of the military resources of Spain, and to the augmentation, composition, discipline and efficiency of the Spanish armies.

For the same purpose it would also be highly advantageous to revise the whole system of the military department, and especially to establish by law, regulations for securing supplies and means of transport for the armies employed in the defence of Spain.

But the source of every improvement must be the efficiency of the executive power, which can never possess sufficient force or activity without the direct assistance of the collective wisdom of the nation, and without the aid of that spirit which must arise from the immediate support of a people animated by equal sentiments of loyalty and freedom.

I have the honour to be, &c.

WELLESLEY.

No. XXXI.

The Marquess Wellesley to the Right Honourable George Canning.

SIR,　　　　　　　　　　　　　　　Seville, Sept. 15th, 1809.

1. On the 4th of September I had the honour to receive your despatch, No. 22, of the 12th of August,* by the messenger Daniel. Not having at that time received any communication from Sir Arthur Wellesley respecting the arrival of the copies of your despatch at the head quarters of the British army, I forwarded to him on the 4th of September the letter of which a copy is enclosed.

---

* See Appendix.

2. On the 5th of September I received from Sir Arthur Wellesley a letter, dated from Badajoz the 3rd of the same month, in which he notified to me the receipt of a copy of your despatch, No. 22, and added his observations upon its contents.

3. On the 7th of September I received from Sir Arthur Wellesley his answer to my letter of the 4th of the same month, and on the 8th I addressed to Don Martin de Garay the note, of which I have the honour to enclose a copy.

4. The substance of his Majesty's commands, as notified to me in your despatch, No. 22, appears to be contained in the following statement. First. The opinion of Sir Arthur Wellesley is to be taken with regard to the expediency of engaging a British army of 30,000 men in the operations of a campaign in Spain; if his opinion should be adverse to such a plan, the Spanish Government is to be distinctly apprized, that the security of Portugal must form the more particular and exclusive object of our attention in the Peninsula, and that the utmost extent of the aid to be afforded to Spain by a British army, is to be confined to that species of occasional concert, which recently took place between the forces under the commands of Sir Arthur Wellesley and of General Cuesta. Secondly. In the event of a determination to employ a British army of 30,000 men in the operations of a campaign in Spain, effectual measures are to be taken previously to the commencement of joint operations, for securing the means of transport, and of constant and regular supplies to our troops. Thirdly. With a view to secure the effectual co-operation of the Spanish army, and (in a case of extremity) the safe retreat of our troops, the supreme command of the Spanish armies is to be vested in the British Commander-in-Chief, and a British garrison is to be established in Cadiz; if those conditions should be deemed indispensable to the security of our operations in Spain on the scale of an extended campaign.

5. The letters which I have had the honour of addressing to you since my arrival at Seville, and the correspondence which has passed between Sir Arthur Wellesley and me, will have already furnished you with sufficient information respecting our sentiments with relation to the first and second articles of your instructions of the 12th of August.

6. You will observe that on the same day of the date of
your instructions, I addressed to M. de Garay a representation of the defective state of the supplies of the British army
acting in Spain; that in consequence of the encreasing distress of our troops, I was not contented with the mere assurances of the Junta, but required satisfactory arrangements to
be actually made for securing provisions and means of movement to the British army, and that, at length finding no satisfaction either in the promises or acts of the Spanish Government, I concurred with Sir Arthur Wellesley in the necessity
of withdrawing his army to Portugal, and of abstaining from
all engagement to co-operate with the Spanish troops within
the territory of Spain.

7. In addition to the total want of supplies of every description, you will have seen that the condition of the Spanish
armies, the failure of concert and co-operation in the generals
and troops of Spain, and the mismanagement of the whole
system of the military department of this Government, opposed insurmountable obstacles to the ultimate success of the
army under Sir Arthur Wellesley. Even if the system of
supplies could have been corrected, the state of the Spanish
army alone would have formed an irresistible motive in my
mind, for withholding from the Spanish Government any expectation of future co-operation, while the same evils should
be left unremedied, and should menace the recurrence of the
same misfortunes on every similar occasion. Sir Arthur Wellesley appears to agree entirely with me in this branch of my
opinion.

8. While the military resources and power of Spain shall
continue in this state of inefficiency and disorder, it is my
decided opinion that no British army of whatever strength
can safely be employed in joint operations with the Spanish
troops within the territory of Spain.

9. The difficulties and dangers of our army in any such
operation, could not be diminished (although they might be
encreased,) by any practicable augmentation of its numbers.
Within the limitation of numbers stated in your despatch
(whether 30 or 40,000 men), a British army, which should
attempt to act in Spain under the present circumstances of
this country and of the enemy, would be exposed to the utmost hazard of total destruction.

10. Although some expressions in your despatch might favour the supposition, that you did not intend to apply to the case of an occasional concert and limited plan of operations in Spain, the same restrictive rules of precaution which are established with relation to a more extended scale of campaigns, an attentive examination of your instructions convinces me, that it was not your intention to permit any movement of the British army into Spain, until the British civil and military authorities should be fully satisfied on all the important points of supply and co-operation. My sentiments and conduct have been conformable to this interpretation of his Majesty's commands.

11. The principles on which I have acted are not confined in their application merely to the case of a general system of joint operation in Spain, which might lead the British army to a considerable distance from the frontier of Portugal. Any advance into Spain even for limited objects, or for purposes merely defensive, would in my opinion be attended with considerable peril, while our army shall be subject to the failure of provisions, of means of movement, and of all adequate support from any auxiliary force.

12. The recent example of the distress of Sir Arthur Wellesley's army, is a sufficient illustration of the necessity of. applying these precautions to all cases, without any exception. Sir Arthur Wellesley entered Spain with a view of acting upon a limited scale of operations, and not with the intention of engaging in a plan of extended campaign: yet the defect of supplies, and of auxiliary support, frustrated the objects even of that limited plan, and exposed the army to great danger. It is indeed difficult to fix the precise point at which the operations of a British army shall cease, when it shall once have entered the Spanish territory, for the purposes even of occasional concert. An operation, of which the original plan may have been defined within narrow bounds, may be extended by unavoidable necessity, and even by success. Difficulties and dangers may spring from success itself; and the occasional extension of a plan, originally limited, may furnish pretexts of complaint to Spain, if any exigency should require our General to revert to the original limits of such a plan. It must be observed that Sir Arthur Wellesley's difficulties commenced at Placencia, within four

days march from the frontier of Portugal, and within a few days after his arrival at Placencia.

13. These objections would necessarily apply with greater force, in proportion to the encrease of the enemy's strength in Spain; it is improbable that any crisis of affairs can occur, in which the enemy's army in Spain will be much reduced below its actual scale, unless he shall be compelled to evacuate Spain altogether. This event would create an entirely new order of things in Europe, and would lead to a new view of the situation of Spain. But the principles which I have stated are applicable to every probable state of affairs in this country; and I therefore submit to you, without qualification, my opinion, that no British army can safely enter this country for the purpose of acting with the Spanish armies, unless some important change shall take place in Spain.

14. With these sentiments I presented my note to M. de Garay, under date the 8th of September; I take the liberty of soliciting your particular attention to that paper, in which I have plainly declared the causes which occasioned the retreat of the British army in the full lustre of its glory, and have added my opinion; that, "until these evils shall be effectually remedied to the entire satisfaction of the British Government, and until other necessary arrangements shall be made for the security of the British troops, no British army can attempt to co-operate with the Spanish armies within the territories of Spain."

15. By these expressions, it was my intention to leave open to future negotiation, all questions respecting the employment of a British army in Spain, the command of the Spanish troops, and the garrison of Cadiz.

16. It appeared to me to be proper at the same time to renew the general assurances of his Majesty's attachment to the alliance, and of his Majesty's intention to afford to Spain every other species of assistance, (excepting that of a British army in Spain,) which might be consistent with the means and interests of the British Government.

17. You will observe, that Sir Arthur Wellesley is of opinion, that in the event of a British army acting in Spain, especially for the defence of the southern provinces, it would be absolutely necessary that the chief command of the Spanish army should be vested in his Majesty's Commander-in-Chief,

and that a British garrison should be placed in Cadiz. I entirely concur in these sentiments, but under the present circumstances, I have postponed all discussion with regard to the command of the Spanish army and the garrison of Cadiz. First. Because I am convinced that in the present crisis of affairs, any such discussion would occasion great jealousy in the minds of those best affected to the British cause, would strengthen the misrepresentations of the French, and of their partizans in Spain; would impair the general confidence of the Spanish nation in our sincerity and good faith, and would induce the people to believe that our army had retreated for the purpose of enabling me to obtain these objects. Secondly. Because the British Commander-in-Chief could not now accept the command of the Spanish troops; and the immediate appointment of a Spanish Commander-in-Chief might preclude all future possibility of introducing a British officer to that command. Thirdly. Because no modification of the command of the Spanish army in any form, in which it could now be granted, would secure either the co-operation or the efficiency of the Spanish army, or remove any of the causes to which the sufferings of our army can justly be imputed. Fourthly. Because the demand of a British garrison for Cadiz would certainly be now refused, and such a refusal might oppose great obstacles to the success of any proposition of that nature upon any future occasion.

18. In obedience to the general tenor of his Majesty's instructions, upon my arrival at Seville my earliest attention was directed to the propriety of abstaining from all unnecessary interference in the internal concerns and interests of Spain; but I had not been many days at Seville before I learnt that his Majesty's army, which had gloriously conquered in the cause of Spain, had been defrauded of every necessary supply; that his Majesty's brave soldiers, wounded in vindicating the independence and glory of Spain, had been abandoned by the Spanish General to the mercy of the enemy; that the Spanish Generals, instead of co-operation, had displayed a systematic spirit of counteraction, and had disconcerted every plan and operation which they were appointed to support ; and that his Majesty's General, (after having compelled the enemy to retreat from a British force of far inferior numbers,) had been himself compelled to re-

treat from the country which he had saved, lest his troops should perish by famine and disease.

19. With such a scene, unexpectedly presented to my view, my duty towards his Majesty, and my respect for the honour of Spain demanded a particular examination of the causes which had produced events so injurious to the interests of the alliance, and so dangerous to the friendship and welfare of both countries.

20. The causes of these misfortunes cannot be justly ascribed to the absolute want of resources in the country, or to any inherent or incorrigible defects in the materials, of which the body of the army is composed; or to any perverse or intractable disposition and temper in the mass of the people.

21. At the time when the determination to resist the usurpation of France broke forth in several of the provinces of Spain, the country was still labouring under the mischievous consequences of a long course of evil government. In the more recent periods of that destructive system, the particular tendency of the administration had been to subvert the efficiency of the army, and to injure the military resources of Spain.

22. These ruinous purposes had been perpetrated with success to a considerable extent, and when the independence of Spain was first invaded by France, the utmost exertion of public spirit was required to call forth the means even of temporary resistance. But although the military resources of the country had been impaired, they had not been destroyed. Great and successful efforts were made by the several provinces, according to their separate plans of resistance; and nothing more seemed to be requisite for the purpose of a successful defence of the whole country, than to combine in one system the means which were to be found in its separate parts.

23. At present, local difficulties certainly exist in some of the provinces, and many of the districts continue to suffer under the consequences of war, or of former mismanagement. But many provinces abound in the means of subsistence and transport. No system however, has been established, by which the deficiencies of one district can be supplied from the abundance of another, nor does any regulation exist, pro-

perly calculated to secure and collect the resources of any
province for its separate defence, and still less for any more
remote objects of active war.   The civil establishments
throughout the provinces, are not properly formed for the
purpose of ascertaining or bringing into use for the service of
the army, either the productions of the soil, or the articles
of transport and conveyance existing in the several districts.
To this want of due regulation and system must be added,
the corruption and even the positive disaffection of many of
the civil authorities in the provinces; in many instances the
strongest evidence has appeared of positive aversion to the
cause of Spain, and of the allies, and of treacherous inclination to the interests of France.

24. The disposition of the people is generally favourable
to the great cause in which the nation is engaged, and the
mass of the population of Spain, certainly appears to contain
the foundations on which a good and powerful government
might be securely established, and the materials of which an
efficient army might be composed.   Among the higher and
middle classes of society are to be found too many examples
of the success of French intrigue.   In those classes may be
traced a disposition to observe events, and to prepare for
accommodation with that party, which may ultimately prevail
in the existing contest.   Many persons of this description, if
not favoured, are not discountenanced by the Government.
From these circumstances, and from the want of any regular
mode of collecting popular opinion, the public spirit of the
people is not properly cultivated, nor directed to the great
objects of the contest.   The people also are still subject to
many heavy exactions, and the abuses and grievances accumulated by recent maladministration, have not yet been duly
remedied or redressed.

25. The population of the country has not yet afforded to
the army a supply of men in any degree adequate to the
exigencies of the country, or to the original inclination of the
people; yet no demand could be made upon the people for
that purpose, with any prospect of success in the present
state of affairs.   But no encrease of the numbers of the
army could be useful, without a total change of the whole
system of its composition and discipline.   These are at present
defective in every branch, and no measures have been adopted,

or appear to be in contemplation, for remedying the abuses of every description, which prevail throughout the whole structure of the army and every stage of the military department.

26. In this condition of the army, it is not surprising that many officers, even in the highest commands, should be notoriously disaffected to the cause of Spain, and of the allies, and should not be duly controlled by the Government. In reviewing the events of the last campaign, it is impossible to imagine any rational motive for the conduct of some of the Spanish Generals and officers, unless it be admitted, that their inclinations were favourable to the enemy, and that they concerted their operations with the French, instead of the British General.

27. The generous resolution of Spain to assert her independence most justly excited the admiration of the world. In considering more deliberately the nature of her original danger, and of the efforts to meet it, reflections arise, which may illustrate the real nature of her present situation.

28. The usurpation of all the rights of Spain did not proceed merely from the violence or corruption of internal Government; it was not merely an act of that character, which in other countries has justified and required national resistance, and against which, that resistance has frequently and happily prevailed. The usurpation of Spain was a great military operation of the most formidable military power on the continent of Europe; it was a contest between two great states, as well as between a depraved government, and an oppressed people. In order to vindicate her independence, it was therefore necessary, that Spain should not only resort to the general spirit of resistance which animated the great body of the people in the separate provinces, but that she should guide and concentrate that spirit, for the indispensable purpose of invigorating her military resources, and of embodying an army, which with the aid of her allies, might enable her to gain sufficient time for the restoration of her monarchy, on a just and legitimate foundation. To this great object, all her efforts should have tended; and in forming a temporary organ to supply the absence of her legitimate sovereign, and the consequent defect of the executive power, she should have combined such principles of council and

action, as might have given to the temporary Government, the entire force of popular opinion, and public zeal. This support was necessary to give due vigour to the regulations, requisite for raising an efficient army in Spain, and supplies to support not only the army of Spain, but the auxiliary force of the allies.

29. The first election of the Central Junta was certainly an apparent step towards the consolidation of the powers of the country. Previously to that event, no point had been fixed for combining the desultory efforts of the several provinces, separated by antient institutions, habits and prejudices, and united only in a common sentiment of aversion to the French yoke. But the constitution of the Supreme Central Junta is not founded on any well understood system of union among the provinces, and still less on any just or wise distribution of the elements or powers of Government. No confederacy of the provinces yet exists; the executive power is weakened and dispersed in the hands of an assembly, too numerous for unity of council, or promptitude of action, and too contracted for the purpose of representing the body of the Spanish nation. The Supreme Central Junta is neither an adequate representative of the Crown, nor of the aristocracy, nor of the people; nor does it comprise any useful quality, either of an executive council, or of a deliberative assembly, while it combines many defects which tend to disturb both deliberation and action.

30. Whether this Government so ill-formed, be deficient in sincerity to the cause of Spain, and of the allies, is certainly questionable. Whatever jealousy exists against the British Government or the allies, is principally to be found in this body, its officers or adherents; in the people, no such unworthy sentiment can be traced; but omitting all question respecting the disposition of the Junta, it is evident that it does not possess any spirit of energy or activity, any degree of authority or strength; that it is unsupported by popular attachment or good-will; while its strange and anomalous constitution unites the contradictory inconveniences of every known form of Government, without possessing the advantages of any.

31. It is not an instrument of sufficient power to accomplish the purposes for which it was formed; nor can it ever

acquire sufficient force or influence to bring into action the resources of the country, and the spirit of the people, with that degree of vigour and alacrity, which might give effect to foreign alliances, and might repel a powerful foreign invader.

32. This is the true cause, at least of the continuance, of that state of weakness, confusion and disorder, of which the British army has recently experienced the consequences in the internal administration of Spain, and especially of her military affairs.

33. The Junta certainly possesses the means of applying to these evils the only remedy, from which any benefit can be expected to arise, although its operation might perhaps be slow and even precarious.

34. The original powers delegated to the Junta, have not been clearly defined, either with relation to time or authority. Much contest has lately arisen on this important question, and as far as I have been enabled to form a judgment upon it, it appears to me, that the question was not a point of distinct attention in many of the provinces at the time of the election of the Junta; but that, whenever it became matter of notice, the formation of the Junta was considered merely as a preliminary step to the assembly of the Cortes, and to the establishment of a more compact form of executive power in the absence of the legitimate king of Spain. It appears also to have been generally expected, that the earliest proceedings of the Junta would have been directed to the redress of the principal grievances, under which the Spanish nation and the colonies have suffered, especially in recent times.

35. In some moments of urgent peril and alarm, the Junta appears to have been impressed with the same sentiments which certainly prevail throughout the nation; and to have considered the primary articles of their duty, as well as the limitation of their right of government to be, the choice of a regency for the due exercise of the executive power, the convocation of the Cortes, and the early redress of existing grievances. Accordingly, they have announced an intention of assembling the Cortes, and have very lately taken steps towards the repeal of some heavy exactions, and promised the repeal of others; and they have repeatedly discussed the question of appointing a regency; but the desire of protracting the continuance of their own authority to the latest pos-

sible period of time, has prevailed over every other consideration. The meeting of the Cortes is delayed to a distant
period of time.* The question relating to a regency has been
often debated, and as often adjourned. No plan has been
adopted for an effectual redress of grievances, correction of
abuses, or relief of exactions ; and the administration of
justice, the regulation of revenue, finance, and commerce, the
security of person and property, and every other great branch
of government, is as defective as the military department.

36. The admission of the Colonies to a share in the government and representation of the mother country, seems to
have been suggested merely as an expedient to confirm the
Junta in the continuance of their present authority, and to
be entirely unconnected with any enlarged or liberal views of
policy or government.

37. Under all these circumstances, the spirit of the alliance,
and the general tenor of his Majesty's instructions, would
have justified me in offering such advice to the Supreme
Central Junta as might be calculated to represent in true
colours, the nature of those dangers which menaced the ruin
of the common cause, and the necessity of resorting to
effectual remedies without subterfuge or delay.

38. But in the course of the last month, M. de Garay
without any previous suggestion on my part, has repeatedly
and anxiously requested my opinion on the state of the Government, especially with relation to the expediency of
appointing a Regency, and of assembling the Cortes.

39. In all these conferences, I have carefully abstained
from delivering any opinion with respect to the claims of any
particular personages to exercise the authority of regent,
during the absence of the king ; with this sole reserve, I have
not hesitated to deliver my opinion in the most distinct and
unqualified terms to M. de Garay.

40. The sentiments which I have expressed, may be comprised under the following heads : First. That the Supreme
Central Junta should immediately nominate (without limiting
the nomination to the members of its own body,) a Council of

* The Proclamation for the Assembling of the Cortes, and the Royal
decrees connected with the state of Spain, will be found at the end of this
despatch.—[ED.]

Regency, to consist of not more than five persons, for the exercise of the executive power, until the Cortes should be assembled. Secondly. That the Cortes should be assembled with the least possible delay. Thirdly. That the Supreme Central Junta, or such members of it, as shall not be of the Council of Regency, shall constitute a deliberative Council for the purpose of superintending the election of the Cortes ; and of preparing for that body with the assent of the Council of Regency, such business as it may be deemed proper to submit to its early consideration. Fourthly. That the same act of the Junta by which the Regency shall be appointed, and the Cortes called, shall contain the principal articles of redress of grievances, correction of abuses, and relief of exactions in Spain and the Indies, and also the heads of such concessions to the Colonies, as shall fully secure to them a due share in the representative body of the Spanish Empire. Fifthly. That the first act of the Regency should be to issue the necessary orders for correcting the whole system of the military department in Spain.

41. These suggestions, originating in M. de Garay's express solicitation, were never committed to writing, nor urged with any greater degree of earnestness, than belongs to the usual freedom of private conversation.

42. M. de Garay listened to me with attention, and expressed his general approbation of my sentiments, signifying only some doubts, with regard to the mode of redressing grievances, and to the particular points comprehended under that part of my observations.

43. At the time when M. de Garay voluntarily opened this discussion, great alarm and agitation prevailed in the public mind in Spain. These sensations have gradually subsided, and with them M. de Garay's solicitude for the early improvement of the government seems to have been relieved. Nor should I have been disposed to renew the subject in any form, had not the accumulated sufferings of our army, and the aggravated injuries and outrages offered to the British alliance, compelled me to intimate to M. de Garay in an official form, the general tenor of those suggestions which he had drawn from me in our private conferences.

44. In my note of the 8th of September, I have therefore declared in general terms, that the interests of the alliance

require an entire change in the military department of the Spanish Government; that no improvement in the system of military administration can be effected, without a previous correction of the weakness and inefficiency of the executive power; nor without a due cultivation of the native resources, a proper use of the intrinsic strength, and a strenuous exertion of the national spirit of Spain; and lastly, that the executive power can never possess authority or force, influence or activity, until it shall be directly aided and supported by the collective wisdom of the nation, and by the loyal energies of the people.

45. I am still ignorant of the effect, which may be produced by this communication; but, if, instead of resorting to the only means, by which Spain can be saved, or faith maintained with her allies, the Supreme Junta should continue to multiply precautions for prolonging the duration of their own power, in defiance of the interests of the monarchy, and of the intentions and wishes of the people, every mischief, and every abuse, under which the country now labours, must be aggravated, and the cause of the enemy must gain hourly strength.

46. No auxiliary force of the allies can enter Spain under such circumstances, with any prospect of advantage, or with any other result, than the certain failure of every military operation.

47. The insurmountable objections, which preclude the possibility of entrusting Spain under her present government, with the aid of an auxiliary British force, must ultimately apply to every other species of assistance, since it cannot be contended, that such a government as now exists in Spain, can be safely entrusted with the management and disposition of the generous and abundant supplies, poured forth by the British Government and nation for the service of a cause, which the government of Spain is no longer able to maintain.

48. The great objects of the alliance between his Majesty and Spain were, to assist the Spanish nation in restoring the independence of the monarchy, and the happiness, freedom, and honour of Spain; and by this just and generous assistance, to accomplish the great political advantage, of opposing an additional barrier to the ambition and violence of France.

49. The spirit of the alliance would be entirely perverted,

if the liberal assistance bestowed by the British Government
and nation should serve only to prolong in Spain the continuance of an order of things, equally adverse to the restoration of the legitimate monarchy, to the happiness, and
wishes of the Spanish nation, and to the prosperity of the
common cause in which the allies are engaged.

ง 50. These observations are made with great reluctance
and pain, under a most serious conviction of their truth, and
of the severe duty which requires me to express my sentiments without reserve. The duration of the present system
of government in Spain cannot fail to prove highly dangerous
to the genuine principles of her hereditary monarchy, by
gradually. establishing habits, interests, and views, inconsistent with the lawful form and order of the government:
the same system would also endanger all the hopes and expectations of Spain. The hopes and expectations of the
body of the Spanish nation are directed with anxious solicitude to some alteration, which, with more attention to the
welfare and feelings of the people, may combine a more just
representation of the crown, a more uniform and concentrated authority, a more effectual and vigorous system of
military administration, and a more cordial co-operation with
the allies.

51. In addition to the sentiments of Spain, when the real
state of the government of the mother country shall be understood in the colonies, the utmost peril is to be apprehended of a violent convulsion in that most important branch
of the empire. Whatever may be the result of the operations of the allies in other quarters of Europe, the French
interests must continue to advance within the Spanish territory, and the whole policy of our alliance must be frustrated,
while the form, character, and conduct of the government
shall be calculated to pervert to the advantage of France,
every succour, which we may afford to Spain.

52. Many instances might be adduced of the abuse and
waste of the supplies of various descriptions with which the
liberality of the British Government and nation has so largely
furnished the government of Spain.

53. The most destructive waste of these supplies has been
occasioned by the defects of the military department, and by
the want of discipline in the army. In the various instances

which have occurred of confusion, panic, and flight among the Spanish troops when in face of the enemy, it has been the usual practice of the soldiers to throw away the arms and cloathing with which they had been provided by the generosity of Great Britain. These of course have generally fallen into the hands of the enemy. In the battle of Talavera, Sir Arthur Wellesley witnessed the flight of whole corps of Spanish troops, who, after having thrown away the British arms and cloathing, plundered the baggage of the British troops, at that moment bravely engaged with the enemy. These calamities and disgraces all flow from one common source; the state of the government of Spain; and all tend to one common end, the benefit of the cause of France.

54. Although deeply impressed with these sentiments, I shall not fail to employ every effort within my power, to maintain the temper of the alliance, and to cultivate a good intelligence with the ministers of Spain, as far as may be compatible with the interests and honour of his Majesty, and with the safety of his Majesty's troops.

55. No demand of any description has been urged by me since my arrival in Spain. My applications to the government have been nothing more than plain representations of the condition of the country, and of the impossibility of permitting a British army to act in Spain, while that condition shall remain unaltered.

56. I am not without hope, (when the Supreme Central Junta shall be convinced of the firm determination of the British Government to withhold all co-operation of the British troops in Spain, until satisfactory remedies shall have been applied to the evils, of which I have complained,) that motives of self interest may concur with the just principles of an enlarged policy, to produce a favourable change in the councils of the Spanish Government.

57. I shall be anxious to receive the advantage of your instructions with reference to the issue of either alternative of the present doubtful state of affairs.

58. In the most unfavourable event, which can be apprehended, I entertain no doubt, that the temper and disposition of the Spanish nation, and the character of the people will prolong the difficulties, which France has experienced in her attempt to subjugate this country. The greatest

obstacle to the deliverance of Spain, is certainly the state of her own government; but even if the mismanagement of those, now entrusted with the conduct of her affairs, should favour the success of the French arms in Spain; much time must elapse before a French government could be established in this country, and many opportunities must open for the improvement of the British interests, with relation to Spain and to her colonies.

59. For the present, the French armies in Spain are in a state of complete inaction; and it does not appear probable that any blow can now be struck to prevent the Spanish Government from accomplishing all the political and military arrangements, which are required, in order to prepare this nation for a more effectual defence of her independence.

I have the honour to be, &c.

WELLESLEY.

[1st Enclosure.]

Translation of a Proclamation for Assembling the Cortes.

THE SUPREME GOVERNING JUNTA TO THE SPANISH NATION.

It is three ages, Spaniards, since the salutary laws on which the nation founded its defence against the efforts of tyranny have been destroyed. Our fathers did not know how to preserve the previous deposit of liberty which had been bequeathed to them; and although all the provinces of Spain successively struggled to defend it, our evil stars, which now began to pursue us, have rendered useless those generous efforts. After having silenced reason and justice the laws from that time forward have been nothing else than an expression more or less tyrannical, or more or less beneficent, of a particular will. Providence, as if to punish the loss of that beautiful prerogative of free men, has sentenced us to be unhappy and paralysed our valour, arrested the progress of our understanding, protracted our civilization, and, after having blinded and exhausted the fountains of prosperity, we have come to that condition that an insolent tyrant has formed a project of subduing under his yoke the greatest nation of the globe, without reckoning upon its will, and despising its existence. In vain have there been some few instances within these three last ages of disasters in which the best directed will of the Princes has attempted to remedy this or the other plagues of the state. In vain the increased illustration of Europe has lately inspired our statesmen with projects of reform both useful and necessary. Buildings cannot be erected on sands; and without fundamental and constituted laws to defend the good already done, and to prevent the evil intended to be done, it is useless for the philosopher in his study, and the public man in the theatre of business to exert himself for the good of the people. The most useful meditations, the best combined projects, are either not put into execution, or if they should be they immediately fall to the ground. To the moment of a happy inspiration succeeds another of an unfortunate one ; to the spirit of economy and order, a spirit of prodigality and rapine ; to a prudent and mild minister, an avaricious and mad favourite ; to the moderation of a pacific monarch, the rage of an inhuman conqueror ; and thus without principles, without an established and fixed principle to which public measures and dispositions can be affixed, the ship of the state floats without her sails, without a helm or direction, until, as has happened to the Spanish Monarchy, it is dashed to pieces on a rock by the hurricane of tyranny.

The evils which are derived from so vicious a beginning cannot be calculated when they are accumulated in such a manner that nothing less than a revolution can destroy them. The Junta itself, in the midst of the power which you have placed in its hands, a power which makes them tremble on account of its unlimited extension, frequently meets, in those ancient vices, insuperable difficulties in the execution of its wishes. If the disorders in the Government for these last twenty years had been less, be assured, Spaniards, that your evils at this moment would not be so great, that our enemies would not enjoy the advantages they have obtained, not over the zeal and prudence of your Government, not over the valour and constancy which every moment are greater in you, but over the ruinous and miserable state to which the many years of arbitrary Government which have been passing over us, have brought us. Thus it is, that when the Supreme Junta took upon itself the supreme authority, it did not deem itself less called upon to defend you from the enemy, than to procure and establish your interior felicity on a solid basis. It announced this solemnly to you from the beginning ; and as solemnly obliged itself in the face of the world to the performance of this sacred duty.

The events of the War prevented at that time the commencing the grand work to which it is now going to put its hand ; and the unexpected commotions which have succeeded one after another, seemed to require the suspension of any other object, and to wait for more serene and tranquil times. But the Junta never lost sight of this grand thought ; the same chain of evils with which fortune, when roused, delights in proving our constancy, is that which precipitated its execution. How otherwise can be recompensed those floods of blood which flow through every corner of the peninsula ? Those sacrifices which at every instant the Spanish Loyalty presents without being ever fatigued by them ; that moral resistance, as universal as it is sublime, which disconcerts and renders desperate our enemies even in the midst of their victories ? He must have a breast of brass who to a people that so magnanimously resists so cruel an enemy should not point out to them immediately a crown of happiness which awaits them as a recompense for their heroic fatigues. When this dreadful contest is concluded, no less glorious for our people, when persecuted by misfortune than when crowned by victory, the Spaniard shall say to himself, with that full pride which his situation ought to inspire, " My fathers left me for inheritance slavery and misery ; I leave to my descendants liberty and glory !" This sentiment of future happiness, which by reflection in some, and by instinct in all, animates you at present, Spaniards, is the same which has made you abhor the former tyranny, which has reduced you to the despicable state in which you see yourselves ; the same which filled you with enthusiasm and with hope when you should be able to destroy it, and raise to the throne that innocent Prince who most sincerely wished to see you happy; the same which gave you valour and boldness to declare war against the most powerful nation, without armies and without resources ; the same, in a word, which inspired you with invincible horror against that tyrant who has heaped upon you all the plagues of misfortune : know then that this institution of happiness shall not be defrauded in its hopes. Let us take from our detractors every pretext for calumniating us ; they say that we are fighting incessantly to defend our ancient abuses, and the inveterate and enormous vices of our corrupted Administration ; but let them know from this moment that your battles, although for independence, are also for the felicity of your country ; let them know that you do not wish to depend henceforward on the uncertain will, or the variable temperament of one man only ; that you do not wish to continue to be the plaything of a Court without justice, under the control of an insolent favourite, or of a capricious woman ; and that on the renewal of the august edifice of your ancient laws you wish to place an eternal barrier between death-bearing despotism and your sacred rights. This barrier, Spaniards, consists in a good Constitution ; to aid and support the operations of the Monarch when they are just ; and to restrain them when he follows evil councils. Without a Constitution all reform is precarious : all prosperity uncertain ; without it all the people are no more than flocks of slaves, put in motion at the order of a will, frequently unjust, and always unrestrained ; without it the forces of the entire society, intended to procure the greatest advantages for all its members, are employed exclusively to satisfy the ambition, or satiate the phrensy of a few, and perhaps of only one.

It is absolutely necessary that you should have a Constitution, by which all the branches which are to contribute to your prosperity shall be solidly secured ; from whence the basis and principles of a social organization, worthy of men like you, may be derived. This Constitution, Spaniards, ought to be the principal object of your toils ; a comfort for the desolation you have suffered ; the reward of your valour, and the hopes of your victories.

It certainly will not present the infamous characters which are contained in the infamous code published by Napoleon at Bayonne, and framed long before in the deposit of his intrigues. With it they wanted to legitimate the most monstrous usurpations known in the annals of the world. With ours it is intended to secure the public prosperity of the state, and the particular one of the citizens performing bonâ fide what all the nation wishes. In that there was not time to deliberate, nor liberty to resist, nor powers to establish. In ours the actual representatives of the nation will excite wise men to expose freely what they think ; they will call them to examine and discuss the same political truths, and the best form of its application ; and the work of their knowledge, their zeal, and their experience, shall be presented for the free sanction of the nation solemnly assembled in Cortes. The insidious forms of the Constitution of Bayonne are not sufficient to disguise the legalised despotism that appears in every part of it. In the Spanish Constitution the public will, lawfully and sufficiently expressed, shall be the law; Government limiting its functions within the terms which nature has pointed out in the political order; the consequences of the one worthy in every respect of the fountain of iniquity from whence they spring, have been the plunder, the perdition, the ruin, and the deplorable desolation of the man and of the people for whose felicity it was said to be intended; the other founded on the basis of virtue, and purchased at the expence of the most glorious efforts of patriotism, will have for its undeniable results the liberty and lasting happiness of the Spanish nation. The Supreme Junta has taken the rudder of the monarchy in the midst of the storm, and will only keep it whilst danger and uncertainty exist, contributing by these direct and principal ways to cast this grand anchor, which so materially contributes to save the country from danger, in doing which it believes that it fills one of its most religious obligations.

This should not be less glorious in the eyes of the nation, and of its political interest, than the extirpation of its enemies, and the triumph of the Spanish arms; and when the day comes that it shall lay down the authority now invested in them, into the hands of that Government which the Constitution shall appoint, it will be for them the most illustrious day of their political existence. Then they will think themselves rewarded for their watchfulness, their cares, and the dangers to which they are subject, by exercising a power to which they were not elevated by ambition, nor called by intrigue, but by the unanimous and determined vote of the provinces of the kingdom, that have sworn to be independent of all foreign dominion, and within themselves free and happy. Such have been the considerations which the Junta had in view in agreeing to the following Decree :

ROYAL DECREE.

The Supreme Governing Power of the Kingdom, considering it to be its primary obligation to free the country from the evils which have until now afflicted it, all which have been occasioned by the arbitrary laws to which it has been subject, pursuing the just and mild intentions of our very beloved King Ferdinand VII. who was desirous to re-constitute the Monarchy, re-establishing in it the national representation of its ancient Cortes, desirous that the nation should take before the eyes of Europe and the Universe, the noble and vigorous acts of a people worthily and legally constituted, desirous that this great work should be performed which the circumstances command, and the heroic sacrifices of the people require, anxious that it should approach to that degree of perfection which men are allowed to obtain when they proceed with good faith and with desire of doing right, has decreed as follows :

1. All wise Spaniards who have meditated on projects of Reform, with respect to the Constitution of the kingdom in general, as well as on the

particular branches of public administration, are invited by the Junta to communicate their ideas with full liberty, and as they may judge may answer best for the good of their country :

2. These writings shall be sent to the Junta through the Secretary's office, within the term of two months from the date of this Decree, and the authors will subscribe their name, or a mark, by which they shall be known in proper time :

3. These writings, after being examined in a summary way, the writers of those, which are found to be really useful by the observations, or by the knowledge they contain, shall be called in order to take part in the Commissions of Reform which shall be immediately created :

4. These commissions shall be presided each by a member of the Junta, and in them will be examined and prepared the works which are to be presented for approbation :

5. The projects approved of by the Junta shall be presented for the national sanction, and from it will receive the character, the authority, and the force of law :

6. The Junta does not anticipate its judgment, nor prepossess the public opinion with respect to these projects, it only believes that it ought to announce from this moment certain principles upon which the wish and desire of the nation has irrevocably resolved, and which nothing that can be written or discussed on the subject of Reform can alter. These principles are reduced to the following :

The Catholic Apostolic Roman Religion, as the only religion of the *State* :

The Constitution of Spain is to be a monarchy hereditary in Ferdinand VII. his descendants, and those called by the law to succeed them :

The nation is to be governed henceforward by the laws freely deliberated and administered :

There shall be a national Cortes in the manner and form which may be established, taking into consideration the difference and alterations which have taken place since the time when they were lawfully held :

Our Americas and other colonies shall be the same as the metropolis in all rights and constitutional prerogatives :

The reform which our legal codes, administration, and recovery of public rents, and every thing belonging to the direction of commerce, agriculture, arts, education, as well as   are to undergo, shall be only and exclusively directed to obtain the greatest ease, and the better illustration of the Spanish people so horridly vexed until now :

7. The general Cortes of the Supreme Monarchy (which has so long been neglected) shall meet together for the first time on that day when the nation shall be legally and solemnly constituted.

[2nd Enclosure.]

Translation of the Proclamation from the Supreme Junta to the Inhabitants of Seville, dated April 9th, 1809.

The Junta of the Government of the Kingdom to the People of Seville.

SEVILLIANS,

The unfortunate events of our arms in La Mancha and Estramadura, by rendering the invasion of Andalusia less difficult, have diminished in your mind the sentiment of security and confidence. The base are already confounded; the cowards appalled; and the profligate, paid by the tyrant, prepare the dagger which they wear to plunge into the heart of the country. A thousand disastrous reports and exaggerated news have been spread, artfully accompanied by specious representations subversive of order, and by suspicions which are as odious as they are contradictory, &c.

But of what do these obscure agitators accuse us, or what do they aim at? Paid undoubtedly by the French, they have no other object than to pervert your opinion, and to precipitate you, Sevillians, into the confusion of anarchy. Do they perhaps impute to us the reverses which we have suffered and the danger of invasion? But have the gusts of storms which make ships founder ever been laid to the charge of the pilot? It would be better to aid him in his anxiety and diligence than to interrupt him with seditious rumours and agitations.

Sevillians, if any one of you has to give an advice that may save the country, reveal it without disguise to Government, which will be the first to put it into execution and to thank you for so great a service. If any one has to complain of, or does not trust to any public officer, let him lay before the Tribunal of Safety his charges, provided they be real, and the offender shall certainly be punished. But no one has hitherto pursued this course, either from a want of ground for accusation, or from want of courage; hence all the processes instituted by this Tribunal have been carried on ex-officio, no particular citizen having lodged any complaint. This was however, the way of usefully evincing the zeal which animates you; but not that to render yourselves the blind and servile instruments of French espionnage, or of the senseless and criminal machinations of some ambitious person.

However, be the origin what it may, the consequences are equally pernicious; and the national Majesty, no less than the security of the state, suffer in a melancholy manner from these scandalous rumours. If therefore any person trusting to the character of mildness and moderation, which have been the basis of the Junta of the realm in the interior administration, means to abuse these virtues for the purpose of destroying the monarchy, such person shall from this moment be considered as a traitor to king and country, as well as guilty of high treason against the nation, and shall be tried as such. His head shall pay for his madness; for the Supreme Junta is far from fearing the outrage and contempt which it is endeavoured to produce by such attempts, it knows that the good and loyal citizens of Seville, the true friends of the salvation of the country and the other provinces, if outraged and despised in their deputies, will either defend or avenge the present Government, which is not the work of one city or one province alone, but of the whole nation.   To dissolve the unity of the state at present residing in the Junta; separate the provinces from each other; deprive us of the aid and relations of our colonies; divest Spain of the consideration of a power; and finally destroy the Spanish empire in order to surrender it to the tyrant, these are the objects aimed at by the infamous persons that corrupt you.   Consider, Sevillians, if there be any crime equal to this !

THE MARQUIS DE ASTORGA, Vice-President.
MARTIN DE GARAY, Secretary-General.

[3rd Enclosure.]

Edict of the Tribunal of Public Security at Seville, April 15th 1809.

In the name of the King our Lord Don Ferdinand VII., and of the Supreme Central Junta of the Government; the Tribunal of the Public Security, &c.

SPANIARDS.—The enemy of the human race, Napoleon Bonaparte, has already found that he cannot conquer Spain by the force of his arms, and he observes with grief and shame that his numerous armies and most valiant soldiers find their graves in our Peninsula; he therefore has recourse to seduction and intrigue in order to attain by these means his wicked ends; he attempts by money, and promises which he will never accomplish, to sow among us division and discord; and he employs for this purpose infamous emissaries, who mislead the minds, deaden the public spirit, and excite distrust of the Supreme and Central Junta, which is the mark of all his arrows, because he cannot corrupt it.   There is no way, however detestable and base, which he does not try for this purpose; and his present object is to disturb the public tranquillity by means of his Agents, who are to place themselves immediately at the head of the partisans whom he unfortunately possesses, and deliver us into his hands to be instantly torn to pieces, and to experience in ourselves, our families and property, the horrors which the band of robbers and assassins, of whom his army is composed, usually exercises.

The Tribunal of Public Safety labours incessantly to discover, chastise, and exterminate, this unworthy race of spies, traitors, and bad Spaniards, who endeavour to mislead and ruin us.   It spares no one; and the inexorable sword of justice is levelled alike against the powerful and the weak.   Some criminals, convicted of this horrible crime, have already paid for their treason with their blood; others of less criminality have been sentenced to the fortress, and confined according to the degree of guilt and conviction likely to result from the suits still pending, among whom there are some public officers.   In the prisons there are likewise several criminals whose processes are carrying on with every despatch, and from the activity with which this important object is pursued, the wicked and the friends of Napoleon will pay on the scaffold, and by other disgraceful punishments, for their abominable conduct.   The most pernicious of all are those, who to divide us, propagate specious falsehoods against the present Government; for this is the safest path chosen by the tyrant, that after destroying the national representation, disuniting the Provinces, and obstructing the relations with America and the foreign Courts, anarchy may be introduced, he become master of our Peninsula, and we all be lost. To remedy this misfortune, which doubtless is the greatest that a Spaniard can suffer, the Tribunal has decreed what is contained in the following articles :

1. Whoever endeavours to raise distrust of the Supreme and Central Junta, and tries to overturn the present Government by popular commotions, or other means that have been reprobated, declares himself guilty of High Treason, undeserving the name of Spaniard, and sold to the tyrant Napoleon.

2. As such he shall infallibly suffer punishment of death, and his estates shall be confiscated.

3. Any person who propagates rumours tending to weaken and soften the hatred which we ought to keep alive against the French armies, composed of infamous assassins and robbers, who only come to pillage and sacrifice us, shall instantly be arrested, tried, and without any remission subjected to the punishment pronounced against him.

4. The name of any person denouncing to the tribunal of public safety crimes of this description shall be kept secret, and he shall be remunerated in proportion, provided they prove well founded.

5. The present manifest is to be fixed up in the usual places of this city, and inserted in the newspapers.

Given in Seville, April 15th, 1809.

D. RAMON NAVARRO,
D. RAMON CALVO,
D. JUAN FERNANDO DE AGUIRRE,
DON JOSEF MORALES GALLEGOS.
By order of the Tribunal,
D. MANUEL JOSEF DE SOUSA RAMIREZ.

[4th Enclosure.]

Don Martin de Garay to B. Frere, Esq.

Seville, May 23d, 1809.

The most Serene the President of the Supreme Junta of the Government has addressed to me the following Royal Decree :

" The Spanish people must come out of this sanguinary contest with the certainty of leaving to their posterity an inheritance of prosperity and glory worthy of their prodigious efforts and of the blood they spill. The Supreme Junta has never lost sight of this object, which in the midst of the continual agitation caused by the events of the war has always been its principal desire. The advantages of the enemy, attributable less to his valour than the superiority of his numbers, called for the exclusive attention of Government; but at the same time they rendered more bitter and affecting the reflection, that the disasters which the nation suffers are solely owing to the circumstance, that those salutary institutions, which in happier times afforded to the state prosperity and force, have fallen into oblivion.

" The usurping ambition of some, and the indolent abandonment of others, reduced these institutions to nothing; and the Junta, from the moment of its installation, solemnly bound itself to restore them. The time is now arrived for taking in hand this great work, and considering the reforms to be made in our administration, which reforms are to be grounded on the fundamental laws of the monarchy that alone are able to consolidate them, while, in order to ensure success the Junta, as has already been announced to the public, are ready to listen to those wise men who wish to impart to it their opinions.

" The Junta, therefore, being desirous that the Spanish nation should appear in the eyes of the world with the dignity due to its heroic efforts, and resolved that the rights and prerogatives of the citizens should be placed beyond the reach of any fresh encroachments, as well as that the sources of public felicity after removing the obstructions which have hitherto impeded them, should run freely the moment the war ceases, and should repair whatever either inveterate arbitrary power has scorched, or the present devastation has destroyed—has decreed as follows :

1. " That the legal and known representation of the monarchy shall be re-established in its ancient Cortes, by convoking the primary ones in the course of the next year or sooner, if circumstances permit it :

2. " That the Junta do immediately proceed to consider about the method, number and class to be attended to under existing circumstances, in convening the deputies to that august assembly; for which end it is to nominate a committee of five of its members, who with all the attention and diligence required by this great matter, shall discuss and prepare every subject and plan, which, after being examined and approved by the Junta, are to be proceeded upon in convoking and forming the primary Cortes :

3. " That independent of this point, which from its urgency was first to be settled, the Junta is to direct its investigations to the following objects, in order to propose them successively to the nation assembled in Cortes :

" Means and ways to support the holy war in which the nation is engaged, with the greatest justice, until it attain the glorious end which it has proposed to itself :

" Means of ensuring the observance of the fundamental laws of the kingdom :

" Means to ameliorate our legislation, abolish the abuses which have crept into it, and facilitate its perfection :

" Collection, administration and distribution of the State revenue :

" Necessary reforms in the system of instruction and public education :

" Method of regulating and keeping up a permanent army in time of peace and war, conformably to the obligations and revenues of the State :

" Method of supporting a navy proportionate to the same :

" The part which Spanish America is to have in the Juntas of the Cortes :

4. " In order to combine the information necessary for such important discussions the Junta is to consult the Councils, the Superior Juntas of the Provinces, the Tribunes, Magistracies, Corporations, Bishops and Universities, and to ask the opinion of intelligent and enlightened persons :

5. " That this Decree be printed, published, and circulated with the accustomed formalities, so that it may become known to the whole nation :"

" You are to take notice of this, and make the needful provisions for its being fulfilled.

The MARQUIS DE ASTORGA."

" Royal Palace of Villa,
   May 22, 1809."
To Don Martin de Garay.

Which Royal Decree I communicate to you, that after circulating and publishing it, the Royal intentions of his Majesty may be fulfilled.   God preserve you many years.

MARTIN DE GARAY.

Royal Palace of Seville,
   May 23, 1809.

No. XLII.

Don Martin de Garay to the Marquess Wellesley.

MY LORD,   Seville, October 3rd, 1809.

I have given an account to the Supreme Central Junta of Government in the Kingdom of the note which your Excellency was pleased to address to me under date the 8th of September last,* in which your Excellency having detailed various reflections and complaints respecting the deficiency of means of subsistence and of transport in the British army, as well as of military co-operation on the part of the Spanish Generals, declares in the name of the British Government that the army commanded by Sir Arthur Wellesley has neither been succoured by the civil authorities, nor aided by the military power of Spain, in any degree sufficient to place it in a condition to fight the French forces which have been opposed to it in the field, and that these motives alone have compelled Sir Arthur Wellesley to retire within the reach of more adequate assistance, and to resume the defence of Portugal, as the only object of his immediate operations ; and his Majesty being informed very much in detail of all which your

---

* See p. 113.

Excellency has been pleased to express on each of the points of which you treat, instructs us to reply to your Excellency, that from the very moment at which the approach to Spain of the English auxiliary army, commanded by General Sir Arthur Wellesley, was made known to the Department of Finance, it has not ceased to give and repeat the most conclusive and urgent instructions, in order that it might suffer no want in the towns which it passed, or where it was cantoned; the constituted authorities being charged to treat it every where in the manner which so worthy and generous an ally merits. To this effect the inhabitants of Estremadura and the Superior Junta of Badajoz were forewarned on the 10th of last June to make the most abundant supplies of all the articles necessary for the subsistence of those troops, and to stimulate the patriotism of the justices, corporations, and individuals of that province, in order that they might contribute to a service so important and indispensable.

The Intendant of the army of Old Castile received the same commission at the proper period with regard to the towns of his district, as did the Junta of Placencia, and other persons of character and reputation, notice being given to all these that they were to correspond with Don Juan Lozano Torres, Minister of the Royal Finance, who was appointed to the said army, and to whom the necessary instructions were given; he was likewise instructed to go and meet it on the frontiers of Spain, as he did, with the proper Commissaries of War, and other persons from the Offices of Accompts, who were to be employed in furnishing the said army with every thing it required. The ministers did not forget to renew this commission incessantly to the Office of General Direction of Royal Provisions before and after the junction of that army with our own; and on the 28th of last June Don Alexandro Garcia Gomez, with others, was commissioned for the purchase of sheep and horned cattle, being furnished with the requisite funds for that and for the supply of wheat, flour, barley, and other articles. Besides these precautions, provisions more than sufficient were collected at all points to subsist that army for the short period during which it could, in the opinion of Government, remain in the desolated and unhealthy towns of Estremadura; since it was supposed that in union with our own it would attack and overthrow the enemy, as happened in the fields of Talavera, by advancing immediately into the lands of Toledo and the country of the Castiles, where, at the distance of four leagues from their position, they would meet with universal abundance, and the towns prepared to satisfy all the wants of the combined armies.

The event has not been so flattering as we might have hoped; the English army retired, recrossed the Tagus, and placed itself in a country where it was least to be expected, according to the plan of the campaign. From the moment at which this retreat was undertaken, General Sir Arthur Wellesley began to require that his army should be provided with all that was necessary, threatening if it were not so to quit entirely the Spanish territory. We endeavoured to tranquillize him on this point by the prompt remittance of various articles, and by the assurance of continuing such remittances. Besides these precautions, a troop of biscuit-makers was sent to place themselves in the neighbourhood of that army and to work in the fabric of that article for the consumption of those troops without prejudice to the establishment of a magazine which had been previously granted of 300 to 400,000 pounds of the same article, which that General had required, and which was to be placed in that situation. A certain number of quintals of salt meat was likewise transmitted to them, which would have been continued to the amount of 1,006 quintals, that quantity having been collected here; 12,000 sheets were likewise sent, and the 1,500 mattresses of wool which had been ordered to be made in the general deposit of clothing, of which part was destined to the use of those troops. Repeated remittances of rice, salt fish, cheese, flour, barley, sheep, and biscuit, were made by the Office of the General Direction of Provisions, and by the Minister of Royal Finance, with the said army, according to the statements which I have the honour to enclose to your Excellency, and which demonstrate the abundance which ought to exist in that army if order were observed in the use and distribution of those articles.

The Department has not been less active in providing mules of burden and carts for the use of the same army. Since the 3rd of last June, long before its entry into Spain, the Superior Junta of Badajoz and the Intendant of the Pro-

vince were instructed to collect the largest possible number
of both.   The Intendant of the army of Old Castile received
the same commission.   Recently after treating with persons
of practice and intelligence on this subject, the commander
of the guards on smuggling in this province, Don Juan
Miguel de Igea, and Don José Antonio Cevallos, were commissioned to procure and remit to that army from all sides
the largest possible number of mules of burden; the proper
commission for carts were given to Don José Fortun; the
Justices being ordered to furnish them with every assistance
whenever the owners of those articles should resist any equi-
table demand, or should decline their aid to a service so important in the critical circumstances of the day.   The result
of these arrangements has been the remittance of two brigades, consisting each of 40 mules of burden, 22 horses of
the same description collected here, 700 mules from Castile
with those which have been transmitted by Igea and Cevallos,
and of which the number is unknown, together with ten brigades of ten each, without taking into account several others.
Your Excellency may be assured that these succours considerably exceed the demands which have been made, and it
cannot be doubted that the supply of provisions has been
continued subsequently to the dates of the said statements.

The Spanish Government proves, by these facts, their vigilance in the fulfilment of the duties which fall to their lot.
Perhaps a deficiency may have been remarked in some one
article, but the blame can never be imputed to them, for they
never could have been expected to collect provisions in a spot
through which the English army should have only passed.
Even after the unexpected determination of Sir Arthur Wellesley to retire from Spain, offers were made to him by the
Commissioners of subsistence in his army, and by persons of
the highest character, to provide him with all that was necessary in the short space of some days, and in fifteen to establish magazines of store for two months.   If this plan was not
accomplished, the reason is, without doubt, the following:—
that Sir Arthur Wellesley, having resolved to retire from
Spain, and such being the deliberate will of your Excellency,
you will perceive in your discretion that it was, as I had the
honour to inform you, an expense which might be spared,
while the nation was compelled to attend with few resources
so many quarters.   Your Excellency will believe that any

hope which would have ensured to the Government a prompt co-operation on the part of the English army, would have inspired the whole impulse of activity which was required for affording assistance to it, and the same would happen at the present time, at the cost of the greatest sacrifices, if we were but assured that those sacrifices would not be fruitless.

With respect to the want of military co-operation on the part of our Generals, of which your Excellency complains, it appears from the War Department, that as soon as it knew the approach of a British army, in aid of our cause, the necessary orders were given to the Captains-General to make all the preparations adapted to the best treatment and convenience of the troops; and the General Don Gregorio de la Cuesta gave information on the 10th of last July, that he had the honour to receive Sir Arthur Wellesley that evening, with whom he was in very good understanding, having agreed with him on the plan of operations, and having informed him that he only waited the ultimate re-union of the troops, and the removal of some difficulties respecting the means of transport, in order to commence those operations, although, in consequence of the movements which the enemy had recently made, he was preparing his army for the passage of the Tietar, to menace his rear and flank.

The good understanding between the two Generals continued, as may be seen in the official note of the 15th from Cuesta, in which he said, that he had agreed with Sir Arthur Wellesley on the movement of the combined armies; the Spanish army to fall on Talavera, while the English army moved at the same time on the left flank, on the road of Escalona. In order that all the armies might make a combined movement, Cuesta was informed, on the 18th, of the instructions which were sent to the Marquis de la Romana, as soon as it was known that Galicia and the Asturias had been evacuated by the enemy. He was likewise informed of the wishes which General Beresford expressed, and the observations he had made respecting the position he should take, in order that he might acquaint General Wellesley with the whole, on the supposition that Beresford would act under the command of that General, with whom Cuesta was to operate in agreement, as he understood that his Majesty desired the preservation of all possible harmony, and that he should pay respect to General Wellesley's opinions. Such have always been the instructions which were sent to that General; and although, on his part, nothing had been left undone for the convenience of the English troops, he gave notice on the 17th, that General Wellesley complained of the want of the means of transport, and that he said, that it was impossible for him to remain in such a condition. As, notwithstanding the best arrangements, it was not easy to provide on the spot for all the wants of an army, which, it was calculated, would bring with it the necessary means of its movement, suitable precautions were taken at this place to provide for its exigencies; and, in effect, an answer was returned to Cuesta, that four troops of cavalry were on the point of departing for Santa Olalla, which, by different routes, and with pressing orders for the Justices, would provide the mules of burden which they could procure, each town being obliged to give up two parts of the three it possessed, with severe penalties for those which resisted or refused; and, in order that they might have no exculpation, the Commander of the troops would carry money to pay for the animals. As it was well known that towns which had been for the most part occupied by the enemy, and had by that means been ruined, could not afford the requisite number of mules, the Intendant of that province was ordered to send to the army the third part of the mules of burden which existed in its towns, the Junta of Badajoz to make every exertion to provide them, and the Commissaries were charged to purchase barley. They sent 500 fanegas for the moment, and proceeded in the plan of sending all the supplies they could meet with. A receipt for the number of mules received, which was given by the English Commissary-General in Talavera, proves sufficiently that these arrangements were not useless.

General Cuesta was also informed, that these arrangements were not to stand in the way of those which he might be able to make of his own accord, with the use of force, in case it was necessary. With the intent of proving to General Wellesley the true desire of the Spanish Government for the assistance of his army, Cuesta was informed to instruct him of the said arrangements, and of the persuasion of his Majesty, that there could be no other motive for the resistance of the towns, of which he complained, but the incapacity in which they had been left by the ravages of the enemy, and

the casual occurrence of harvest-time. His Majesty was in
some degree tranquillized by information from Cuesta, that,
on the 18th, the armies were in motion, and, on the 22d,
that they were in the neighbourhood of the enemy, who had
fortified himself at the bridge of the Alberché. Neither
these, nor other previous circumstances were, unfortunately,
sufficient to tranquillize the mind of his Majesty, since, on
the 27th, a note was presented which your Excellency transmitted from General Wellesley, dated from Talavera, declaring the want of provisions and of the means of transport
which was suffered by the army under his command; while
the Spanish army lived in abundance, and even the French
prisoners and their horses. This note was sent to General
Cuesta, with orders not to omit any precaution which could
conduce to the prompt succour of those troops; and that he
should give information of the cause of the deficiency, after
the very active measures which had been taken. Cuesta
replied to this order on the 1st of August, saying, that he
thought the note, at least, very much exaggerated with
respect to the abundance in which the Spanish army lived,
with its French prisoners and their horses. That the Spanish
army patiently endured the scarcity occasioned by the want
of money and the rapidity of the marches, and that there
neither was, nor had been, any one French prisoner who
possessed a horse; that the Spanish cavalry had consumed
barley, when it could be procured, and that herbage had
been its general nourishment; that there had been several
days on which it had been scarcely possible to give out to
the troops a ration of a quarter of a pound of bread, and
that such a life is far from a life of abundance; that the
English army never had suffered such scarcity, and that he
individually had received no information of its wants, as there
was a Spanish Commissary for that army, absolute in his
powers, and that he collected provisions by means of his own
Commissaries; that for this reason he had sent for the Intendant Commissary, in order to take information on this
branch, and to assist him in all the arrangements which depended on himself; and he found, that he had never been
able to know the number of rations which the English army
required, nor that which it consumed, while he assured
Cuesta, that it was at least double of that which was wanted.
That he could not obtain receipts for the towns, or the Com-

missary, of the articles furnished. That, having offered to pay all, as they received it, they had not done so up to that period, nor had chosen to accept contracts for flesh, of which offers had been made to them; that in such circumstances, and having perceived the disorder and insubordination which prevailed, he had called together the said Intendant Commissary, with the Intendant and Purveyor of the Spanish army, in order to consult with them on the most expedient manner of checking those faults and deficiencies; and they agreed that the towns on the left should be destined for the English army, and those to the right for the Spanish, by means of Spanish Commissaries from both Intendants; that the necessary escorts should be given for the security of the provisions, and that, with those that could be procured, the English troops should be attended to, in preference, although they might not come from their district, and that he would endeavour to come to an agreement with General Wellesley, that, on his part, order in the accounts and all possible economy might be introduced.

After the glorious battle of Talavera, in which our allies gave such signal proofs of valour and interest in the just cause which we defend, General Cuesta sent advices, dated the 29th of July, that the enemy had left two corps of considerable numbers in sight, that he had advanced his vanguard to observe them, and that in the meanwhile his army rested in columns while some provisions were procured, and the English, employed in relieving the wounded, were placing themselves in a condition to follow them; that he had given orders to the towns of the district to furnish them with all the provisions they could collect.

His Majesty, unwilling to rely on these arrangements alone for the supply of provisions and means of transport for the armies, thought fit to nominate Señor Calvo, a member of the Supreme Junta, who with the full powers that were given to him was enabled to arrange all necessary points for the best provisionment of the same. His nomination was made known to General Cuesta on the 1st of August, together with the royal order of the same date, which was sent to the justices of the places on the route from this capital to Talavera, Badajoz, and Placencia, to send without any excuse all the provisions they possessed by post, and with an understanding that commissioners were to be named to seize those which were kept back.

When intelligence was received that Marshal Soult was marching to the Puerto de Baños, General Wellesley applied to Cuesta to reinforce that point, and although in his opinion with small advantage, he said that he had despatched the fifth division with 300 horse, in order to impede the passage of Soult, if it arrived in time; notwithstanding his expectation that General Beresford, with 15,000 men, would harass and intercept him; or that, at all events, that General would retard the march of Soult. Nothing of this kind happened; for, General Beresford not having appeared, and the Spanish troops which covered the Puerto de Baños, finding themselves alone, were compelled to retire towards the Tietar, and the enemy arrived at Placencia. On this account, Cuesta agreed with Sir Arthur Wellesley that the English army should march against Soult, and the Spanish remain in Talavera. General Wellesley marched; but Cuesta knowing afterwards, by intercepted letters, that Soult was ordered to reach Placencia, and there to direct his attack against the English, and this being confirmed by a movement of Victor, it was his natural opinion, on a consideration of data so solid, that the English not being alone sufficient to oppose 25 or 30,000 men, which according to the very intercepted letters he must suppose Soult to have, it was his obligation to hasten to the aid of his good ally, General Wellesley, either to prevent his defeat, or if that disastrous event happened to prevent himself (Cuesta) from being placed between Victor and Soult, with a certainty of the same lot, and being well assured that if he remained in Talavera that same destiny awaited him. Determined by these considerations to march on the 3d, he joined the English army at Oropesa, a circumstance which surprised him, as he supposed him to be in search of the enemy, who was then in Navalmoral, and still more was he surprised to find General Wellesley resolved not to attack Soult, suspecting that he had more forces than every account gave to him, and declaring that he would not engage without having a secure retreat; for which reason he was projecting to take up a position on the other side of the Puerto del Arzobispo. Cuesta replied to him, that the enemy had not a force sufficient to resist both armies; that being now united they could without difficulty give him the law, and that by a retreat to the Puerto a free passage would be allowed to him to reinforce Victor.

General Wellesley being posted at the bridge altered his position to the Mesa de Ibor. Afterwards he passed with his army to Deleytosa, having his vanguard at the Puerto de Almaraz; and Cuesta on the 9th passed to the Mesa de Ibor and Tresnodoso. On the 11th he proposed to General Wellesley the formation of a general magazine at Truxillo, where the necessary supplies might be equitably distributed to both armies. This proposal was repeated by General Eguia immediately after he took the command; and it being agreed to, Commissaries were named on the 15th for both parties, to regulate the articles of subsistence in Truxillo and their distribution, although with a preference in favour of the English. The Commissaries were employed in the said regulation, and their exertions were so effectual, that they provided the British army with all it required, of which General Wellesley was informed by Eguia. The former, however, having complained on the 17th of the want of provisions, forewarned the latter to prepare his troops to occupy the ensuing night the positions which were covered by the English, unless he was completely succoured on that very day, and his subsistence was assured for the future. This resolution so sudden, so peremptory, and so perilous in these circumstances caused the greatest pain to General Eguia, who endeavoured to use forcible arguments for convincing General Wellesley; but all was useless. In this critical situation he, however, gave the orders to the Commissaries for supplying the exigencies of General Wellesley. They fulfilled their commissions so well, as is proved by the certificate given by Lieut.-Colonel William Waters, the Commissary of General Wellesley, that he says, that furnaces and other articles had been furnished; that a daily statement of their magazines was presented to them; that the choice of the existing supplies was left to them; and they declare that they had informed their General-in-Chief of the whole. This and the statement of the supplies given on the 21st and 22d, and still more the result of the demands, and the preparations to meet them for the future, prove that their subsistence was secured as far as possible.

Notwithstanding this circumstance, that General Wellesley was informed that the 300 mares for which he had applied would be purchased; that we had 700 mules which should be sent towards the completion of the 1,100 for which he had applied; that two brigades of carts were on the march, the remainder being to follow until the 100 were completed; he drew away on the night of the 19th of August the troops which he had near the Puerto de Almaraz, and on the 20th he commenced his march towards Portugal.

The greatest diligence and toil was likewise employed in this place to supply the English army with every necessary; and having transmitted to the Section of War the note of your Excellency, in which, among other points, you treat of the means of subsistence, I was assured that the ideas of your Excellency were greatly in conformity with the directions of the regulation which was at the point of being formed, with the variation of one point only, and I enclosed it to your Excellency in order that you might be pleased to express your opinion respecting it.

The precautions for the supply of every necessary to the army of General Beresford were not less continued or energetic, although the Chargé d'Affaires of his Majesty at Lisbon sent accounts of the want of provisions which he experienced. This, however, is by no means wonderful; for, having altered his route without giving information to the Duque del Parque, as he declared, he could not easily meet with the necessary subsistence, particularly in a country which had been so much overrun by the enemy. The Duque however conferred in Ciudad Rodrigo with Beresford. The Intendant of that army came to an agreement with the Commissary of General Beresford's army respecting the supply of rations which the latter required, and afterwards on the 11th of August, when the same General agreed with the Duque to vary the position of his army, they smoothed the difficulties which presented themselves for the supply of provisions arising from the desolation of that country and the scarcity of the season. The Duque del Parque continued to assist Beresford in consequence of the pressing orders which had been sent to him; and Chone, Commissary of the army, having presented himself before the Duque, he gave him a part of the articles destined for the provisionment of that place to such an extent, that having given up all the wheat which he had for his cavalry, he found himself for two days in great distress for its maintenance. He provided him likewise with the most expeditious means for securing to the Portuguese troops in the town, of the neighbourhood, and on their route, the rations, carts, and beasts of burden which they have needed ; but he would not consent to give him, as he solicited, a considerable part of the magazines of that place, they being absolutely necessary to him and less than sufficient.

The Duque sent word on the 17th of August that General Beresford, alledging the want of provisions, was projecting a retreat to Portugal, although every imaginable exertion had been made to procure provisions in such manner, that the agents have returned from some quarters with superfluity ; that although it is certain that some delay has been experienced in some situations, it has been occasioned by the sudden alterations of the routes, for which orders had been despatched, and provisions have been addressed, as it was impossible to convey them by the post with the celerity with which the positions were varied.

He has notwithstanding despatched Commissaries, with the most express orders for all towns to send to the Portuguese army all in their power and possession; but the disorder with which they have of their own will seized various articles has caused the consumption in two days of provisions sufficient for four.

With a desire of satisfying your Excellency, questions were put to General Cuesta respecting the wounded English who remained in the hospitals of Talavera, after the retreat of the said General; he answered, that some died before the departure of the armies ; that the situation of others was so critical, that humanity did not allow of their removal; that the greater part had been conveyed to Oropeza, by an arrangement of General Wellesley, with the succours which had been requested of him, and which were given, in preference to the Spaniards, in such a manner that the English Commissary was very well satisfied, and returned thanks; that besides a considerable number of wounded marched away on foot; and lastly, that when on the 4th his vanguard left Talavera, he was assured by the Commandant, Zayas, that he had seen the Hospital of St. Augustin evacuated and closed, which hospital had been occupied by the English; and that the officers of the Royal Finance answered to him, under their signatures, that they had realized all the supplies in the midst of the scarcity of mules and carts.

It is very difficult, after the foregoing facts, to answer punctually the complaint of want of co-operation in the Spanish Generals, while cases and facts are not pointed out. The orders which exist in the power of the Generals will prove their instructions to maintain the greatest harmony with our allies, to respect their opinions, and to concede all they could, to any extent but that of causing any grievous evil to their country. Such are the orders which have been repeatedly given, and if we speak from the despatches of the Generals, we read in those of Cuesta of the 2d July, that an English officer informed him from Placencia that the British army would pass from Zarca la Mayor to Coria and Placencia, and requested him to have a bridge thrown over the Tietar, for its passage by the Bazagona, and that in consequence he ordered an engineer and workmen to reconnoitre the spot, and to make a report of the work. In another of the 4th, he said, that the English vanguard was at Zarca la Mayor, and that an English Commissary having proved to him that a provisional bridge over the Tietar was requisite for the junction of the two armies, the workmen and utensils necessary for constructing it with all haste departed on the following day, although the river is fordable. In another of the 5th, he said, that the Commissioner Don Joseph O'Lawlor having explained to him, from Zarca la Mayor, that General Wellesley conceived it to be expedient that the Spanish troops which occupied Placencia, should pass to the Puerto de Baños, immediately after the arrival of his army in that place, for which purpose he offered engineers and artillerymen with the corresponding train, and he would then make arrangements for the sending to the Puerto de Baños the troops necessary to defend it, together with those which were in Ciudad Rodrigo. In another of the 7th, he said, that he had information of Soult's entry into Zamora on the 29th, and that he was expected to join Victor; that if it was attempted by Baños, he would re-inforce that point with the troops he had on the Tietar; if by Puerto Pico, he had written to Wilson to advance to Arenas with his vanguard. In another of the 15th, he said, that he had agreed with General Wellesley on the movements to be made by the combined armies. Lastly, on the 1st of August, he said, in another despatch, that at the earnest request of Sir Arthur Wellesley, although against his own opinion, he sent the fifth division with 300 cavalry towards Placencia, and the Puerto de Baños, to impede the passage of Soult if it arrived in time; although he hoped, that General Beresford with his 15,000 men would harass and intercept him.

These, among many others, are data justifying not only the co-operation but the spirit of union, concord, and energy in the Spanish Generals and Government towards our allies. It appears that there can be no greater deference towards them, nor can it be proved in a more conclusive manner than by acting at the pleasure of our allies against our own opinion, and for the sole purpose of giving satisfaction to the English Generals. The latter may be able, perhaps, to cite some cases in which the Spaniards have not agreed with them; but neither does the want of absolute complaisance prove the idea or spirit of disunion, nor is all which is claimed practicable on every occasion, but in whatever manner it may be, the Spanish Generals shall answer it to their Government, if the allies point out to them the cases, and manifest the concerted plans which were abandoned suddenly at the most critical moments of the campaign; since the section of the war has no information of them, and in the meanwhile co-operation and concord on its part appear to be proved by the foregoing observations. Cuesta was instructed to treat with General Wellesley respecting the future destination of the troops of the Marquis de la Romana, with reference to the expressed opinion of General Beresford. Cuesta did so; and, having declared on the 23d of July that he was of Beresford's opinion, it was resolved that Romana with all his disposable troops should take up a position in the Carhajales, a spot proposed by Beresford to whom it was communicated, through the Chargé d'Affaires of his Majesty in Lisbon. Cuesta was answered, that in consequence of General Wellesley's opinion, orders were given to that effect. From the preceding accounts there can remain no doubt that the departments of war and finance have given with diligence and promptitude all the orders which were requisite for supplying the allied armies; that it has been repeatedly recommended to our Generals, not only to preserve a good understanding with those of his Britannic Majesty, but to respect their opinions; that in effect these instructions have been so well observed, that we have acted on all occasions according to those opinions, and that on the part of those departments all has been activity, and no labour has been spared in attaining the end.

His Majesty moreover instructed me, that the plan which your Excellency was pleased to transmit to me, dated the 21st of August, for improving the system of transport, and the mode of supplying the British army employed in Spain, should be immediately adopted; the suitable orders were given for carrying it into effect, for establishing the magazines, and for making the supplies of every necessary article, without sparing any expence in the maintenance of the said army, with the supposition of its stay in Spain.

Notwithstanding all these circumstances, Sir Arthur Wellesley has persevered in removing his troops from this country; but whatever may be the plans of that military chief, he can never say, that the inaction or the small degree of zeal in the Spanish Government has forced him to vary those which that Government expected from so generous an ally, who had inspired the enemy himself with fear and respect.

This is the exposition which I am instructed by his Majesty to lay before your Excellency, in reply to your two notes of the 30th of August and 8th of September last, and for your satisfaction with regard to the complaints which your Excellency has detailed in the same; and his Majesty hopes, that in the facts which are related, your Excellency will perceive the energy with which the Spanish Government has endeavoured to correspond to the generous efforts of its intimate allies, and the sincerity with which it promotes every thing which can contribute to draw closer the bonds of good friendship and firm alliance which it has contracted with his Britannic Majesty and the English nation; with these principles, and with the supposition of a decided co-operation, and the formation of a sincere and solid plan of campaign for the armies of the three nations, his Majesty will not only listen to the opinion of General Wellesley with the greatest

respect and distinction, but, without losing an instant, will
so arrange as to put in motion all the resources which the
country offers; possessed with the most ardent desires to
gain our liberty and independence, and to destroy our cruel
and perfidious enemy; desires, which have been effectually
proved during the course of a struggle of more than a year
so unequal, and so worthily sustained by the Government,
whose constancy neither the greatest misfortunes, nor the
diminished hopes of the feeble aid of the greater part of
the nations of Europe, nor the most seductive offers, nor the
intrigues of the ill-intentioned, have had the power to shake
for a single moment.

His Majesty hopes that the day has arrived on which this
magnanimous nation is doomed to reap the fruit of its perseverance, and of the generosity of his Britannic Majesty.
Her armies, however feeble they may be represented, when
united with the valiant English and Portuguese, are more than
double those which the enemy retains in Spain at this day.
Let us not give time for those to be reinforced. Let numbers
and a sincere desire to drive them from the Peninsula supply
the want of some articles, which time will be able to provide.
Let all combine in one plan, and the Government in the name
of the nation offers to its allies the greatest energy in its
arrangements, and the greatest efficacy in its succours.

Your Excellency likewise remarks, that to the intent
"that these offers may be realized, it were necessary to
revise the military system, and above all, that in order to
make any progress, it were indispensable to give energy and
efficacy to the executive power, which can never possess sufficient force or activity, without the direct assistance of the
collective wisdom of the nation, and without the aid of that
spirit which must flow from the support of a people animated
with equal sentiments of loyalty and liberty."

No person knows better than your Excellency, what serious
consideration is requisite on this subject in the present circumstances; since, through the channel of your Excellency,
the Government has been informed of the desire of some
persons to introduce novelties, by the use of means which are
not only reprobated by the laws, but which might bring down
irreparable injury on the good cause which both nations
defend with so much glory. And your Excellency is so

deeply convinced of this truth, that when you had been informed of those projects, your communications to the Government, and your individual actions for frustrating them,
have so largely contributed to that end, that the Government
cannot consider them with indifference, and omit giving to
your Excellency in return for them the most express thanks.*

The Spanish nation, after having seen her kings perfi-
diously torn from her bosom, abandoned to herself, her
capital, with the tribunals of justice, being occupied by the
enemy found that she was compelled to reflect on her own
condition, and on the state of abandonment in which she was
placed; and exerted the right which her situation gave,
formed a Government, to which all classes of the State have
sworn allegiance and have shewn obedience.   This plain
narrative is a complete proof, how important and necessary it
is to seek for means of conciliating the plan of a reform with
the different interests which must concur in effecting it, and
to deliver the common cause from evils greater than those we
are desiring to avoid.   Such is the intention of Government,
and such has been its occupation for many days; its situation
is by no means common, and if it succeed in the object, as it

* These expressions refer to the following extraordinary circumstance.
A person came to the hotel of the British Embassy at Seville and desired
to speak privately with the Ambassador.   Being admitted, he detailed
distinctly to the Marquess Wellesley the whole plan of a conspiracy for the
seizure of the persons composing the Supreme Junta then assembled at
Seville, and for the appointment of a Regency in the place of the existing
Government.   The Ambassador, finding that the conspirators intended to
carry their plot into execution on the next day, detained the informant,
and immediately proceeded to the office of M. de Garay, and communicated the whole to him.   The informant had named some persons of the
highest rank as being likely to favour the conspiracy.   The Marquess Wellesley, as soon as he had seen M. de Garay, went to each of those persons,
and prevented their taking any part in the plot.   The Junta took the necessary precautions; and the plot, which had certainly been formed, was
frustrated.

The Junta on this occasion expressed great gratitude; and M. de Garay
offered the Order of the Golden Fleece to the Marquess Wellesley, which
his Lordship declined, stating that, " he could not accept that high honour
from an authority, whose conduct towards the interests of Spain and of
the Alliance he could not approve."   The Order of the Golden Fleece had
before been offered by the Supreme Junta to his Majesty George the Third,
who had declined the offer.—[ED.]

desires, without convulsions and without intestine dissensions, which it would scarcely be possible to escape in any other manner, and which moreover would throw the nation into the hands of our enemy, it will be enabled to give this instance, in addition to so many others of prudence and moderation; and to our faithful and generous ally the king of Great Britain, a testimony of what he may expect from a Government which has known how, in the midst of its calamities, to maintain itself with firmness and energy, and to keep aloof from the evils which others have suffered, because they did not act with the same caution and deliberation; and to your Excellency, of the value which it places on your enlightened wisdom, and your exertions, which spring from a desire that our affairs may be conducted to the most successful conclusion.

I have the honour to be, &c.

MARTIN DE GARAY.

No. XLIII.

The Marquess Wellesley to Viscount Wellington.

MY LORD,   Seville, October 17, 1809.

1. In my despatch of the 19th of September, I had the honour to communicate to your Excellency my letters, (No. 4 and 5,) to Mr. Secretary Canning.

2. Among the enclosures in No. 5, was a copy of a note, under date the 8th of September, to M. de Garay. I now have the honour of enclosing a copy of that note for your Excellency's reference.

3. I also enclose a copy in the original, and translation of the answer which I have received to that note from M. de Garay. Although the answer is dated on the 3d of October, I did not receive it until several days after that date. I request your Excellency to give your attention to those passages in this paper which refer to the provisions and means of transport furnished to the British army under your command, to the co-operation and general conduct of the Spanish Generals and troops, and to the causes which occasioned the movement of your army towards the frontier of Portugal.

I shall be happy to receive the advantage of your observations upon these points, before I return my reply to the various extraordinary mis-statements with which this paper abounds.

Towards the conclusion of the paper, M. de Garay refers to a transaction which occurred at Seville during the last month. A plan had been formed in this town for seizing the persons of the principal members of the Supreme Junta, for subverting by force the existing Government of Spain, and for substituting in its place, by the same violent means, a Regency to be chosen by the persons engaged in the plot. This project having come to my knowledge, I immediately communicated it to the Government, and, by a timely inter-position of my personal influence, I prevented the acts of vio-lence which had been meditated against the Supreme Junta.

I have the honour, &c.

WELLESLEY.

No. XLIV.

The Marquess Wellesley to Don Martin de Garay.

SIR, Seville, October 24th, 1809.

The condition to which the British army was reduced by the internal state of Spain during the last campaign, com-pelled me to submit to your Excellency the representations contained in my note of the 8th of September.

Your Excellency is fully informed of the urgent motives of public duty, which induced me to solicit the attention of the Government of Spain to those circumstances in the state of the country, which menaced destruction to the common cause, and rendered the co-operation of the British army impracti-cable.

The danger to which the interests of the alliance were ex-posed required from me a plain exposition of the evils which had occasioned such a calamity, and of the remedies which might be derived from an early interposition of the wisdom of the Spanish Government.

With this view I suggested the necessity of strengthening and amending the frame of the Government, by concen-trating the executive power in a more compact form, and by resting that power on the direct support of the collective wisdom of the nation, and on the immediate aid of a due representation of the several estates of the realm.

In offering these suggestions to your Excellency's consideration, my intention was not to transgress the bounds of amicable counsel, or to interfere in the independent exercise of the judgment of the Spanish Government.

The Supreme Central Junta, through your Excellency's intervention, had repeatedly and earnestly solicited me to assist in promoting the efforts of Spain, by recommending the direct co-operation of the British army. In answer to these solicitations, I pointed out: First, The causes which had frustrated the spirited endeavours of the British army in the last campaign. Secondly, The only practicable means of placing Spain in a condition to receive the benefit of that species of assistance which she most anxiously desired.

The Supreme Central Junta has recently given much consideration to these important questions, and has determined that it is necessary to concentrate the executive power, and to assemble the Cortes without delay.

Much time, however, has already elapsed, and the peril becomes more imminent, while the true bulwark of defence remains incomplete.

Your Excellency has been pleased to imform me, that the Supreme Central Junta is occupied in the election of a Committee of seven of its members, to whom it proposes to delegate the military branch of the executive power, with some reservations. The appointment of such a committee cannot be deemed a concentration of the executive power; it is, in fact, a subdivision of the executive power, which, instead of activity and vigour, must tend to produce additional delay, counteraction, and weakness in the operations of the Government. To concentrate in the hands of seven persons the military department of the executive power, while all the other departments of the Government shall remain in the whole body of the Junta, is to separate one essential branch of the executive power from the main body of the Government, and to detach from the whole a part essential to its combined strength.

Unity of council and of action (the main source of vigour and activity) cannot be secured unless the several branches of the executive power be united. The strength of each branch essentially depends on mutual aid and reciprocal connexion; nor can any branch of the executive power, severed from the rest, possess the same degree of force which belong to it, when combined in the general and connected system of executive government, and where each part contributes to the strength and efficacy of the whole.

I cannot therefore expect that even the military department will gain any degree of alacrity or promptitude by this new separation from the general frame of the executive government, nor can I hope that any concentrated strength will result to the remaining departments, from a mere division of power which breaks the collective force of the entire administration, without any benefit either to the departments which continue in the hands of the Junta, or to that which is taken from them.

The Military Section of the Supreme Junta, was, perhaps, a more convenient instrument of administration; and it possessed the advantage of a more compact form, as its number was less than that of the proposed committee.

In every view, the division of the Junta into sections for the despatch of business, is less objectionable than the positive separation of a branch of the executive power from the Government. If the proposed committee could be considered as a new form of executive power, or a new executive council of Regency, the number of its members would constitute an insuperable objection to its structure.

The executive council should not consist of more than five members at the utmost; if limited to three members, a strong hope might be entertained of its efficiency; but the new committee is not an executive council, it is a mere military commission, with limited powers.

It is my duty to declare to your Excellency, that the appointment of this committee affords me no confidence in the promised correction of any of those evils of which I complained in my note of the 8th of September, nor furnishes any security to the British army, in any operation within the Spanish territory.

Your Excellency has further been pleased to inform me, that it is intended to issue the summons for the assembly of the Cortes on the 1st of January, and that the assembly is actually to meet on the 1st of March 1810.

Your Excellency's communication authorizes me to use on this most interesting point, the same freedom of amicable counsel, which I have already exercised respecting the nominal concentration of the executive power.

The intention of assembling the Cortes was announced in the month of May 1809; it will be difficult to persuade the world that all the necessary regulations with a view to that important event, might not have been completed before the month of March 1810. I am well aware of the absolute necessity of preparing the principal rules and orders for the regular despatch of business in the Cortes, before that Assembly shall meet, but it would have been highly desirable that the utmost degree of expedition should have been used in calling the aid of the Cortes to support the executive power, in the great work of delivering the Spanish nation from the French usurpation, and of restoring the independency of the monarchy, together with the prosperity and happiness of the people.

These objects are inseparable from the interests of the alliance; and it is therefore with the deepest regret, that I witness any course of proceedings, tending to procrastinate those improvements in the condition of Spain, which alone can enable her to receive the auxiliary armies of Great Britain.

Your Excellency is fully apprized of my sentiments, with respect to the exigency of the present crisis in Spain. My solicitude for the stability of the alliance has already induced me (under your Excellency's encouragement) to explain distinctly principles and opinions, which cannot be satisfied by the present course of proceedings. I take the liberty of referring your Excellency to a paper, which I had the honour of communicating to you confidentially, some time ago, and of which I now request you to make any use that you may deem advantageous to the public service. In that paper I did not express a wish to see the military branch of the Government separated from the main body of the executive power, under the direction of a committee of seven members; but I submitted to your Excellency the expediency of uniting every branch of the executive power in the hands of a council, to consist of not more than five persons, and to be selected either from the body of the Junta, or from the nation at

large, with reference, exclusively, to the character and qualifications of the persons to be elected.

I recommended that this Council of Regency should exercise the executive power, until the Cortes should be assembled.   Secondly, That the Cortes should be assembled with
the least possible delay.   Thirdly, That the Supreme Central Junta, or such members of it as should not be of the
Council of Regency, should constitute a deliberative Council,
for the purpose of superintending the election of the Cortes;
and of preparing for that body, with the assent of the
Council of Regency, such business as may be deemed proper
to submit to its early consideration.   Fourthly, That the
same act of the Junta by which the Regency shall be appointed, and the Cortes called, shall contain the principal
articles of redress of grievances, correction of abuses, and
relief of exactions in Spain and the Indies, and also the heads
of such concessions to the Colonies, as shall fully secure to
them a direct share in the representative body of the Spanish
empire.   Fifthly, That the first act of the Regency should
be, to issue the necessary orders for correcting the whole
system of the military department in Spain.

Your Excellency will judge whether the communication
which I had the honour to receive from you last night (respecting the nomination of a Committee of seven members,
and the assembly of the Cortes on the 1st of March 1810)
accord in any degree with my anxious solicitude for an
improvement in the general condition of Spain, and whether
it would be consistent with my declared sentiments, to offer
to your Excellency, any expectation of the co-operation of
the British army in Spain, while every evil of which I have
complained remains without hope of remedy.

With the most sincere respect, and with sentiments of the
highest esteem and consideration,

I have the honour to remain, Sir,
your Excellency's most obedient,
and faithful servant,
WELLESLEY.

No. XLV.

The Marquess Wellesley to Don Martin de Garay.

SIR,　　　　　　　　　　　　　　　Seville, October 29, 1809.

I have the honour to acknowledge the receipt of your Excellency's note under date the 28th instant.

I return your Excellency many thanks for the official communication of the success obtained by the Spanish troops, under the command of the Duque del Parque; and I request your Excellency to present my respectful congratulations to the Supreme Central Junta on an event so honourable to the arms of Spain, and so interesting to the common cause.

Your Excellency has taken this occasion to repeat the desire so often expressed by the Central Junta, within the course of the last month, for the services of the British and Portuguese forces in Spain.

Upon this point, I must take the liberty of referring your Excellency to my notes of the 8th of September and 24th of October, in which I have stated distinctly the reasons which prevent me from recommending any such operation to the Commander-in-Chief of the British forces.

Your Excellency is pleased to observe, that Great Britain has derived little advantage from the late expedition against the French naval force in the Scheldt. Your Excellency will permit me to remind you, that, according to the most authentic information which has been received from France, and with which your Excellency is fully acquainted, a considerable French army, actually advanced to the vicinity of Bayonne, for the purpose of reinforcing the French troops in Spain was recalled, in consequence of that expedition. I cannot therefore concur with your Excellency in opinion, that the expedition to the Scheldt has proved entirely fruitless to Great Britain; since the first effect of that armament was so beneficial to the cause of Spain, by occasioning a powerful diversion of troops, intended to reinforce the enemy in this quarter.

It is unnecessary to renew the assurances of his Britannic Majesty's sincere desire to aid the cause of Spain by every species of assistance, compatible with the interests and honour of his own kingdom, and consistent with the principles of the alliance.

His Majesty however, has not engaged to permit his troops to operate in Spain, under circumstances which must lead to their certain destruction, without any benefit to his ally.

I have the honour to be,

with the highest consideration
and esteem, Sir, &c.

WELLESLEY.

No. XLVI.

Lord Wellington to the Marquess Wellesley.

MY LORD,   Badajoz, 30th October, 1809.

I have had the honour of receiving your Excellency's despatch of the 17th instant, containing a copy of your note to M. de Garay of the 8th of September, and a copy of his note in answer to your Excellency of the 3rd of October.

I am not surprised that M. de Garay should endeavour to attribute to the irregularities of the English Commissariat, the deficiencies of supplies and means of transport experienced by the British army in its late service in Spain, I am not disposed to justify the English Commissariat where they deserve blame; but I must think it but justice to them to declare, that the British army is indebted to their exertions for the scanty supplies it received.

From some of the statements contained in M. de Garay's note, it would appear that the British army had suffered no distress during the late service; others have a tendency to prove that great distress was suffered at a very early period by both armies; particularly the quotation of a letter from General Cuesta, of the 1st of August, in answer to a complaint which I am supposed to have made, that the Spanish troops and *their prisoners* were better supplied than the British army. The answer to all these statements is a reference to the fact, that the army suffered great distress for want of provisions, forage, and means of equipment; and although that distress might have been aggravated, it could not have been occasioned by the inexperience or irregularity of the English Commissariat.

I know nothing of the orders which M. de Garay states were sent by the Government to the different Provincial Juntas, to provide provisions and means of transport for the British army on its passage through the different towns in the provinces. If such orders were sent, it was obvious that the Central Junta, as a Government, have no power or influence over the Provincial Juntas and Magistrates to whom their orders were addressed, as they produced no effect; and the supplies, such as they were, were procured only by the requisitions and exertions of the English Commissaries. But it is obvious from M. de Garay's account of these orders, that the Central Junta had taken a very erroneous view of the operations to be carried on by the army, and of the provision to be made for the troops while engaged in those operations. The Government provided, by their orders, for the troops only while on the passage through the towns, relying upon their immediate success, and making no provision for the collection of one body of not less than 50,000 men, even for one day. At the same time that they were guilty of this unpardonable omission which paralyzed all our efforts, they rendered that success doubtful by countermanding the orders given to General Venegas by General Cuesta, and thus exposing the combined armies to a general action with the enemy's concentrated force. The effect of their orders will appear more fully in the following detail:—

As soon as the line of my operations in Spain was decided, I sent a Commissary to Ciudad Rodrigo, to endeavour to procure mules to attend the army, in concert with Don Lozano des Torres, that city and its neighbourhood being the places in which the army commanded by the late Sir John Moore had been most largely supplied. M. de Garay expresses the astonishment of the Government that the British army should have entered Spain unprovided with the means of transport, notwithstanding that a few paragraphs preceding this expression of astonishment, he informs your Excellency, in the name of the Government, that they had given orders to the Provincial Juntas of Badajoz and Castile (at Ciudad Rodrigo) and the Magistrates, to provide and supply us with the means which of course they must have been aware that we should require. No army can carry on its operations if unprovided with means of transport; and the British army was, from circumstances, particularly in want at that moment.

The means of transport commonly used in Portugal are carts drawn by bullocks, which are unable, without great distress, to move more than 12 miles in a day, a distance much shorter than that which the state of the country in which the army was to carry on operations in Spain, and the nature of the country would oblige the army to march. The number of carts which we had been able to bring from Portugal was not sufficient to draw our ammunition, and there were none to carry provisions.

Having failed in procuring at Ciudad Rodrigo, and in the neighbourhood, the means of transport which I required, I wrote to General O'Donaghue, on the 16th of July, a letter in which, after stating our wants and the failure of the country in supplying them, I gave notice, that if they were not supplied, I should discontinue my co-operation with General Cuesta, after I should have performed my part in the first operation which we had concerted, viz. the removal of the enemy from the Alberché; and if not supplied as I required, I should eventually withdraw from Spain altogether. From this letter of the 16th July, it will appear that I called for the supplies, and gave notice that I should withdraw from Spain if they were not furnished, not only long previous to the retreat across the Tagus of the 4th of August, but even previous to the commencement of the operations of the campaign.

Notwithstanding that this letter of the 16th of July was communicated to the Central Junta, both by Mr. Frere and General Cuesta, the British army has to this day received no assistance of this description from Spain, excepting twenty carts which joined at Merida, ten on the 30th of August, and ten on the 2nd of September; and about 300 mules of about 500, which were hired at Bejan, and joined at a subsequent period. None of the mules stated to have been hired and despatched to the army from Seville, or by Igea or Cevallos, or the two brigades of forty each, or the horses have ever joined the British army, and I conclude that they are with the Spanish army of Estremadura, as are the remainder of the (100) ten brigades of carts which were intended and are marked for the British army.   But none of these mules or carts, supposing them to have been sent from Seville for our use, reached Estremadura till after the 21st of August, the day on which, after five weeks notice, I was obliged to separate from the Spanish army.

It is not true, therefore, that my resolution to withdraw from Spain, as then carried into execution was " sudden," or ought to have surprised the Government; nor does it appear to have been perilous from what has since occurred in this part of Spain.

I ought, probably, on the 16th of July, to have determined to suspend all operations till the army should be supplied with the means required ; but having on the 11th of July settled with General Cuesta a plan of operations to be carried into execution by the armies under the command of General Venegas, General Cuesta, and myself respectively, I did not think it proper to disappoint General Cuesta.   I believed that General Venegas would have carried into execution that part of the plan of operations allotted to his army, although I was afterwards disappointed in that expectation ; and I preferred that the British army should suffer inconvenience, than that General Venegas' corps should be exposed alone to the attack of the enemy ; and, above all, I was induced to hope that I should be supplied.

Accordingly I marched on the 18th of July from Placentia ; the soldiers carrying on their backs their provisions to the 21st, on which day a junction was formed with General Cuesta's army, and from that day to the 24th of August the troops or their horses did not receive one regular ration.   The irregularity and deficiency both in quality and quantity were so great, that I considered it a matter of justice to the troops to remit to them, during that period, half of the sum usually stopped from their pay for rations.

The forage for the horses was picked up for them by their riders wherever they could find it, and was generally wheat or rye, which are considered unwholesome food ; and the consequence was, that, exclusive of the loss by engaging with the enemy, the army lost in the short period of five weeks not less than 1,500 horses.

I have no knowledge of what passed between General Cuesta and Don Lozano des Torres, and the Intendant of

Provisions of the Spanish army. I never saw the latter gentleman excepting twice; the first time on the 22nd of July, when he waited upon me to claim for the Spanish army 16,000 rations of bread which had been brought into Talavera, and had been sent to my quarters, and which were delivered over to him, notwithstanding that the British troops were in want; and the second time on the 25th of July, when he waited upon me also at Talavera, to desire that the ovens of that town might be delivered over for the use of the Spanish army, they having moved to St. Ollalla, and the British army being still at Talavera. This request, which was not complied with, is an example of the preference which was given to the British troops while they were in Spain.

The orders stated to have been given by the Central to the Provincial Juntas and Magistrates were not more effectual in procuring provisions than in procuring means of transport. In the interval between the 15th and 21st of July the British Commissaries had made contracts with the Magistrates in the different villages of the Vera de Placentia, a country abounding in resources of every description, for the delivery at Talavera, on different days before the 24th of July, of 250,000 rations of provisions. These contracts were not performed; the British army was consequently unable to move in pursuit of the enemy when he retired on that day; and I conclude that the French army have since subsisted on these resources.

The British army never received any salt meat, nor any of the rice or other articles stated to have been sent from Seville for their use, excepting to make up the miserable ration by which the men were only prevented from starving during the period to which I have adverted, nor was it attended by the troop of biscuit bakers, nor did it enjoy any of the advantages of their labours, nor was the promise of 400,000 pounds of biscuit ever performed. These are notorious facts which cannot be disputed, of the truth of which every officer and soldier in the army can bear testimony. I assure your Excellency that not only have the supplies furnished to the army under my command been paid for whenever the bills for them could be got in, but the old debt due to the inhabitants for supplies furnished to the army under the command of the late Sir John Moore have been discharged ; and I have repeatedly desired the Spanish agents, and others acting with the army, and the different Juntas with which I have communicated to let the people know that all demands upon the British Government which could be substantiated would be discharged.

I beg to refer your Excellency to my despatches of the 21st of August, No. 12, for an account of the state of the magazine at Truxillo on the 20th of August; of the state of supplies and provisions at that period Lieut.-Colonel Walters had, by my desire, made an arrangement with the Spanish Commissariat for the division of the magazine at Truxillo between the two armies ; and he as well as I was satisfied with the principle and detail of that arrangement. But if the British army received only one third of a ration on the 18th of August, and only one half of a ration on the 19th, not of bread, but of flour ; if the horses of the army received nothing, and if the state of the magazine at Truxillo was such as at that time to hold out no hope, not of improvement (for it was too late to wait for improvement) but of a full and regular supply of provisions and forage of all descriptions, I was justified in withdrawing from Spain. In point of fact, the magazine at Truxillo, which under the arrangement made by Lieut.-Colonel Walters was to be the sole source of the supply to both armies, did not contain on the 20th of August a sufficiency to supply one day's demand upon it.

But it is said that M. de Calvo promised and engaged to supply the British army ; upon which I have only to observe, that I had trusted too long to the promises of Spanish agents, and that I had particular reason for want of confidence in M. de Calvo, as at the moment he was assuring me that the British army should have all the provisions the country could afford, in preference to, and to the exclusion of the Spanish army, I had in my possession an order from him (of which your Excellency has a copy) addressed to the magistrate of Guadalupé, directing him to send to the head-quarters of the Spanish army provisions which a British Commissary had ordered to be prepared and sent to the magazines at Truxillo, to be divided between both armies, in conformity to the agreement entered into with the Spanish Commissaries by Lieut. Colonel Walters.

As the state of the magazine at Truxillo was the immediate cause (as far as the want of provisions went) of my withdrawing from Spain, I beg to observe to your Excellency that I was not mistaken in my opinion of its insufficiency; as if I am not misinformed, General Eguia's army suffered the greatest distress in the neighbourhood of Truxillo, even after that part of the country and the magazines had been relieved from the burthen of supporting the British army.

In respect to the conduct of the operations in Spain by the Spanish general officers, many things were done of which I did not approve; some contrary to my expectations, and some contrary to positive agreement.

M. de Garay has stated that the orders to the Marquis de la Romana were framed in conformity with suggestions from Marshal Beresford; and thence he infers that the operations of that corps were approved of by me.

The Marquis de la Romana was still at Corunna on the 5th, and I believe as late as the 9th of August; and the armies of Estremadura retired across the Tagus on the 4th of August. This reference to date shews that there was and could have been no connexion in the operations of those different armies. In fact I knew nothing of the Marquis de la Romana's operations, and till I heard on the 3d of August that Marshal Ney's corps had passed through the mountains of Estremadura at Baños and was at Naval Moral, I did not believe that that part of the enemy's army had quitted Astorga, or that the Marquis was at liberty, or had it in his power to quit Gallicia.

Marshal Beresford's corps was collected upon the frontiers of Portugal in the end of July, principally for the purpose of forming the troops; and it was hoped he would keep in check the enemy's corps under Soult, which was at Zamora and threatened Portugal; that he would act as a corps of observation in that quarter, and on the left of the British army; and I particularly requested Marshal Beresford to attend to the Puerto de Perales. But I never intended and never held out any hope to the Spanish officers, that the corps under Marshal Beresford could effect any operation at that period of the campaign, and never was a party to any arrangement of an operation in which that corps was to be concerned.

In the cases in which measures were carried on in a manner of which I did not approve, or which I did not expect, or contrary to the positive agreement, those who acted contrary to my opinion may have been right; but still they acted in a manner of which they were aware I did not approve, and the assertion in the note that the operations were carried on with my concurrence is unfounded.

I expected from the communications I had with General Cuesta, through Sir Robert Wilson and Colonel Roche, that the Puerto de Baños would have-been effectually occupied and secured; and at all events that the troops appointed to guard that point, upon which I was aware that all the operations, nay, the security of the army depended, would not have retired without firing a shot.

It was agreed between General Cuesta and me on the 11th of July that General Venegas, who was under his command, should march by Trembleque, Ocaña, Puerto Dueños, to Arganda near Madrid; where he was to be on the 22d and 23d of July, when the combined armies should be at Talavera and Escola. This agreement was not performed, and the consequence of its non-performance (which had been foreseen) occurred; viz. that the combined armies were engaged with the enemy's concentrated force. I have heard that the cause of the non-performance of this agreement was, that the Central Junta had countermanded the orders which General Venegas had received from General Cuesta; of which countermand they gave us no notice. I shall make no observation upon this proceeding, excepting that the plan of operations as agreed upon with me was not carried into execution by General Venegas in this instance.

It was agreed by General Cuesta, on the 2d of August, that when I marched against Soult on the 3d he would remain at Talavera. That agreement was broken when he withdrew from Talavera, in my opinion, without sufficient cause. And it is also my opinion, that he ought not to have withdrawn, particularly considering that he had the charge of my hospital, without my consent. I do not conceive that if General Cuesta had remained at Talavera it would have made any difference in the result of the campaign. When Soult added 34,000 to the numbers already opposed to the combined armies in Estremadura, the enemy were too strong for us; and it was necessary that we should retire across the Tagus. But if General Cuesta had held the post of Talavera according to agreement, I should have been able to remove my hospital, or at least to know the exact situation of every individual left there; and I think that other disadvantages might have been avoided in the retreat.

When adverting to this part of the subject, I cannot avoid to observe upon the ambiguity of language used in the note, respecting the assistance afforded by General Cuesta to remove the hospital from Talavera. That assistance amounted to four carts on the 4th of August at Oropesa. In the subsequent removal of the wounded, and of the men subsequently taken sick, we had absolutely no assistance from the Spanish army or the country. We were obliged to lay down our ammunition, which was delivered over to the Spanish army, and to unload the treasure, and employ the carts in the removal of the wounded and sick, at Truxillo in particular, assistance which could have been afforded was withheld, on the 22d and 23d of August, M. de Calvo and Don Lozano des Torres being in the town.

In respect to the refusal to make movements recommended by me, I am of opinion that if General Bassecourt had been detached towards Placentia on the 30th of July when I recommended that movement, and if the troops had done their duty, Soult would have been stopped at the Tietar, at least for a sufficient length of time to enable me to secure the passage of the Tagus at Almaraz, and here again the hospital would have been saved.

He was not detached however till the 2d, and then I understood from M. de Garay's note, that it was General Cuesta's opinion that the movement was useless.

It could not have been considered as useless by General Cuesta on the 30th, because the proposition for making a detachment from the combined armies originated with himself on that day; and it could not have been considered as useless even on the morning of the 2d, as till the evening of that day we did not receive intelligence of the arrival of Soult at Placentia. A reference to the date of the period at which the General considered this detachment as useless would have been desirable.

I cannot account for the surprise stated to have been felt

by General Cuesta upon finding the British army at Oropesa on the 4th of August. The army had left Talavera
on the morning of the 3d, and had marched to Oropesa,
six leagues or twenty-four miles on that day, which I conceive a sufficient distance for a body of men which had been
starving for many days before. The accounts received,
on the evening of the 3d, of the enemy's position at Naval
Moral, and of his strength, and of General Cuesta's intended
march on that evening, leaving my hospital to its fate, were
sufficient to induce me to pause and consider our situation,
and at least not to move before daylight on the 4th, shortly
after which time General Cuesta arrived at Oropesa.

Upon considering our situation at that time, it was evident
to me that the combined armies must retire across the Tagus,
and that every moment's delay must expose them to the risk
of being cut off from their only remaining point of retreat.
A battle, even if it had been successful, could not have improved our situation; two battles or possibly three must have
been fought and gained before our difficulties, resulting from
the increased strength of the enemy in Estremadura, could
be removed. I did not consider the British army, at least,
equal to such an exertion at that moment. It is unnecessary
to make any observation upon the Spanish army; but the
occurrences at Arzobispo a few days afterwards shewed that
they were not equal to any great contest.

M. de Garay complains of the alteration in the line of our
operations, and of the sudden changes in the direction of our
marches, to which he attributes the deficiency of supplies,
which in this part of the note he is disposed to admit that
the British army experienced. I know of but one alteration
in the plan of operations and in the direction of the march,
which was occasioned by the circumstances to which I have
just referred.

When intelligence was first received of the arrival of the
enemy at Placentia, and of the retreat without resistance of
the corps appointed to guard the Puerto de Baños, my intention was to move towards Placentia, to attack the enemy's
corps which had passed through the Puerto. That intention
was altered only when I heard of the numbers of which that
corps consisted; and when I found that by General Cuesta's
movement from Talavera, the rear of the army was not

secure, that the only retreat was liable to be cut off, and that the enemy had it in their power and at their option to join or to attack us in separate bodies.

It could not be attributed to me that this large reinforcement was allowed to enter Estremadura, or that we had not earlier intelligence of their approach.

The Puerto de Baños was abandoned without firing a shot by the Spanish troops sent there to guard it; and the Junta of Castile, if they knew of the collection of the enemy's troops at Salamanca, sent no notice of it; and no notice was in fact received till the accounts arrived that the enemy had ordered rations at Fuerte Noble and Los Santos, and they arrived on the following day. But when the enemy arrived at Naval Moral, in Estremadura, in such strength, and the post of Talavera was abandoned, the Central Junta will find it difficult to convince their country and the world that it was not expedient to alter the plan of our operations and the direction of our march.

But this alteration, instead of aggravating the deficiency of our supplies, ought to have alleviated our distresses, if any measures had been adopted at Seville to supply the British army, in consequence of my letter of the 16th of July. The alteration was from the offensive to the defensive; the march was retrograde, and if any supplies had been prepared and sent, the army must have met them on the road, and must have received them sooner. Accordingly, we did meet supplies on the road, but they were for the Spanish army; and although our troops were starving at the time, they were forwarded untouched to their destination.

I have sent to Marshal Beresford a copy of that part of M. de Garay's note which refers to the supplies for the Portuguese army under his command, upon which he will make his observations, which I propose to forward to your Excellency. I shall here therefore only repeat, that the want of magazines, and the apathy and disinclination of the magistrates and people in Spain to furnish supplies for the armies, even for payment, were the causes that the Portuguese army, as well as the British army, suffered great distress from want, while within the Spanish frontier.

Till the evils of which I think I have reason to complain are remedied, till I shall see magazines established for the supply of the armies, and a regular system adopted for keeping them filled, and an army upon whose exertions I can depend, commanded by officers capable and willing to carry into execution the operations which may have been planned by mutual agreement, I cannot enter upon any system of co-operation with the Spanish armies. I do not think it necessary now to enter into any calculations to shew the fallacy of M. de Garay's calculations of the relative numerical strength of the allies, and of the enemy, in the Peninsula; if the fallacy was not so great as I am certain it is, I should be of the same opinion respecting the expediency of co-operating with the Spanish troops. But if the British and the Portuguese armies should not actively co-operate with them, they will at least do them no injury; and if M. de Garay is not mistaken, as I believe he is, in his calculations of numbers, and if the Spanish armies are in the state of efficiency in which they are represented to be, and in which they ought to be to invite our co-operation, the deficiency of 36,000 men, which the British and Portuguese armies might add to their numbers, can be no objection to their undertaking immediately the operations which M. de Garay is of opinion would give to his countrymen the early possession of those blessings for which they are contending.

I have the honour to be, &c.

WELLINGTON.

No. XLVII.

The Marquess Wellesley to Don Francisco de Saavedra.

SIR,   Cadiz, November 8, 1809.

The note from M. de Garay, under date the 3d of October, containing his Excellency's reply to my note of the 8th of September, has been communicated to Lord Viscount Wellington, of whose observations I have the honour to enclose a copy.

From the remarks of the Commander-in-Chief of the British army, it will appear that the exertions of the Spanish Government, described by M. de Garay, however active and sincere, have been entirely fruitless.

Whatever orders may have been issued at Seville for the

supply of provisions to the British army, for the security of its means of transport, or for the co-operation of the Spanish general and armies, the fact is, that the British troops neither received adequate means of subsistence nor of movement, nor sufficient aid of any description, in the course of the last campaign.

The detailed statements, contained in the enclosed letter from Lord Wellington, leave no doubt of this fact. It is for Spain to judge, whether the cause of this calamity is to be found in her Government, in its officers, or in the state of the country.

It is neither my duty nor my inclination to exhibit criminal charges against any civil or military officer in the service of Spain If the facts stated by the British Commander-in-Chief should appear to demand enquiry into the conduct of any individual, it is to be supposed, that the Government of Spain will institute the necessary process, without requiring the British Ambassador to undertake the invidious office of criminal accusation.

It is sufficient for me to have ascertained the existence of the evils, which I have repeatedly submitted to the consideration of the Spanish Government, and when the active operation of the British army in Spain is again solicited by the Spanish Government, I am compelled to require the correction of those evils, before I can consent to recommend any such operation to the British Commander-in-Chief.

M. de Garay has attempted to insinuate, that the British Commander-in-Chief was actuated, in his retirement towards the frontier of Portugal, by some motives different from those which had been publicly declared.

M. de Garay charges me with a deliberate determination to urge the retreat of the British army from Spain. These insinuations are entirely void of foundation.

M. de Garay also states, that the British army has abandoned Spain. This assertion is grossly and manifestly erroneous. Your Excellency is sufficiently informed of the anxious solicitude manifested by Lord Wellington and myself to maintain such a position in Spain, as might effectually protect the Southern Provinces and the City of Seville; and your Excellency knows, that the British army, for upwards of two months, has actually occupied a position upon the river Guadiana, nearly the same as that earnestly recommended by M. de Garay himself.

It is unnecessary to remind your Excellency, that ever since the 31st of August, the British army has been stationed from Badajoz to Merida, and, occupying that station, has accomplished the defensive purposes originally intended. It will remain for M. de Garay to explain by what argument he can now justify the assertion, that the British army has abandoned Spain.

The discussion which has lately arisen respecting the difficulty of furnishing provisions for the British army at Badajoz, has sufficiently proved the anxiety of the Commander-in-chief to make every reasonable sacrifice to the security of Spain. On the other hand, your Excellency must recollect the recent attempts which have been made at Badajoz, to compel our army to retire from that position.

If the distress of our army, and the want of provisions, or the necessity of defending Portugal, had compelled Lord Wellington to retire within the Portuguese frontier, I trust that the justice and liberality of the Spanish character would still have vindicated the British Commander-in-chief from the imputations which are insinuated in M. de Garay's note.

At the conclusion of M. de Garay's note, his Excellency is pleased to advert to the suggestion, which I had intimated, of the advantage which might be derived from an early effort to improve the administration of military affairs in Spain, by concentrating the strength of the executive power, and by connecting its activity and vigour with the public spirit of the people, and with the collective wisdom of the nation.

In this intimation, it was not my intention to suggest any course of proceeding essentially different from that which the Government had already announced to Spain, as absolutely necessary to her complete deliverance from the enemy, and to her permanent happiness and glory.

An executive power wisely constituted, and deriving its authority and strength, not only from its more compact form, but from the support of the people, and from the good-will of the nation, would afford the most certain protection against all projects of innovation or seditious mischief; as well as the most powerful security for the independence of the monarchy, and for the general union and tranquillity of Spain.

My duty towards my just and virtuous Sovereign, as well as towards the Government to which I am accredited, required that I should discountenance any project which might come to my knowledge, of effecting alterations in the existing public authorities of Spain by violent or irregular means.

For a mere act of duty, I claim no acknowledgment from the Spanish Government; but, on the other hand, I trust that from my endeavour to avert the dreadful consequences of conspiracy and tumult, no inference will be drawn to prevent or to delay the correction of those evils which menace the welfare and honour of Spain, and the efficacy and stability of her alliance with Great Britain.

With the highest respect, &c.

WELLESLEY.

APPENDIX

OF

OFFICIAL AND PUBLIC DOCUMENTS.

A.

Mr. Secretary Canning to the Marquess Wellesley.

(Extract.)

Foreign Office, June 27th, 1809.

I enclose to your Excellency a copy of the treaty of peace, friendship and alliance between his Majesty and Spain, concluded here in the month of January of the present year.

The stipulations of this instrument are so clear and simple as to require little to be said in explanation of them. I, however, think it my duty to accompany the communication of it to your Excellency, with such a statement of the reasons upon which the different articles are founded, as may serve to guide your Excellency hereafter in any discussion which may possibly arise, respecting either the effect of the treaty itself or any ulterior negotiations to be founded upon it.

I have first to state to your Excellency, the motives upon which it was thought right, by his Majesty, to give to his Majesty's connexions with Spain the form of positive treaty.

These motives are to be found partly in the obvious and natural adherence to that ordinary course by which the conclusion of a state of hostility between two countries, and the restoration of a state of peace are uniformly consigned to a written record and agreement; but partly also to the peculiar circumstances of the case, which while they made the negotiation of a treaty with a Government in the state in which that of Spain was, and still continues peculiarly difficult, rendered it at the same time peculiarly important that the extent of his Majesty's pledges and undertakings, with respect to Spain, should be accurately defined, and should be compensated in a certain degree by reciprocal obligation.

The sudden and simultaneous burst of resistance to French tyranny and oppression, which broke out in the different kingdoms and provinces of Spain, afforded as little opportunity as there was inclination for weighing minutely the terms and conditions on which assistance was to be afforded by this country to an effort, the character and tendency of which were such as at once to demand all the assistance that could be afforded to it.

This assistance therefore was given at once, largely and unconditionally, without any other question than how it could be most beneficially applied.

But it soon became necessary that the desultory and divided efforts of the separate provinces, which were perhaps best adapted to the beginning of such a war, inasmuch as they were calculated to distract the attention and dissipate the force of the enemy, would when that enemy recovered from his first surprise, and was enabled to concentre his force and act upon system, become wholly inadequate to an effectual and continued resistance.

It was therefore of the utmost importance that a Central Government should be formed; and the temptation of a closer and more regular relation with Great Britain was held out (perhaps not without effect) to induce the Spaniards to hasten the formation of such a Government.

What might have been the decision of his Majesty in respect to the establishment of such more intimate relations with the Spanish Government, if it had assumed a shape and adopted principles decidedly different from those of the ancient monarchy, is a question which it is fortunately not necessary to discuss.

The early and unanimous adoption on the part not only of the Juntas, but of the people throughout Spain, of those principles which reconcile loyalty with a spirit of independence, and a desire to maintain their country free, with a determination to uphold its laws and its legitimate sovereignty, left nothing to be questioned on this head, and made it matter of undoubted policy to encourage a Government founding itself on such principles, by early acknowledgment and by the offer of an intimate connexion.

This was of itself a sufficient motive for the conclusion of a treaty which should define, in precise terms, the relation between Great Britain and the existing Government of Spain. But further, as both nations were engaged in war against France, it was clearly desirable that the two Governments should be not only so firmly but so publicly united, as to make any attempt to divide them, by separate peace, hopeless; and to give to each in the most indisputable manner, and according to the formal practice of nations, the right which his Majesty took upon himself to exercise on the overtures from Erfurth, of claiming the admission of the other to any negotiation with the common enemy.

It remains for me to point out to your Excellency, such parts of the articles of the treaty as require any particular notice.

In the first article, the stipulation for " an entire and lasting oblivion of all acts of hostility done on either side, in the course of the late wars in which they have been engaged against each other," though an ordinary stipulation in treaties of peace, was peculiarly desirable in this, from the remembrance and resentment which were understood to be cherished by some of the leading statesmen in Spain, with respect to the manner in which the last war was begun; a transaction entirely justifiable under its circumstances, but of which, in the actual relation of the two countries, it was undoubtedly more advisable to avoid the discussion than to establish the propriety.

The second article has the effect of confirming and making reciprocal an engagement which his Majesty had gratuitously taken by his order in council of the 4th of July 1808, for the restoration of all Spanish vessels captured after that period.

The justice and generosity which dictated his Majesty's conduct on this occasion are happily so far rewarded, as that the only cases which have yet arisen under this article (the stipulations of which appeared, and were believed to be perfectly gratuitous on the part of his Majesty) are two cases of captures of British vessels in the ports of Spanish America, the particulars of which captures your Excellency will find in my correspondence with Mr. Frere, and for the release of which vessels your Excellency will follow up the applications which Mr. Frere will, no doubt, have made, founding yourself on the faith of this second article.

The third article, in addition to the general engagement of his Majesty for assistance to Spain, and that of Spain not to cede any territory to France, of which I have already spoken, contains a promise in his Majesty's name, not to acknowledge " any other King of Spain, and the Indies thereunto appertaining, than his Catholic Majesty Ferdinand VII. his heirs, or such lawful successor as the Spanish nation shall acknowledge."

The object of this stipulation is to avoid the inconvenience of his Majesty being called upon to decide between the conflicting claims of the candidates for the crown of Spain, in the event, not wholly out of probability, of Ferdinand VII. and his immediate family being removed by death.

Into the examination of this question it is not necessary now to enter ; but the treaty could not have defined the successor whom his Majesty was to profess his readiness to acknowledge, without either deciding this question or qualifying the engagement, as it is here qualified, by reference to the previous acknowledgment of the Spanish nation.

The fourth article is framed on the obvious policy of connecting the efforts and interests of the two countries, and of preventing any arrangement between Spain and the common enemy, to which his Majesty should not be a party, or which, if concluded without his participation, should not release his Majesty from his engagement.

I reserve what I have to say on the separate articles annexed to the treaty for another despatch.

APPENDIX B.

Mr. Secretary Canning to the Marquess Wellesley.

My Lord,   Foreign Office, 27th June, 1809.

The first separate article annexed to the treaty of peace, friendship, and alliance between his Majesty and Spain is of the utmost importance, and relates to a subject upon which it will be necessary that you should act with the greatest delicacy, but at the same time with the utmost vigilance and circumspection.

This article was added to the treaty, because it was foreseen that the securing of the fleets of Spain and of France, in case of such reverses as might expose the ports of Spain to the occupation of a French army, would be matter of great difficulty on account of the jealousy manifested by the Spaniards whenever it has been proposed to introduce a British force into any of the maritime fortresses ; and at the very moment when this article was in negotiation, the fate of Ferrol and of the ships in that harbour sufficiently evinced the necessity of such a precaution.

This article by making public the object for which alone British troops could be introduced into Cadiz or Carthagena, and the pledge of good faith implied by such publicity, that the occupation if permitted would not be abused to any other purpose, would, it is hoped, secure the consent of the Spaniards to their introduction in case of absolute necessity or of confessedly approaching danger.

But at all events, on the faith of this article his Majesty has a right to require that every preparation which can previously be made for the removal of the fleets on such an emergency shall be diligently made by the Spanish Government itself. Accounts have been received here which represent the precautions already taken as very inefficient for this purpose ; and as being apparently calculated rather to resist an attack from the sea, than to facilitate the withdrawing of the ships from within the reach of a force which may occupy Cadiz.

Your Excellency will have an opportunity on your landing at Cadiz of verifying these representations ; and, if you find them true, you,will not fail to remonstrate against a neglect so prejudicial to the interests of both countries, and against an appearance of mistrust so little merited by his Majesty's disinterested conduct towards Spain.

You will take the earliest opportunity of making the same enquiries with respect to Carthagena, and will report to me as early as you conveniently can the result of your enquiries for his Majesty's information.

I am, &c.
GEORGE CANNING.

APPENDIX C.

Mr. Secretary Canning to the Marquess Wellesley.

(Extract.)

Foreign Office, 27th June, 1809.

The second separate article annexed to the treaty of peace, amity, and alliance between his Majesty and Spain, refers to a future treaty to be subsequently negotiated for the specification of the nature and amount of the succours to be afforded by his Majesty to the Spanish Government.

The Spanish Government has not pressed the negotiation of such a treaty ; and there is no reason on his Majesty's part, in the present state of Spain and of Europe, for wishing to recal their attention to it.

The circumstances in question necessarily resolve themselves into, 1st. arms, ammunition, clothing, &c. 2d. Pecuniary assistance ; 3d. Military co-operation.

With respect to the objects comprehended under the first denomination of assistance, arms, stores, and clothing, &c. the absence of any specific engagement has not prevented and will not prevent his Majesty from furnishing such supplies as have been or may be required for the Spanish armies, to the utmost possible extent : but this is obviously a species of assistance not susceptible of minute and accurate specification before hand.

The ground on which his Majesty's consent to make it the subject of treaty was obtained, was no other than to gratify the desire expressed by the Spaniards, that all the expenditure of Great Britain on their account should be considered rather in the nature of loan than of gift, and that therefore some record might exist of the value of the articles for which they would stand indebted to his Majesty.

The enclosed letter will put your Excellency in possession of the amount of articles actually furnished to Spain. But I am not to instruct your Excellency to revive the question of valuation and repayment, or to recur to it on any other occasion, or for any other purpose, than for that of insisting that the amount of the value of these stores shall be taken into account in any statement of subsidiary aid from this country to Spain whenever (if ever) the government of Spain shall voluntarily require such a statement to be made out.

The supplies in kind are not only the most convenient, but in fact the only mode by which his Majesty's subsidiary aid to Spain could, under the present circumstances of the world, be continued to any considerable extent.

Among these supplies, at the same time, it is necessary to make an exception with respect to the article of muskets, the power of supplying which is unavoidably limited by the amount of the stock in hand, and the extent of the means of manufacturing them in this country.

2. My despatches to Mr. Frere of the   will have shewn
to your Excellency that the extent to which it was proposed to engage for pecuniary assistance, if a treaty on this subject had been negotiated, was ten millions
of dollars, including in that sum the specie which was consigned to Mr. Frere at
the time of his departure, and sent to Cadiz, amounting to about two millions
three hundred thousand dollars, or about five hundred thousand pounds sterling,
and including also the value of arms and stores sent to Spain from the period of
the installation of the Central Junta.

Since these instructions were given, however, a variety of circumstances have
concurred to render the execution of them at once unimportant and impracticable.

1st. The influx into Spain of specie from America, which has fortunately made
Spain in a great degree independent of external assistance.

2dly. The continued dearth of specie in this country, which makes the exportation even of a very small sum a matter of the most serious difficulty and embarrassment.

So much have these two circumstances together changed, or rather inverted the
relative situations of the two countries, that we must now (and until a supply of
specie can be obtained from America) rely in a great measure upon the Spanish
Government for silver to pay the expences of our army in the Peninsula, purchasing that silver by bills on the Treasury ; with respect to which operation
I shall have occasion to speak to your Excellency more particularly in another
despatch.

3dly. In the third place, the breaking out of the Austrian war, while it has relieved Spain in a considerable degree from the immediate pressure of the enemy,
has created a new demand upon the pecuniary resources of this country ; a demand which it would be impossible to meet in any degree if so large a portion of our disposable means had been appropriated by treaty to the use of
Spain. It is on this account a great satisfaction, not only that no positive stipulation has been made, but that the feelings of the Spanish Government with regard
to Austria have been found to be such as to induce them to consent, that any
consideration of their convenience should be postponed to that of the more pressing and urgent necessities of the court of Vienna.

This statement your Excellency will have seen expressed in a late despatch of
Mr. Frere, as what he collected from M. Garay in his conversation upon the
subject of a loan proposed here by Don Pedro Cevallos. The amount of the
loan which Don Pedro Cevallos proposed to raise was, as your Excellency will
have seen, no less than ten or twenty millions, not of dollars but of pounds
sterling.

The extravagance of this proposal, if it is not to be considered merely as an
unauthorized effort of zeal on the part of Don Pedro Cevallos himself, affords a
proof how little satisfactory the more limited aid of ten millions of dollars would
have been likely to prove to the Spanish Government.

It is on this ground, therefore, as well as on others, fortunate, that that suggestion has not been brought forward as the basis of a treaty ; and your Excellency will find in the amount of Don Pedro Cevallos' proposal and its consequent impracticability, as well as in the wants of the Austrian Government, and
the immense importance of that diversion to Spain, sufficient reason for avoiding
to entertain any discussion for a precise or definite pecuniary engagement on the
part of his Majesty at the present moment.

You will, however, not decline to receive any proposition which may be made
to you on this subject for the purpose of transmitting it home ; and you will (as

already instructed) profess his Majesty's readiness to continue his supplies in kind, to the utmost extent that Spain can require and this country can furnish.

But your Excellency will understand it to be generally a most desirable and important object to teach Spain to rely upon her own pecuniary resources ; and particularly so at the present crisis, when not only the wants of Austria (as already stated) are infinitely beyond what this country can relieve, but when the very successes of that power may at any moment, by encouraging other nations of the Continent to rise against France, produce new calls upon the liberality of Great Britain, which it is as much the interest of Spain herself, as of Germany, of Great Britain, and of all Europe that we should be enabled to answer.

3. The third species of assistance, and that to which the stipulations of treaty have been more particularly applicable is that of military co-operation. Your Excellency will be aware, that the treaty of January was concluded and signed at a time when we were yet uncertain as to the issue of Sir John Moore's campaign ; that accounts had been received here from that commander of the unfriendly reception of his army by the Spaniards, and of what appeared to him the general want of spirit in the Spanish nation, and the utter hopelessness of the Spanish cause.

In this state of things it was determined not to hazard another British army in Spain, without such previous stipulations for its reception, and for its secure retreat in case of necessity, as might effectually prevent the repetition of similar causes of complaint, and of the disasters which were then apprehended.

The war in the north of Spain then appearing hopeless, the admission of British troops into the fortress of Cadiz was the condition stipulated for the transfer of the British army to the south.

Your Excellency will have seen in the correspondence which has been submitted to your perusal the progress of the discussions on this subject, and the difficulties which were started by the Junta with respect to the admission of British troops ; difficulties which must be admitted to have been not wholly imaginary.

You will have observed, however, that these discussions have been conducted on both sides without the smallest degree of ill-humour ; and that although the result was not to admit a British force, and consequently not to send a British army to the south of Spain, there is no ground to apprehend that this result has produced in Spain any alienation from this country, and it certainly has produced here no diminution of interest for Spain.

In this state of things, a treaty for adjusting the terms of military co-operation has become unnecessary.

APPENDIX D.

Mr. Secretary Canning to the Marquess Wellesley.

My Lord,   Foreign Office, June 27th, 1809.

The additional article to the treaty of peace, friendship, and alliance, which additional article was signed on the 21st of March, defers the negotiation of a treaty of commerce till a more favourable opportunity, but stipulates in the mean time for mutual facilities to be afforded by temporary regulations on principles of reciprocal utility.

I have, therefore, only at present to desire that your Excellency will make it your business to ascertain and collect all the different regulations or orders which may have be n passed since the institution of the Central Junta, in favour of British commerce, and transmit them to me with such observations as may occur or be suggested to your Excellency by Mr. Duff, or others his Majesty's consuls or commercial agents in Spain ; and that, with a view to future arrangements, you should lose no opportunity of endeavouring to do away the prejudices which exist with respect to the restrictions upon the intercourse with the Spanish possessions in America.

I am, &c.
GEORGE CANNING.

APPENDIX E.

Extract of the Instructions to the Marquess Wellesley, K. P.

June 27th, 1809.

You will exert your utmost endeavours to maintain the best understanding with the Spanish Government, and to satisfy them of the deep and lively interest which we take in the welfare of Spain, and in the success of the cause in which the Spanish nation is engaged.

You will profess our earnest desire to fulfil to the utmost extent all the duties of our alliance with the Spanish Government, and to assist them in bringing the war to a fortunate conclusion, by the restoration of their lawful Sovereign, and the establishment of a just and sufficient security for the independence and integrity of the Spanish monarchy.

You will avoid any appearance of a desire to interfere, unnecessarily, with the internal concerns and interests of Spain. But as in the issue of the present momentous contest, in which the interests of the two countries are inseparably blended, much, if not every thing, must depend upon the vigour and energy with which the persons at the head of affairs in Spain call forth and employ the resources of that country ; as the opportunity now presented for such exertions as may place the country in a state of absolute security, is one of which the utmost advantage ought to be made, both in point of military activity and political and civil arrangements ; as the Central Junta itself has recently evinced its own conviction of the necessity of extraordinary diligence and attention to these important objects ; and as they have uniformly professed a desire to receive the assistance and advice of the British Government in every point of common interest, you will not decline any occasion of offering a fair and unreserved opinion upon such questions, either of a political or civil nature ; or of urging in the strongest manner such arrangements as may appear to you necessary for the effectual prosecution of the war on the part of Spain, and for the administration of the internal affairs of the Government in the manner the most conducive to the welfare of the nation, and to the preservation of the monarchy. You will, at the same time, be perfectly aware of the suspicions which might be excited, and of the disadvantage which might arise to the common cause, and to the harmony of the two Governments, if there should appear any thing too authoritative in the manner of delivering such opinions as you may feel yourself called upon to deliver, and you will, in your discretion consult the jealousy natural to a new Government, and to a delegated and unconfirmed authority.

In matters of internal Government, and in questions of commerce, you will avail yourself of any proper occasion, generally, to recommend a more enlarged and liberal policy than has heretofore been acted upon in Spain, strongly recommending, however, that whatever changes it may be thought right to introduce in the system by which the Government of Spain has been carried on, should be well weighed and digested previously to the actual assembling of the Cortez, so as to be propounded to them for their adoption, with the previous sanction and authority of the Junta, rather than that the whole of so vast and complicated a subject should be thrown loose before that Assembly, without any settled plan by which their deliberations may be guided.

You will observe, that the removal of such grievances or restrictions on political and personal liberty as the Junta may already have made up their minds to recommend, if granted soon, would tend to give weight and energy to the authority of the Government; whereas if all such boons are deferred to the Assembly of the Cortez, the intermediate period may witness the decline of the popularity and authority of the Junta, and therewith impair the means of carrying on the war with effect, and maintaining the kingdom against the usurpation of the enemy.

APPENDIX F.

Mr. Secretary Canning to the Marquess Wellesley.

(Extract.)

Foreign Office, June 27th, 1809.

The instructions with which Sir Arthur Wellesley has been furnished (copies of which are herewith enclosed) leave to that Commander a latitude to pursue his operations into Spain, so far as may be not inconsistent with the defence and security of Portugal. In exercising this discretion he will of course concert his movements with the Spanish General nearest to the Portuguese frontier. He will be directed to keep your Excellency constantly informed of all his movements; and your Excellency will, in any such case, procure from the Spanish Government such instructions to be given to their General as may aid Sir Arthur Wellesley's plan, and secure the cordial co-operation of the two armies. But these points are of too partial a nature to require the negotiation of a regular treaty for their arrangement.

The case for any negotiation of such a kind, could only arise, if at any future period, an operation upon a larger scale should be undertaken by a British force in Spain, for the purpose of clearing the Peninsula altogether of French force; and establishing, after the accomplishment of that object, such a system of military defence as should not only afford a permanent security to the frontiers of Spain, but enable the Spaniards, in some supposable events, to carry their arms beyond the Pyrennees, and become themselves the assailants.

The period for such an undertaking is certainly not yet arrived, and the destination of the disposable military force of this country, at the present moment, to other objects more immediately connected with the war on the continent of Europe, and calculated to operate a diversion in favour of Austria, will probably be considered by the Spanish Government itself as of more instant necessity and more obvious advantage.

Should the efforts of Austria unfortunately prove unavailing, or should they, on the other hand, so far succeed as to leave the force of this country free for more distant operations; in one or other of these cases, the necessity or the temptation might arise for the employment of a large British force in Spain. But it is only in one or other of these cases that your Excellency can be authorized to hold out any expectation of an augmentation of the British army now in the Peninsula, beyond such reinforcements as are already destined for it; (a statement of which is herewith enclosed) or of an extension of its operations beyond the limits assigned in Sir Arthur Wellesley's last instructions.

But with a view to any such larger operation (if the occasion for it should arise) it is obvious that it would be necessary to enter into previous and positive stipulations, such as might prevent the inconveniences, the complaints and recriminations which attended Sir John Moore's Expedition. With this view, as well as for the purpose of a more effectual service, in the interval, the new and more perfect arrangement of the Spanish army, and especially the delegation of the whole command to one responsible head, would be in the highest degree expedient and desirable. It was intimated some months ago, that there would be no indisposition to confide the command of the Spanish army to a British General. This cannot be required, nor while General Cuesta remains in command, does it seem likely that it should be offered; but if obtained, it would probably afford the best chance of remedying all inconveniences, and would be, above all things, likely to ensure that promptitude and unity of action by which alone any very extended and important operation, such as I have above described, could be successfully carried into execution.

Your Excellency will therefore direct your attention to these objects; though without giving any pledge of such an operation being carried into effect at any time, and with a direct acknowledgment that a diversion in aid of the war in Germany, must necessarily, for the present, command the immediate attention of the British Government.

In the mean time the diminished strength of the French armies in Spain, and the impossibility under which Buonaparte evidently must be of reinforcing them, afford such opportunities for the success of those partial and desultory attacks for which the Spanish armies, in their present state, are peculiarly fitted, as to afford a reasonable ground of hope, that until the turn of affairs in Germany shall be more decided, the Spaniards will not only be enabled to maintain the contest with advantage, but to gain ground daily against an enfeebled and disheartened enemy, and to prepare the way for those more large and effectual operations which may be undertaken hereafter.

APPENDIX G.

Mr. Secretary Canning to the Marquess Wellesley.

My Lord,   Foreign Office, June 27th, 1809.

I enclose to your Excellency a list of all the Agents civil and military employed in the service of his Majesty in Spain; to all of whom instructions will be given to correspond directly with your Excellency (sending copies of their letters home in cases where their proximity to England affords the means of their intelligence being received here more speedily than through your Excellency), and to attend to your Excellency's suggestions and directions to the extent of even returning home, if at any time your Excellency shall think it necessary for the public service so to direct.

                                   I am, &c.
                                   GEORGE CANNING.

APPENDIX H.

Mr. Secretary Canning to the Marquess Wellesley.

July 18th, 1809.

Your Excellency will at the same time, without exciting any expectations of any immediate reinforcement of the British army in the Peninsula, endeavour to ascertain on what footing a British army would be received in the interior of Spain, and whether there would be any disposition to confide the chief command of the Spanish forces to the Commander-in-Chief of a British auxiliary army.

The accounts which have been received here of the dispersion of General Blake's corps, and of the consequent resignation of that officer, of the intended recall of the Marquis de la Romana, and of the jealousy entertained by the Junta with respect to the designs of General Cuesta, appear to leave no officer of great note or possessing much confidence, in the way of such an arrangement. But your Excellency will understand that you are not to suggest, much less to solicit it, but merely to receive and transmit home for his Majesty's consideration any solicitation or suggestion which you may receive from the Spanish Government upon this subject.

APPENDIX I.

Mr. Secretary Canning to the Marquess Wellesley.

MY LORD,   Foreign Office, August 12th, 1809.

I have delayed some days sending off this messenger in expectation of receiving some direct information from the Austrian head quarters.

Nothing however has yet been received which throws any light upon the armistice, or reconciles the contradictory rumours respecting the causes which led to that transaction, and the consequences which may be expected to follow it.

Notwithstanding the want of authentic information, however, as there can be no doubt of the fact of the armistice having taken place, and as the terms are such as indicate the sense of over-ruling necessity, under which it must have been concluded, I cannot encourage your Excellency to give credit to any of those reports which represent the cessation of hostilities as merely matter of mutual convenience; and the war as likely to be renewed.

Even if the ground for such belief were more substantial than it is, I should be loth to induce your Excellency to hold out any such expectation in Spain : where the disposition to rely upon every thing rather than its own exertions is unfortunately so strongly marked in all the proceedings of the Supreme Junta, that even if there were a chance of a renewal of the contest between Austria and France, it would be in the highest degree desirable to take advantage of the alarm created by the armistice to stimulate the Spanish Government to those efforts by which alone (whatever be the fate of the other countries) Spain itself can be saved.

I have the honour to be, &c.

GEORGE CANNING.

APPENDIX K.

Mr. Secretary Canning to the Marquess Wellesley.

(Extract.)

Foreign Office, August 12th, 1809.

The change which has been produced in the state of affairs, under which your Excellency's instructions were prepared, by the disastrous result of the last battle between the Austrian and the French armies, and by the armistice which has followed them, will naturally have directed your Excellency's attention to that part of my despatch, No. 4, which prescribes the language to be held by your Excellency in respect to the employment of a British army in Spain.

Your Excellency was there informed, that it was only in the case either of complete failure of the efforts of the Austrian arms against France, or on the other hand of such decided success on the part of Austria as should relieve us from all necessity of co-operation with that power, and should set the armies of this country free for distant operations, that your Excellency " could be authorized to hold out any expectation of the augmentation of the British army in the peninsula, beyond the reinforcement then actually under orders, or of the extension of its operations beyond the limits assigned in Sir Arthur Wellesley's last instructions."

Unhappily there is so much reason to believe the former of these two cases to have arisen, that it now becomes my duty to furnish your Excellency with more precise instructions on the subject of military co-operation.

APPENDIX L.

Mr. Secretary Canning to the Marquess Wellesley.

(Extract.)

Foreign Office, August 12th, 1809.

The question which first arises is, whether the state of things in Spain be such as that a British army of 30,000 men, acting in co-operation with the Spanish armies, or in conjunction with them, could be reasonably expected either to effect the deliverance of the whole Peninsula, by the expulsion of the French armies now in Spain, or to make head against the augmented force which Buonaparte may now be enabled to direct against that country?

Upon this question your Excellency will receive the opinion of Sir A. Wellesley, to whom a copy of this despatch is transmitted; and who is instructed to lose no time in communicating with your Excellency upon it.

If the opinion of Sir A. Wellesley shall be that, with so limited a force as 30,000 men, offensive operations in Spain on an extended scale could not prudently be attempted; if he shall conceive that the utmost object to which such an army would be adequate, is the separate defence of Portugal; and that Portugal will be best defended by confining his operations within the limits of his present instructions, your Excellency will then only have to state to the Spanish Government, if questioned by them upon the subject, the nature of the instructions under which Sir Arthur Wellesley now acts, and the impracticability of going beyond them.

o

You will observe that, after the refusal of the Junta to admit a British garrison into Cadiz, the attention of the British Government was more particularly and exclusively turned to the security of Portugal; and that to that object we consider ourselves as bound, by the confidence which the Portuguese Government has reposed in us, especially to direct our efforts in the Peninsula.

That the security of Portugal does not necessarily confine the British army within the frontier of that kingdom; nor preclude its co-operation with the Spanish armies, so long as the course of that co-operation is not such as to lead to the leaving Portugal uncovered; the recent co-operation of Sir A. Wellesley with General Cuesta is a sufficient proof.

But this species of occasional concert your Excellency will state to be the utmost extent of the aid which, under the circumstances here described, Spain is to expect from a British army.

If, on the other hand, Sir A. Wellesley shall entertain the opinion, that with an effective British army of 30,000 men, combined with the Spanish and Portuguese armies, it might be possible either to expel the French from Spain, or to resist even their augmented numbers, with a reasonable prospect of success; if he shall think that Portugal itself would be best defended, in the end, by making the defence of that kingdom a part of a system of general operations throughout the Peninsula; the next question which will then arise, and upon which your Excellency will also receive the opinion of Sir Arthur Wellesley, is, as to the conditions which it may be necessary that your Excellency should obtain from the Spanish Government as preliminary to entering upon any concerted system of joint military operations.

Such preliminary arrangements would be most highly desirable, were it only with a view to prevent the recurrence of those inconveniences which were experienced in the last campaign, and of the complaints and recriminations which arose from them. But the reports received from Sir A. Wellesley of what has taken place between him and General Cuesta, and of the state of the country through which he has passed; the want of any settled plan of any arrangement either for moving or for provisioning an army, render it absolutely indispensable.

Upon all these points at least, a clear distinct understanding must be established; and the Spanish Government must be distinctly pledged to furnish the means of moving the army, and of supplying it regularly with provisions.

This is not intended to be done at the expence of the Spanish Government (though so far as the means of moving go, that might perhaps be reasonably expected): but that the provisions and means of transport should be forthcoming on the demand, and at the expence of the British army, is so essential, that unless arrangements to this effect are not only promised, but actually made by the Junta, to the satisfaction of your Excellency and of Sir Arthur Wellesley, there is an end at once of any question of co-operation, and Sir Arthur Wellesley will be instructed to withdraw his army to Portugal.

In addition to this indispensable preliminary, which admits of no doubt or qualification, are two, with respect to the requiring of which your Excellency will be guided by Sir A. Wellesley's opinion.

The first of these conditions is that which was proposed to the Spanish Government before the disastrous events in Gallicia, and at the time when it was intended to transfer the services of Sir John Moore's army to the south of Spain; viz. the occupation of Cadiz by a British garrison.

The object of this demand was, as well to provide for the security of the British army, in case of their being compelled to retreat before an overpowering superiority of numbers, as to ensure the Spanish and French ships, in the harbour of Cadiz, from falling into the hands of the enemy.

The second condition is one which has never yet been proposed to the Spaniards, but which they themselves authorized one of their officers to propose to General Moore ; viz. the confiding the command of the Spanish army to the Commander of the British army.

Sir Arthur Wellesley will report to your Excellency his opinion how far, under the present circumstances, and with a view to such a plan of operations as he might think it expedient to carry on, the occupation of Cadiz would be essentially impor‑ tant to the safety of a British army engaged in general operations in Spain ; or how far the possession of the Tagus, and the present improved military state of Portugal, may make. it less necessary to press this condition upon the Spanish Government, supposing them to continue to manifest the same repugnance to it as before.

In the event of Sir Arthur Wellesley's being of opinion that the occupation of Cadiz is essentially important to the safety of the British army, your Excellency is to decribe it to the Spanish Government as a condition *sine quâ non* of the employ‑ ment of the British army in Spain.

But if Sir Arthur Wellesley's opinion should be, that this measure is not neces‑ sary in a military point of view, then, although the other object which was in contemplation when the demand was originally made, viz. the safety of the Spanish and French ships in the harbour of Cadiz, is one of such magnitude that your Excellency is never to lose sight of it, and is to employ every effort of reasoning and of persuasion to induce the Junta to adopt such measures with respect to those fleets as may, in the worst extremity, disappoint the designs of the enemy ; yet your Excellency is not on this ground alone to make the admission of a British garrison into Cadiz a condition *sine quâ non* of the employment of a British army in Spain.

With respect to the second condition, the Spaniards offered the supreme com‑ mand of their armies to Sir John Moore. Mr. Stuart was present when this offer was made by Mr. Caro to the British General, and was declined. But with respect to this condition, your Excellency will be so far guided by the opinion of Sir Arthur Wellesley as not to press it, if Sir A. Wellesley, from reasons which his local knowledge and experience of the conduct of Spanish armies may suggest, should think it not advisable. Your Excellency will, nevertheless, even in that case, take care to leave the question so far open, that if in the course of his co‑operation with the Spanish generals, Sir A. Wellesley should find reason subsequently to change his opinion upon the subject, there may be no difficulty in making the demand hereafter.

If, on the other hand, Sir A. Wellesley deems this arrangement to be highly desirable, your Excellency is to make it a condition *sine quâ non*.

If the command is not to be in the British General, your Excellency is to press with redoubled earnestness for the appointment of a Generalissimo to the Spanish armies ; the mischiefs arising from divided and independent commands becoming every day more apparent.

It is to be understood distinctly, at the same time, that in no case is the British commander to place himself under the orders of the Spanish generalissimo, much less of any Spanish general commanding a separate army.

Independently of the other obvious considerations arising out of the past expe‑ rience of the conduct of the Spanish commanders, which would of themselves preclude such an arrangement, the nature of the engagements with Portugal would make it entirely impracticable. When the Government of Portugal placed their armies under British command, it certainly was not with any expectation that the British general himself should act in subordination to another commander.

The result of these instructions is :—

First :—That if Sir A. Wellesley's opinion shall be against the engaging a British army of 30,000 men in a campaign in Spain on any conditions whatever, your Excellency should take an opportunity of putting an end to any expectation of such an aid, which may be entertained by the Supreme Junta.

Secondly :—That, if on the contrary, Sir A. Wellesley, shall give an opinion favourable to the employment in Spain of a British army of 30,000 men, on all or any of the conditions hereinbefore described, your Excellency shall immediately proceed to require of the Spanish Government that the most effectual measures shall be taken for placing at the disposal of the British general such means of transport as he may describe to your Excellency to be necessary for the movement of his army ; and for securing to him a constant and regular supply of provisions ; and your Excellency will take care to have satisfactory evidence that these measures are actually put in train, before any joint operation is commenced.

With respect to the other two conditions, if Sir A. Wellesley thinks either or both of them indispensable, your Excellency will require both or either of them accordingly. If, on the other hand, Sir A. Wellesley should not deem it necessary to insist upon the admission into Cadiz as matter of precaution for the safety of the British army, your Excellency is not to make that admission a condition *sine quâ non* of British military co-operation.

If Sir Arthur Wellesley's decision shall be against requiring the supreme command of the Spanish armies, your Excellency is not in that case to make the demand.

I have only to add, that your Excellency is not to enter into any pledge as to the duration of the service of the British army in Spain : and, with respect to the Portuguese army, your Excellency is not to undertake, as matter of course, that they shall act with the British army in Spain, but merely that the good offices of the British Government shall be used with the Portuguese Regency to induce them to agree to such an employment of their forces.

Sir Arthur Wellesley will be instructed to write to your Excellency without delay on all the points of this despatch, and your Excellency will lose no time in informing me of the result of his report, and (in the event of its being favourable to the employment of the British army in Spain) of the steps which your Excellency may have taken upon it, and of the disposition which the Spanish Government may show to adopt whatever conditions your Excellency may have had to propose to them.

Your Excellency shall hear from me again as soon as we have the means of judging more precisely of the amount of force which will be actually disposable for the reinforcement of the army in the Peninsula. But it appeared not expedient to wait for that more precise information, before your Excellency was put in possession of those considerations, and directed eventually to take those steps, on the result of which it would depend, whether the services of a British army should, under any circumstances, be extended to Spain.

APPENDIX M.

Mr. Secretary Canning to the Marquess Wellesley.

(Extract.)

Foreign Office, August 12th, 1809.

Although it is not thought right to make the employment of the British army in Spain, if in the opinion of Sir Arthur Wellesley it can be employed there with a reasonable hope of contributing to accomplish the great objects of the deliverance of the Peninsula, or in offensive operations upon an extended scale, absolutely contingent upon the admission of a British garrison into Cadiz, yet your Excellency will be aware of all the importance of obtaining the consent of the Junta to this admission, at any favourable opportunity, and you are to spare no pains for effecting this object.

Whatever hopes may be entertained of a successful struggle, or at least of a protracted resistance on the part of the Spaniards, it is impossible to contemplate the force which may soon be brought against them, or to look back upon the examples of treachery which have marked some former periods of the contest, without feeling it to be matter worthy of the utmost precaution, that a fortress of such importance, and interests so vital as those which are connected with Cadiz, should be put beyond the reach either of the fate of war or of the intrigues of the disaffected.

At any moment when these arguments can be pressed with advantage, your Excellency will not fail to use them ; and if, by these or any other arguments, you can obtain the consent of the Junta, your Excellency is authorized to promise an adequate British garrison for Cadiz, independently of the army under Sir Arthur Wellesley.

For EU product safety concerns, contact us at Calle de José Abascal, 56–1°,
28003 Madrid, Spain or eugpsr@cambridge.org.

www.ingramcontent.com/pod-product-compliance
Ingram Content Group UK Ltd.
Pitfield, Milton Keynes, MK11 3LW, UK
UKHW010344140625
459647UK00010B/810